Adobe Master Class:
Illustrator Illuminated

**Ted Padova and
Barbara Obermeier**

Adobe Master Class: Illustrator Illuminated
Barbara Obermeier and Ted Padova
Copyright ©2003 by Barbara Obermeier and Ted Padova
Additional copyright information is on page 325-6.

This Adobe Press book is published by Peachpit Press.
For information on Adobe Press books, contact:
Peachpit Press
1249 Eighth Street
Berkeley, California 94710
510-524-2178 (tel), 510-524-2221 (fax)
http://www.peachpit.com

To report errors, please send a note to errata@peachpit.com
Peachpit Press is a division of Pearson Education
For the latest on Adobe Press books, go to
http://www.adobe.com/adobepress

Editors: Kelly Ryer, Serena Herr
Development Editor: Nancy Peterson
Technical Editor: Conrad Chavez
Production Coordinators: David Van Ness and Hilal Sala
Interior Design: Maureen Forys, Happenstance Type-O-Rama
Cover Design: Aren Howell
Cover Management: Georgia Vaughan
Compositor: Maureen Forys, Happenstance Type-O-Rama
Production Assistant: Chris Gillespie, Happenstance Type-O-Rama
Permissions Assistance: Rebecca Ross
Index: Joy Dean Lee

ISBN 0-201-77573-5
9 8 7 6 5 4 3 2 1
Printed and bound in the United States of America

Dedication

From Ted Padova
For Tanya

From Barbara Obermeier
For Gary and Kylie

Acknowledgements

The authors would like to thank our two managing editors, Serena Herr and Kelly Ryer, who continually supported our production delays. We could ask for no more support than they provided. We both concur that we had the best managing editors we've worked with to date; and now that it's over, we'd love to do it all again.

We wish to offer a special thank you to development editor Nancy Peterson, who pushed us to add the drama in each artist's biographical description that made the entire work much more interesting. Nancy's keen eye kept us on track and she tweaked the words so it could be comprehensible to you.

We additionally wish to thank the people in the background at Peachpit Press like David Van Ness, Rebecca Ross, Maureen Forys (for the super interior design of the book), the editors, and production team.

A special thanks to Marjorie Baer, the awesome Executive Editor at Peachpit, who always manages to come up with refreshing book ideas and does such a great job bringing together the right projects, authors, and editors.

Through his careful review and added research, Conrad Chavez insured technical accuracy. He went beyond a technical reviewer's responsibilities and researched everything from the technical points to the proper use of phrases and wording. Thanks Conrad—super job.

Thank you to our mutual friend and colleague Ted Alspach of Adobe Systems for coming forth and writing the foreword. Ted put his pressing schedule aside to review the work and add his kind words.

We extend much appreciation to our fifteen artists who took valuable time from their demanding schedules to answer questions, provide artwork, and follow up with many last minute details. We kept going back for more, and the artists responded to every request without complaint. Some of our best moments were spending time with this group.

Foreword

Adobe Illustrator is a part of everyone's lives nowadays, even if they have no idea what Adobe Illustrator is. Because Illustrator has become the industry-standard graphics software (pretty much every design firm, ad agency, and print shop uses it), Illustrator artwork has penetrated our lives to an extent that most people just aren't aware of. The next time you walk down an aisle in your neighborhood grocery store, look at the hundreds of packages on the shelves; almost all of them have been designed in Illustrator. All forms of advertising, from billboards to movie posters are either created by or at the least touched by Illustrator.

That's why this book is so fascinating—the artwork covers a broad range of what can be done in Illustrator. Even more amazingly, most of the artwork was created using Illustrator exclusively. When you start adding all the other tools in a creative designer's arsenal, like image editing, page layout, digital video, and Web software, Illustrator becomes the corner-stone for a creative process. This book provides insight and instruction on how the creative workflow happens with Illustrator as a predominant player.

At Adobe, we strive to provide cutting-edge technology and tools to allow users of our software to express their creativity in as many ways as possible. This book is a testament to that goal.

Ted Alspach
Group Product Manager, Illustration Products
Adobe Systems

Contents

Introduction

This is a different kind of Illustrator book. If you want a tips-and-tricks book or a comprehensive reference for using the program, you'll need to keep browsing the shelves for another publication. But, be aware—other software books tend to overlap in content. What this book offers you is a unique look at Illustrator and how professional artists use the program to earn their livings.

When Peachpit contacted us about writing an *Adobe Master Class* book, both of us were involved in writing other books. We discussed the project between ourselves and concluded that a little publication like the one you're holding would be a snap and we could push it out the door in no time. After all, what could be difficult about getting some artists together to collaborate on such a project?

It took more than five months to get *Illustrator Illuminated* to production. What we thought would be a little side job took many hours of researching artists, contacting people who produce refreshing and new perspectives on art a al Adobe Illustrator, and many fascinating conversations with a group of very talented people. The more we delved into the project, the more time we spent searching out a broad range of artists, distinctive in their techniques and varied in their methods.

As we searched through the Internet, talked with colleagues, and held discussions with formative artists, we were determined to include people who work both within and outside the United States. The artists featured in this book work in the United States, Canada, England, Japan, South Africa, Australia, Denmark, and England. Bringing an international group of artists together gave us an understanding of how culture can impact artwork.

We begin each chapter by describing a little background about the artist and how they came to choose their profession and, ultimately, adopt a computer and Illustrator as their illustration tools. Understanding the education, work history, and accumulated awards each artist has mounted is interesting, but the real value in each biographical sketch lies in the description of how each artist relates to their clients, acquires a new project, and develops concepts for the artwork they create. We tried to get inside the head of each artist and walk you through the steps they use to spark a new idea, fulfill their client's requests, and produce a piece that is both artistically enriching and useful.

To offer you technical information about Illustrator, we added a sidebar in each chapter that covers a technique used by each artist. Look over the sidebars and find out how artists use some particular feature in Illustrator. In each sidebar, we provide you with a tip or technique related to the way the masters work.

If you have the skill to work effectively in Illustrator and you struggle with design concepts, this book is for you. If you want to add a few tips to your arsenal of Illustrator methods, this book is for you. If you're a beginning artist, then the combination of studying the masters and learning their approaches for new design projects will be a valuable asset. Regardless of where you are in computer illustration, you can find something valuable in the pages ahead.

 If you think we've left something out or you wish to see something added in the next revision then please let us know. Ted can be reached at ted@west.net and Barbara can be reached at barbobie@dcninternet.net.

NO ORDINARY BIRD

CANTON

广東市集

MARKET

Chapter 1

The Illustrator Way of Thinking

The style of artwork created in Illustrator varies widely.

About Adobe Illustrator

From its humble beginnings through its many iterations, Illustrator has grown to levels of sophistication that can boggle the most complex minds. With more than 25 palettes, over 70 tools, and more than 250 menu commands, this vector art drawing program can do almost anything an artist could want.

In the real world, however, artists rarely exploit Illustrator to take advantage of all its power. The artists profiled in this book, for instance, sidestep many of the features, preferring to pick and choose the tools they need to get the job out the door. Professional artists earning a living from the work they produce in Illustrator aren't necessarily interested in poking around new whiz-bang features. Instead they choose tools based on familiarity and short learning curves. A few artists use newer features introduced in the most recent version of the program, while many gravitate to tools and features introduced in Illustrator's initial release.

Tiffany Larsen begins with a sketch and scans the drawing. She works in Illustrator on one monitor while she views the sketch on another.

Sarajo Frieden uses the Paint Brush and Pen tool much as she uses analog tools for fine art drawings such as this one.

To more clearly understand how a professional artist uses Illustrator, this chapter covers some basic principles on how artists begin an assignment and take it to the final stages. In the pages ahead you'll learn how some of the pros in this book get inspired for a project, what they consider the most useful Illustrator features, and many practical tips on avoiding printing problems.

Beginning an Illustration

Although their techniques vary according to personal taste and interest, the single common ingredient for all our artists is a fundamental understanding of art and design. With all of Illustrator's capability, a drawing doesn't become art unless the user has spent some time studying art.

While the artists profiled in this book have successfully embraced the computer as a creative tool, many have not abandoned their fine art skills. Artists such as Tiffany Larsen and Sarajo Frieden often draw and paint, even if it's just for personal projects. They say they do so because they need to: The work they perform in Illustrator is an extension of the kind of work they do using traditional methods. Extending fine art work to computer illustration only makes their work stronger, providing an organic quality that is often lacking in computer-generated art.

For many artists the most crucial stage in creating art comes before ever launching Illustrator and beginning a drawing: the concept development stage. Almost all the artists in this book religiously follow a specific series of steps to develop a concept, although the steps are unique to each artist. Martin French starts with a period of concentrated study, involving research, listening to music, and studying master artists' illustrations. Nick Diggory puts some distance between himself and the project for a while when he steps away and goes fishing. Daniel Pelavin's is a method of creative procrastination—he intentionally postpones making first drafts

Daniel Pelavin draws 40 to 50 sketches within a few hours for each project. From the sketches, he chooses 10 to 12 drawings to send to the client. He uses the final drawing as a template to begin the project.

Michael Bartalos uses sketches as templates for each new project. In this figure, the original sketch is for a design for panels completely covering a school bus.

until the night before a deadline to give his unconscious mind time to work away. The ways to develop a concept may vary wildly from artist to artist, but giving this stage the emphasis that it's due is as important as developing good techniques in Illustrator.

Tracing Templates

Adobe Illustrator is the avant-garde tool for illustrators and artists. However, most of our artists rely on traditional methods before grabbing Illustrator's Pen tool, often making thumbnail sketches and rough drawings. In many cases, artists scan the roughs and then send them to the client for approval. It may be a single sketch or a handful of sketches selected from as many as 40 to 50 thumbnails.

When a client approves a concept, artists typically use thumbnails or rough sketches as templates in Illustrator. Only a few artists start a project by launching Illustrator and using paths and objects to begin a new drawing.

The first version of Illustrator was designed so that artists could trace templates with the Pen tool. After all the upgrades and product revisions, the program is still designed to work this way. Some artists use templates as a basis for their illustration, others use them only for reference, feeling that it can constrict their creativity.

Managing with Layers

One Illustrator feature that almost every artist uses is layers. Layers allow the artist to concentrate on a single element or group of elements without distraction from the composite.

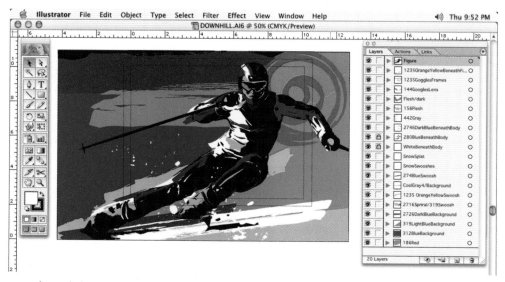

Using layers helps Martin French easily select objects to apply color fills and strokes.

The artist can more easily modify or eliminate an element if it isn't working. And it affords great flexibility in managing the illustration because the artist can view, lock, rearrange, and print elements separately.

The Ubiquitous Pen Tool

Master artists working in any vector art program have developed great skill at using the Pen tool. Some may gravitate to the Pencil tool, but even with a stylus, the Pen tool is still the precision instrument needed to polish a drawing. The artists in this book developed their Bézier-curve drawing skills by tracing drawings —many of them—until the Pen tool became a familiar friend.

The one tool in the first version of Illustrator that still looks, feels, and works the same as it does in Illustrator 10 is the Pen tool. Its intimidating little icon tested the patience of the first Illustrator users and still keeps some artists away from its non-intuitive approach to freehand illustration. Yet, once you understand and master the Pen tool , it will probably become the one you use most frequently.

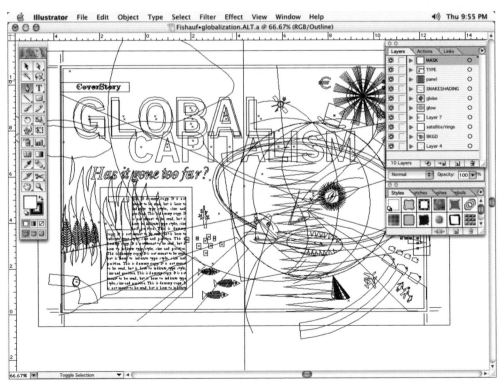

In the hands of an experienced artist such as Louis Fishauf, you get complex paths created with the Pen tool in every drawing.

Avoiding Printing Problems

During the entire process of building a design—from the beginnings of developing a concept, to drawing, to introducing illustrative lines with fills and adding type characters—the eventual output format is a constant consideration for the artist. Through experience with service centers and print shops, many artists have learned the limitations of printing Illustrator files. Therefore, one of the most important considerations for an Illustrator artist is what kind of output will be obtained from which kind of printing device (such as composite color or color separations output to a film setter, platesetter, or large-format inkjet printer).

If you have the luxury of sending all your files to the same vendor, you're fortunate. That makes it easier to get feedback on what works and what doesn't. Unfortunately, commercial artists serving different clients often need to deal with many different vendors using many different devices. Therefore, it's helpful to observe some general guidelines for all printing devices.

Excessive Points on Paths

At one point or another, too many points on a path can present imaging problems on the most sophisticated printing devices. Some artists use companion programs such as Adobe Streamline to automatically trace sketches. Often the artist's auto traces are used as templates and are ultimately deleted from the file before it goes to print. Automatically tracing images can add too many points to a path, so use care if using the auto trace tool in Illustrator or other programs, including Adobe Streamline. Since it's easy to smooth paths or eliminate excessive points in Illustrator, these are good methods to use when using auto trace and the Pencil tool.

You can also create excessive points on paths when converting type to outlines. For artwork such as logos, editorials, book and magazine covers, and posters there may be short passages of type. With limited type in a drawing, converting the type to outlines typically doesn't present a problem, even on older RIPs (Raster Image Processors) and printing devices. However, if you create a large-format design with an extraordinary amount of body copy and convert the type to outlines, you may experience problems. Not converting type to outlines reduces the complexity of a drawing and the amount of time required to print the file.

Transparency

Files containing transparency often present imaging problems on devices with Level 2 and earlier RIPs and non-Adobe PostScript RIPs. To eliminate problems you may need to flatten transparency or save your Illustrator artwork as an EPS file with an earlier version compatibility, such as version 8 or below.

To preserve transparency in files that can be printed to PostScript 3 devices, you need to be certain that the file format supports transparent effects. Most imaging centers typically print Illustrator files from applications other than Illustrator for better page control and other print attributes. More often than not, your Illustrator files will wind up in a page layout program, such as Adobe InDesign or QuarkXPress, where the separations are printed. Although Illustrator 9 and 10 save EPS files with both true transparency and flattened data, QuarkXPress 5 uses the flattened data in an imported EPS. If imaging technicians save your Illustrator files as EPS in order to import the artwork in a separating program, it will be the technician who decides which attributes to use in the saved EPS document. To insure the file is prepared properly, make sure you're the one who saves files as EPS or as PDF, taking the file-conversion job away from the imaging center.

Setting Frequencies

Traditional process-color separations are usually not a problem when printing separations at the local service center. If some colors in a process-color job have been applied as spot colors, the imaging center can globally convert spot colors to process if necessary. If you

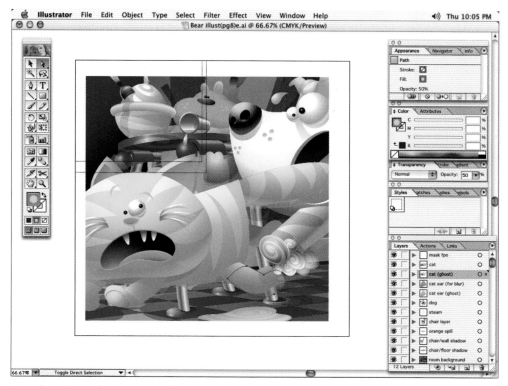

Russell Benfanti often rasterizes Illustrator art in Adobe Photoshop to eliminate potential printing problems with transparent Illustrator objects.

instruct technicians to print your files with a specified halftone frequency, they should be able to adhere to your instructions and deliver the proper output.

Files designed for spot color separations are a little more tricky. If you work with a service center and have confidence in their ability to output the files according to your instructions, you can deliver the Illustrator document to the service center and be done with it. If, on the other hand, you work with a new service center and aren't certain about their ability to properly print a file, you may wish to embed all your frequencies and angles directly in the Illustrator document.

Rasterizing Stubborn Files

If an Illustrator file won't print on a specific device, you have one last resort: rasterizing the vector objects. You can do this within Illustrator itself. Or you can rasterize by opening the Illustrator file in Photoshop, where you can specify the color mode and image resolution when you open the file. Once converted to a raster image, the complexity of the vector objects is eliminated and you often experience no printing problems with the file. Above all, make sure that you supply the proper resolution for the output device when you rasterize an Illustrator file.

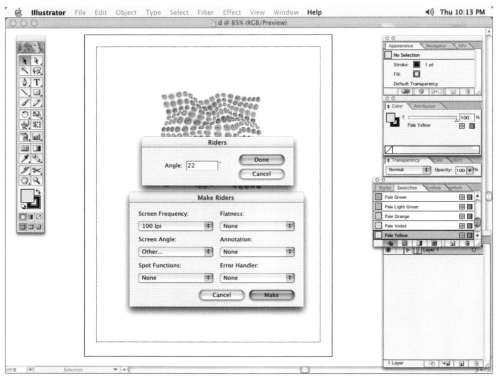

When using custom frequencies and angles, you can embed these attributes using the Riders plug-in from the Utilities folder. Copy the file to the Illustrator Plug-ins folder and relaunch Illustrator.

Looking Forward

Many artists featured in this book use a variety of traditional media—graphite, ink, acrylic, oils, and color pencil. They are skilled at using a number of tools, allowing them to express their creativity unhampered. For most artists, computer graphics is an extension of a talent developed from fundamental analog skills and education rooted in traditional methods.

The artists have distinctive ways of using Illustrator and each favors different Illustrator tools, but they have one trait in common: each employs a personal method for creating a concept before launching Illustrator. The background and biographical information about the artists in the following chapters will help you get a feeling for how they develop concepts and what methods they use to spark new ideas. We also feature walkthroughs of specific projects, detailing the artist's journey from concept through completion and submission to the client. As a final bonus, take a look at the sidebars, which contain Illustrator techniques to help you become more proficient in using this program.

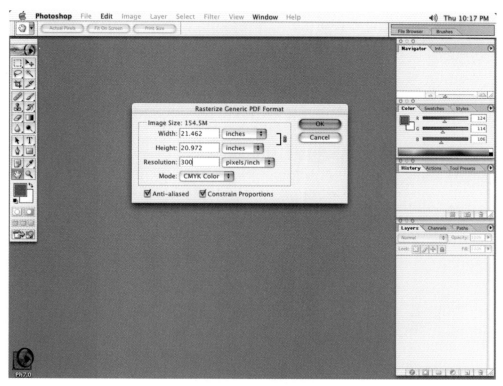

When rasterizing Illustrator files in Photoshop or using the Illustrator Rasterize command, be certain to supply the proper resolution.

Chapter 2
Technical Illustration

Artist
Alan Raine
Technical Illustrator, Graphic Designer
Cheshire, England
www.alanraine-graphicillustration.co.uk

Project
Technical illustration of a hoist

Client
Street Crane Company, a heavy equipment manufacturer

Illustrator Tools and Techniques
Pen Tool, Transformation Tools, Guides, Layers, Transparency

Opposite: Powersite | Ozone Systems, brochure drawing

Alan Raine
An Isometric View

For Alan Raine, it was a matter of survival for him to convert his hand-drawn, traditional illustrations to computer-generated artwork. His customers increasingly wanted digital art. "I found a company that dealt in liquidated stock and I managed to pick up a complete computer system quite inexpensively. The hardware came with Adobe Illustrator 3.1 and Photoshop 2.0, plus an assortment of digital imaging applications. I just learned as I went along and found adapting to computer illustration to be fairly easy. Illustrator was ideal for my purpose and it fitted in well with most of my clients, who were also going along the Apple Mac road. We used to help each other out and pool information. In short order, I became the Illustrator expert!"

Becoming a professional freelance technical illustrator requires a formal education in the field and some qualified on-the-job experience. Fortunately for Raine, he had both. He left Barnfield College in Luton, England in 1975 with a degree in Technical Illustration and a

Gutter | PLC Advertising Agency, product brochure illustration for a plastics company

concentration in Technical Drawing. After doing technical drawing for several British companies, he moved to Wolfsburg, Germany. There he spent two years at an agency that primarily produced technical drawings for Volkswagen. "It was a good experience," he proclaims. "If you were good enough, you survived. If you weren't, you were shown the door. I found my feet and came out of it with a lot of confidence. The only reason I left was I got married and needed to return to England."

"I often produce sketches on paper to get an idea of the perspective. Then, I create a perspective template—a 3-dimensional box around a scanned photo of the product, using perspective vanishing points. This is ultimately the basis for the whole illustration."

Upon returning to England in 1983, Raine went freelance and has worked as an independent technical illustrator ever since. His clients have included companies such as Ableworld,

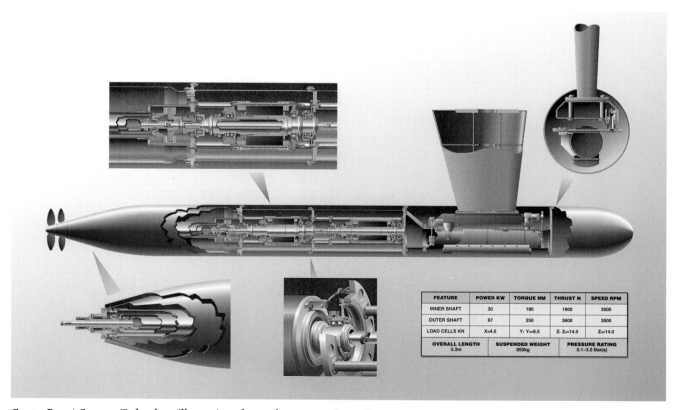

FEATURE	POWER KW	TORQUE NM	THRUST N	SPEED RPM
INNER SHAFT	30	180	1800	3500
OUTER SHAFT	67	250	3600	3500
LOAD CELLS KN	$X=4.0$	$Y_1 Y_2=8.0$	$Z_1 Z_2=14.0$	$Z_3=14.0$

OVERALL LENGTH	SUSPENDED WEIGHT	PRESSURE RATING
5.3m	850kg	0.1~3.0 Bar(a)

Contra Prop | Cussons Technology, illustration of an underwater testing unit

Aintree Racing Driver's School, Beldam Crossley, British Gas, *Classic Cars Magazine*, Cussons Technology, Daryl Industries, Deva Tap Company, Dri-Sil Technics, IGS Gmgh, Ozone Systems, Rolls Royce Motors, R.W. Salt Communications, and Street Crane.

Drawing technical illustrations on a computer was both a curse and a blessing for Raine. "The cost of the equipment and current software eats into my profits. When I illustrated using traditional tools, the number of changes provided to clients was only one or two. There was always a limit to what you could change, due to damage to the working surface that would always show up on final artwork. Now projects undergo changes for as long as it takes to get client approval. However, the computer has helped me gather information—especially since the advent of the Internet. The real beauty of computer-generated artwork is that it can be changed to suit a multitude of purposes without losing quality."

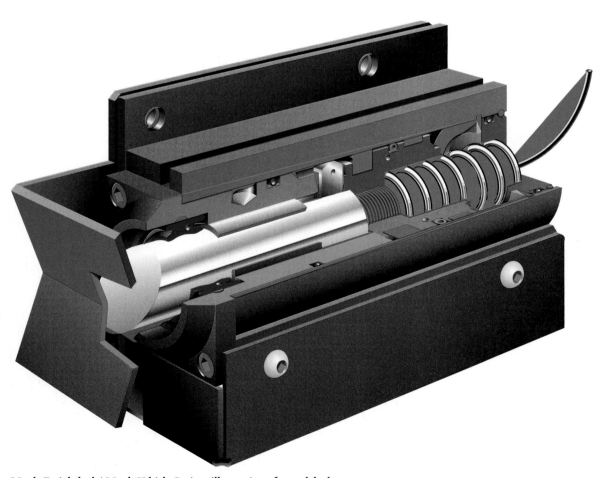

Maple Freightlock | Maple Vehicle Society, illustration of a truck lock

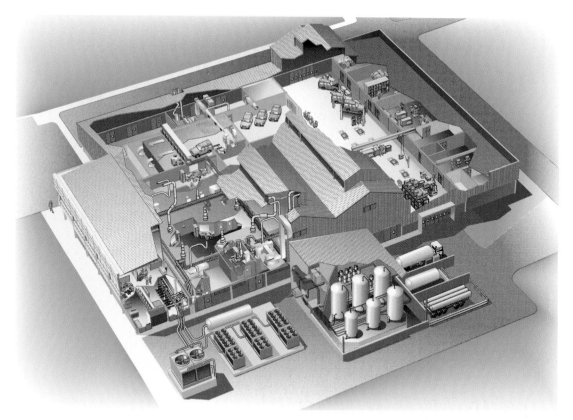

Test Centre Cutaway | Cussons Technology, cutaway illustration of an engine development test plant

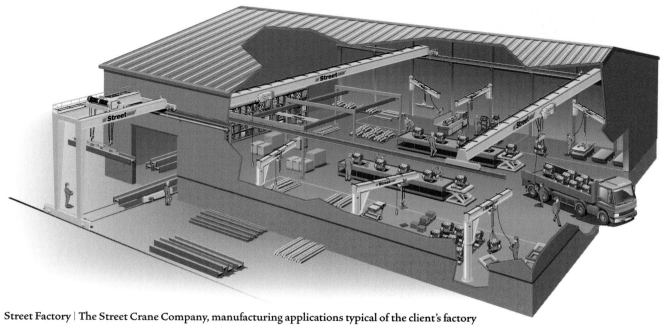

Street Factory | The Street Crane Company, manufacturing applications typical of the client's factory

Raine has a number of regular clients, for whom he creates illustrations for product brochures, advertisements, packaging, and instructional manuals. For these clients, developing concepts comes from an intimate knowledge of the client and the client's products. His illustrations are prescribed by clients in meetings and instructions are straightforward with little need to create a unique design concept. His challenge comes in determining the exact view of a product. "It takes a great deal of thinking to determine the best view. I often produce sketches on paper first to get an idea of the perspective. Once I decide on the right view, I create a perspective template. I make a 3-dimensional box around a scanned photo or plans of the product by using perspective vanishing points and create a template, which is ultimately the basis for the whole illustration."

MONDIALE 00
Silverstone Formula THE CONCEPT

A modern single seater car constructed with a very rigid space frame chassis using the Ford 1800 or 2000cc Zetec engine. It can be run using wings and Formula 3 size wheels and tyres.

Alternatively it can be offered in a more simple configuration without wings and using Formula Ford type wheels and tyres. This slightly less sophisticated specification could have the power output reduced accordingly.

Race Car Proposal | Mondiale Racing Cars, race car design prototype

Walking Boot | Ron Hill
Sports Clothing, used in
brochures and advertising

Screw Conveyor Cutaway |
Vibrair, Ltd., illustration for
brochure

4500 Class Locomotive | an illustration for a series of books on locomotives

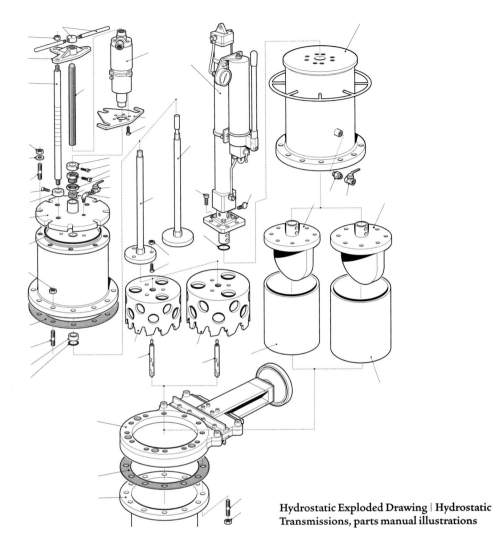

Hydrostatic Exploded Drawing | Hydrostatic Transmissions, parts manual illustrations

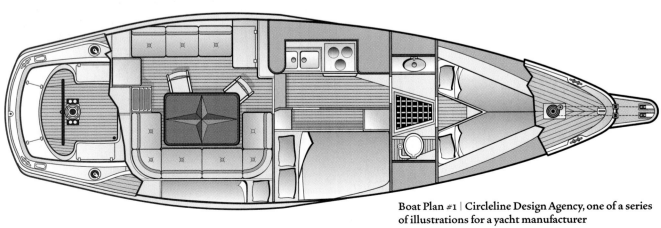

Boat Plan #1 | Circleline Design Agency, one of a series of illustrations for a yacht manufacturer

When he acquires a new client, there is considerably more work involved in a project. "I spend much time getting a thorough brief of the client and the products they manufacture. I often visit a client's facility and take photos with a digital camera. I collect engineering drawings and samples of any artwork available. Often clients can't visualize the final product, so I take my research materials and go off and produce the artwork that I envision meeting the client's needs. Once I have created the basic structure of an illustration, I start to add detail and color. Often, how much I put into a project depends on the budget and time available. But sometimes I go a little overboard and end up offering more detail than the client expected."

"The thing I like best about working in Adobe Illustrator is that I can produce technical illustrations in ways similar to those I used when I was originally trained. Being able to create a drawing and then slightly modify it in seconds without loss of quality is brilliant. I can still be creative and now, with bigger hard drives, faster processors, and stronger links with Photoshop, I can produce stunning images and see-through technical illustrations."

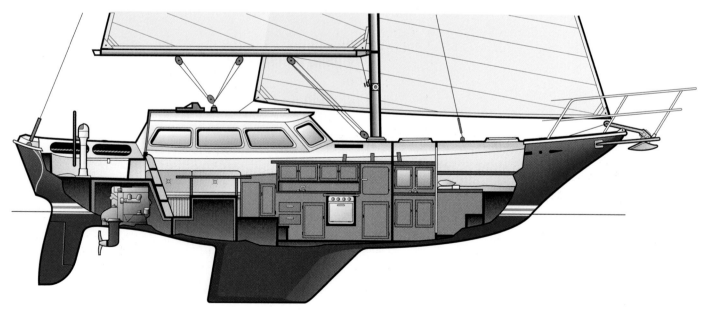

Boat Side Cutaway | Circleline Design Agency

Salt Cover | R.W. Salt Communications, product catalog cover

The Project

The Street Crane Company of Chapel-en-le-Frith, England needed a technical illustration of a hoist. Raine went to the Street Crane factory armed with a camera and sketchpad. The company, however, used CAD design systems and was able to give Raine detailed construction drawings. In addition, Raine and the crew at Street Crane Company played around on the CAD system and rotated the drawings until they found the view that would show the parts that were most visibly important—the gearbox, brake, and drum/cable assemblies. The managing director also wanted, in his words, "a sexy-looking hook."

Although the hoist was still at the design stage without a complete prototype, certain parts were already available. In addition, existing similar components gave him an idea of how things worked. Raine photographed these components and then went through construction drawings with the company's engineers to glean as much information as possible.

Raine then went away and started the work. Using a rough printout of the 3D CAD image, he worked out the perspective. Says Raine, "The managing director didn't want to make the

unit look big, but he wanted it to look compact, so I didn't put too much harsh perspective on it. I produced a rough outline drawing in Illustrator and faxed a copy to Street Crane. They agreed on the view and I proceeded with the artwork." Raine sent preliminary drawings of various parts of the hoist to the engineers. "I wanted to check if the components were correct and also to find out areas where I couldn't work out how it fitted together!" After about three to four weeks, a first draft of the entire illustration was ready. Raine sent a PDF file for approval before he went to the presentation meeting with the client to see if there were any modifications. Fortunately, a few tweaks were all that was required. Street Crane asked Raine if he could produce a second image of the hoist, without any cutaways. The illustrations were originally for a company brochure, but they have also been used in advertising, manuals, and as exhibition material.

"Now with bigger hard drives, faster processors, and stronger links to Photoshop, Illustrator enables me to produce stunning DTP images and see-through technical illustrations. If I could have one more tool it would be an Eraser tool that could erase vector shapes."

—ALAN RAINE

The Steps

Step 1: Creating the initial perspective lines. Once Raine got approval on the view of the hoist, he launched Illustrator and created a new A4 size, CMYK file. He then created a horizon line and two vanishing points that were the basis for the perspective of the illustration. He put the perspective lines on a separate layer. Raine says, "I often have to tinker with this until I am satisfied that the perspective is how I want it." (**Figure 16**)

Step 2: Creating the box in perspective. Raine was given two-dimensional CAD printouts to use as references. Using those printouts, he created a box around each side elevation. He then placed them into a perspective box in his illustration, using the lines from the vanishing points. He created this perspective box on its own layer (**Figure 17**).

Step 3: Making a grid. Says Raine, "A good way to accurately project information from the drawings to the illustration is to create a grid. Divide the sides of the perspective box by drawing guidelines from corner to corner. Where they cross is the center of the square. Keep doing this until you have your grid. By laying a similar grid over the reference elevations, you can find other information, such as center points and distances." (**Figure 18**)

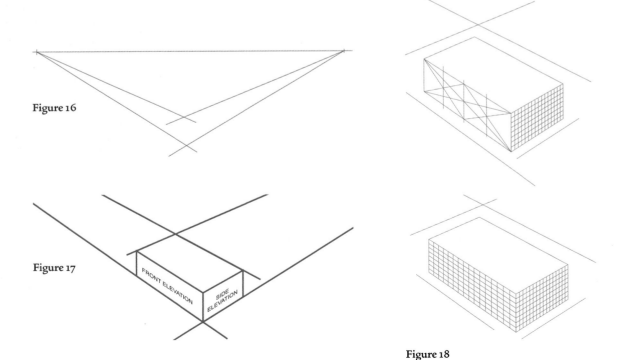

Figure 16

Figure 17

Figure 18

Step 4: Starting the illustration. After establishing his perspective base, Raine began the illustration. Due to the stacking-order nature of Illustrator—in which some elements get hidden—Raine tends to work on the front elements first, making his way to the rear elements. "I tend to work from the front going to the back to save having to draw everything. In this case, I started with the frame." Using the grid to find dimensions, he grabbed the Pen tool (his tool of choice), drew the nearest part of the frame first, and put it on its own layer. Like many other artists, Raine uses a Wacom tablet and stylus pen. "I start off in outline view to get the accurate shape, then when I'm happy with the shape, I add color." Raine mixed a few different shades of process yellow, using the CMYK sliders in the Color palette. For the front of the frame he created a gradient, which he mixed using two shades of dark yellow in the Gradient palette (**Figure 19**). He stored the colors and gradient in the Swatches palette.

Step 5: Completing the frame. Raine finished constructing the main frame in a similar manner. Projecting from the 2D reference drawings onto the perspective grid, he drew the remaining shapes of the frame in Outline view, refined the shape, and then mixed and added color (**Figure 20**). Says Raine, "It was necessary to tweak existing colors so that things would stand out. I wasn't too concerned about the rear of the frame, as I knew a great deal of it would be covered by the cable, drum, and other parts."

Step 6: Creating the drum and cables. Next, Raine drew the drum and cables. On a new layer, he created the first cable and then copied and pasted a second cable. He moved it into position and then adjusted it slightly for perspective. Raine repeated the process until the cable was complete (**Figure 21a**). On another layer, he drew the drum and created a gradient to mimic the exposed polished metal of the drum. He also saved the metal gradient in the Swatches palette (**Figure 21b**).

Step 7: Drawing the motors. Raine then created a new layer and drew the first motor (**Figure 22a**). The second red motor had to be drawn on the frame layer, since it would be hidden behind the frame. After drawing the motors in Outline view, he mixed several gradients, using shades of process red, and filled the shapes (**Figure 22b**).

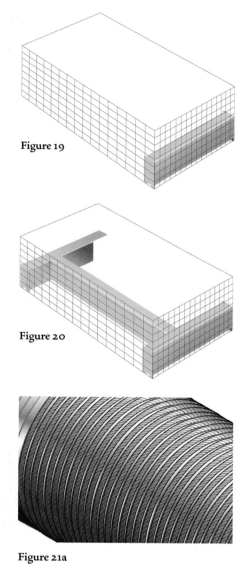

Figure 19

Figure 20

Figure 21a

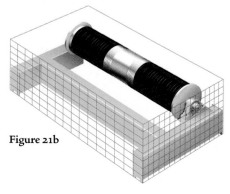

Figure 21b

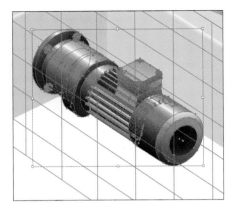

Figure 22a

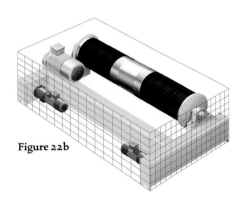

Figure 22b

Step 8: Adding the gearbox and brake assembly. Moving on, Raine added the complex gearbox and brake assembly (**Figure 23a**). "This was the awkward bit. The proposed gearbox was not available to view and I had only a very rough 3D-CAD printout as a guide. So, I photographed a similar box and adapted it to suit this application. It is also outside the perspective box, so I kept the perspective accurate by using the lines from the vanishing points." After creating the components, Raine filled the gearbox shapes with the process yellows he used earlier and with gradients he mixed using the Gradient palette. For the shapes of the brake assembly, he used shades of process burgundy and a couple of new gradients as well (**Figure 23b**).

Step 9: Creating the hook and pulley assembly. "I cheated a little with the hook, as I had already drawn it before on several other jobs and it only needed tweaking a bit to get it in the correct perspective. I had to cheat a little with the pulleys and cables too, as they were partially hidden by the frame, so I moved them to a more convenient position—artistic license." (**Figure 24a**) Raine also created the rear of the main frame. He filled all components with solid process colors or gradients (**Figure 24b**).

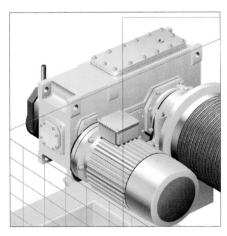

Figure 23a

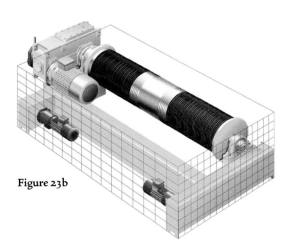

Figure 23b

Figure 24a

Step 10: Completing the hoist. With the main illustration of the hoist complete, he added the remaining details, such as the Street Crane logo, screw covers, and shadows. Raine did not use transparency for his shadows, instead he carefully crafted his shadow gradients to give the illusion of transparency. He removed the perspective grid and vanishing points and saved his final file. Raine then printed a high-quality color proof. "I feel it is worth producing a good quality color print at this stage, as it will show more clearly where the colors don't match or where they need to be strengthened or lightened." After reviewing the proof, he adjusted the color where needed. Raine presented the proof to the client, who asked only that he alter the cable slightly. After this final adjustment, Raine delivered the electronic files and final color proofs to the client of both this hoist (**Figure 25**) and the original cutaway version (**Figure 26**).

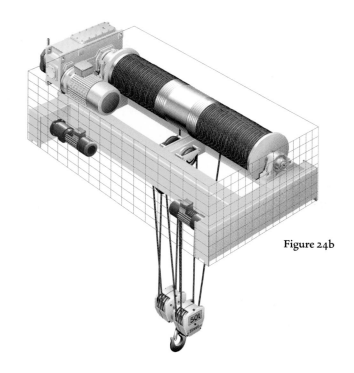

Figure 24b

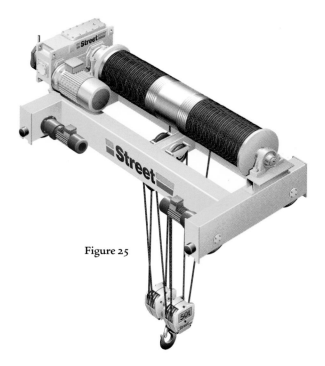

Figure 25

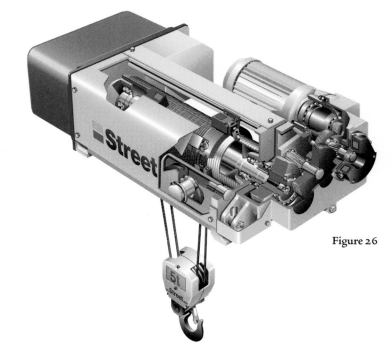

Figure 26

Creating Isometric Drawings

The most common type of drawing created by technical illustrators—whether the drawing is for automotive, machinery, architecture, or similar industries—is the isometric view, or *pictorial view*, as it is often called.

Whereas other types of designers and illustrators often rely on freehand sketches, technical illustrators like Raine create precise templates, using geometric lines fixed to a horizon and vanishing points. To begin a new drawing, Raine first decides on the view of his illustration in relation to the horizon, then creates two vanishing points for the basis of his drawing.

Isometric drawings contain three axis points: the x, y, and z axes. The z axis is almost always a vertical line while the x and y axes are drawn from the two vanishing points. The most frequently used convention for isometric drawings is a 30-degree angle for both the x and y axes (**Figure 27**).

To create a template for a drawing similar to Figure 27 below, you start with a horizon line. This line might extend well beyond the Illustrator page, depending on where you want the two vanishing points. Copy the horizon line (Command or Control-C) and paste the line in front (Command or Control-F). Be certain to select both anchor points if they are not already selected. Select the Rotate tool, press the Option or Alt key, and click on the left anchor point. The Rotate dialog box opens (**Figure 28**).

Enter –30 for the angle and click OK. Press Command or Control-F again to paste another copy in front of the horizon line. With the line selected, press Option or Control and click with the Rotate tool on the right anchor point. When the Rotate dialog box opens, enter 30 for the angle. At this point you have two lines that will be used for the base of the x and y axes (**Figure 29**). Note: you can use the scissors tool to clip the lines to fit the corners of the object as shown in the figures here.

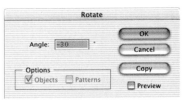

Figure 28

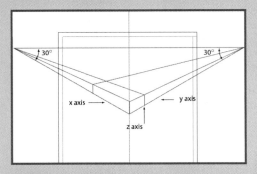

Figure 27

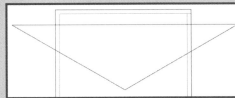

Figure 29

Draw a vertical line where you want the center of the view and make a guide from the line by selecting View > Guides > Make Guides. Select the Direct Select tool and click on the bottom anchor point on one of the 30-degree lines. Press the Option or Alt key and Shift-drag the anchor point up to duplicate the line. (Be certain only the anchor point you're moving is selected and the opposite anchor point remains deselected to rotate the line on an axis.) This position is arbitrary. Move the line to where you want the top of the cube (or building). Repeat the same steps for the other 30-degree line and move the anchor point to the same position as the first movement (**Figure 30**).

Repeat the same steps to duplicate two more lines to form the left and right rear of the top of the cube. Draw two vertical lines to form the left rear and right front sides (**Figure 31**).

Raine likes to work with a grid. To create a grid for the sides of the object, he draws guidelines from corner to corner on each plane. Where the guidelines intersect is the middle of the plane; he draws a vertical line at the midpoint (**Figure 32**).

He repeats the process to find the midpoint between the ends and the new vertical lines. He draws additional vertical lines at each new midpoint and continues this process to create the horizontal and vertical guidelines (**Figure 33**).

After you create the perspective and grid, double-click the Layer palette, and select Template. Lock the template and you're ready to draw objects conforming to an isometric view.

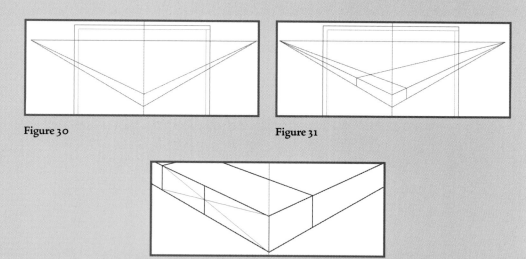

Figure 30

Figure 31

Figure 32

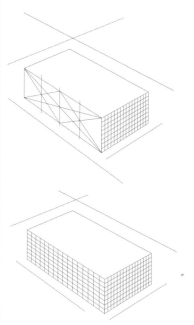

Figure 33

Chapter 3
Children's Illustration

Artist
Russell Benfanti
Clarence, New York
Designer, Illustrator, Art Director
www.benfanti.com

Project
Illustrations for *The Chair Where Bear Sits,* Winslow Press

Client
Winslow Press

Illustrator Tools and Techniques
Pen Tool, Layers, Gradients, Masks, Transparency, Blur Filters

Opposite: Clyde | ipicturebooks

Russell Benfanti
Love of Children

Early in his career Russell Benfanti needed to make a decision—become a designer or, in his words, "a real illustrator." To the joy of many children, he chose the latter. Benfanti's work is published in numerous children's books, on product packaging, magazines, television shows, and just about anything else for children and young adults. You can see his children's illustrations in recent publications, such as *The Chair Where Bear Sits* (Winslow Press) and *Hide, Clyde* (ipicturebooks). His clients include Milton Bradley-Hasbro for package designs such as *Cootie, Ants in the Pants, Don't Break the Ice,* and *Don't Spill the Beans.* He has illustrated artwork for Pizza Hut, Brunswick Kids, Aussie Land shampoos, Fisher-Price, Hasbro, Frito-Lay, and many others.

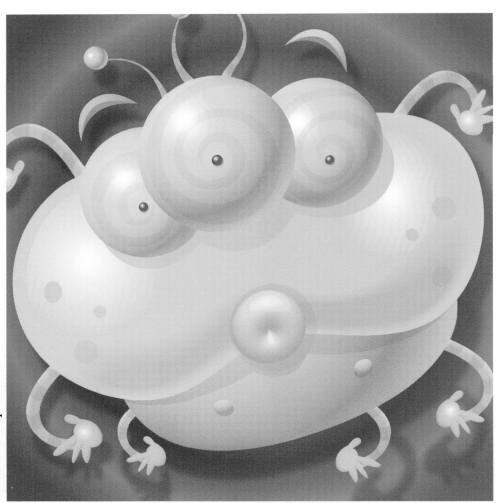

Yellowbloat | self-promotion

When Benfanti began his career as an artist, the word was out that designers were paid regularly while illustrators earned an occasional income. So, at first, Benfanti did what seemed most practical—he pursued a career as a designer, starting out with a major in design at the State University of New York at Buffalo. His first love was illustration, which was his minor.

"I try to get clients to provide me with a sketch of what they're envisioning. I hate guessing, and even the most crude napkin drawings provide information that's too difficult to describe verbally."

After finishing school Benfanti worked as a freelance designer, though he dislikes the term. "The word *free* seemed to conflict with the business side of the profession," he says.

Octopus' Garden book study | **Byron Preiss Visual Communications**

Mendola cover | self-promotion

But business was what was needed to sustain his lifestyle, so Benfanti worked a few years with a design firm before opening his own studio. "We partnered with local companies on all types of projects. It was fun, but I had to have a chameleon-like illustration style. The market was too small for me to specialize in one style of illustration. Clients would call and say 'I know you can illustrate—but can you do this style?'" He would always say yes, even if he had no idea how to do it, and figure out how to do it afterwards.

As a designer, though, he found it dissatisfying to develop the initial concepts for a job, and then have to hand the project off to *real illustrators*. Clients thought that if he needed to design for a living, he couldn't be that good at illustration, he says. Eventually, he decided to specialize his style and make the jump from working designer to aspiring illustrator. His rationale: "If creative directors want a photograph, they hire a photographer. If they want a copywriter, they hire a copywriter. If they want an illustrator...well, you know."

Workbook (apple) | self-promotion

AdSource | self-promotion

To maintain a steady income, Benfanti kept some design clients while beginning his illustration career. And rather than just hunt for illustration jobs, he decided to start a company that led to a successful career as an illustrator and businessman with a long-term emphasis on children's illustration.

Benfanti started working on a Mac IIci in 1989. The agency where he was working decided to bring in Macs with those powerful 68000 processors and a whopping 16 MB of RAM. The coolest thing he found was this little program called Adobe Illustrator 88 that soon went to version 3.0, and shortly thereafter settled down at version 3.2. He didn't feel comfortable learning all the necessary computer skills at the office, so he decided to make a purchase for home use. He got a Mac IIsi with 12 MB of RAM, a 100-MB hard drive, and a StyleWriter printer on a special sale for only $5,000.

Benfanti's been working with every version of Adobe Illustrator since version 88. Today he says, "The computer is my ultimate tool. I still doodle on paper and I still create 'roughs.' But my style and approach depend on technology. Overall, working digitally gives the illustrator much more control over the flow of work and its ultimate production. I used to have to rely on so many other disciplines to complete a project. Now I can control all the aspects in a project that I care to and never be afraid of revisions." To effectively control his illustrations on a computer, he now uses a dual 500-MHz Macintosh computer with 1.37 GB of RAM.

Sheep | Concordia House Publishing

Groovy Tubes *Bug Blast* book | Innovative Kids

Every project he creates is different in one way or another. However, he always begins by asking clients to produce a rough thumbnail sketch of the work they want. "I generally try to get a client to provide me with a sketch of what they're envisioning. I hate guessing, and I find that even the most crude napkin sketches provide information that is sometimes just too difficult to describe verbally."

From the rough illustrations provided by the client, he develops conceptual sketches. "I still generally doodle out a pencil sketch for myself, but rarely present it to a client. I find pencil sketches leave too much for interpretation." He uses the scanned pencil sketches as templates in Illustrator and quickly roughs out a color sketch. The first round of sketches includes rough composition and a color palette that he'll use in the final artwork.

He generally saves the roughs as JPEG or PDF files and sends them via email to the client. Clients, such as book publishers, can drop a work-in-progress into their layouts.

Cootie | Milton Bradley/Hasbro

Mat used with a Hasbro novelty compound product | Hasbro

JustBee | self-promotion

He believes the clients have a better sense of comfort knowing the designs are in process and they won't have to anxiously wait for the final delivery. Benfanti rarely sends a pencil sketch to a client, preferring to show them color layout comps. He finds that it's easier for his clients to visualize the end product and it makes the whole process more enjoyable for them.

Changing an illustration midstream is a necessary evil for illustrators. This is perhaps one reason Benfanti is so fond of a program like Adobe Illustrator. He's sensitive to his clients' needs. "I know many designers and art buyers feel their control of the process is limited, so I try to remain as flexible and accommodating as possible," he says. "We rarely meet face to face, and I know when they contract me there's a lot of blind faith in my abilities to pull off something that makes them look good, let alone the possible embarrassment they face if I screw up. Communication throughout the process is critical. Changing as you go is much easier than starting over once you've finished."

Cootie Group anniversary packaging | Milton Bradley/Hasbro

When the final artwork is ready, Benfanti sends his files via FTP, email, or sometimes overnight on CD-ROM. "The process is much faster than ever before—some projects span weeks; some are completed literally within hours of the first contact with a client."

What's the most difficult part of the process for Russell Benfanti? "Being able to watch TV while I'm doing it," he jokes. "Actually, I think it will always be the same issue—managing the process. Knowing what I've just proposed will take 20 to 30 hours, but only having 8." What he enjoys most in Illustrator 10? "I've fallen in love with some of the new 'Photoshop' functions, like the transparency and blur tools. Much of my style in the past was based on artificial transparency. This was quite challenging in previous versions, but now I find myself almost giggling at how easy it is to accomplish those things."

Hide, Clyde cover | ipicturebooks

The Project

The art director at Winslow Press was looking through *The Workbook*, saw Benfanti's ad and loved his style. He contacted Benfanti's agent, who asked if Benfanti would be interested in illustrating a 16-page children's book. Up to that point he had done some book illustration for Scholastic, but nothing that was considered a high-end "trade" book. Benfanti reviewed the copy for the story and then met with the publisher for a brainstorming session. Since the client was already sold on the look and feel of the illustrations, based on his style, they cut him loose to start the project. The entire project took approximately 400 hours. Each complete illustration took an average of 15 to 25 hours, with the pace accelerating as he went along. Benfanti finished all of the illustrations, exported them as PDFs, and sent them to Winslow for approval. The final files for output, due to their large size, were burned on CDs and mailed to the client. In addition to using the illustration for the book, Winslow Press also took Benfanti's layered files and produced Flash animations for their Web site.

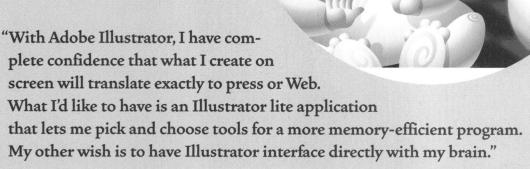

"With Adobe Illustrator, I have complete confidence that what I create on screen will translate exactly to press or Web. What I'd like to have is an Illustrator lite application that lets me pick and choose tools for a more memory-efficient program. My other wish is to have Illustrator interface directly with my brain."

—RUSSELL BENFANTI

The Steps (Entire Illustration)

Step 1: Develop digital comp. The book Benfanti illustrated is unique in that the entire story takes place in one room. He adds another element to the room on every page of the book. For example, the book begins, "This is the chair..." It then goes to, "This is the tray that hooks to the chair..." From there it evolves to, "This is the bowl that's put on the tray that hooks to the chair..." and so forth. The perspective from which the reader is viewing the room may differ, but it is still the same room with the same elements in the same positions (**Figure 15**). "Everything stays static in the illustrations, except for the cat and dog who are creating the action. It is almost a freeze-frame effect."

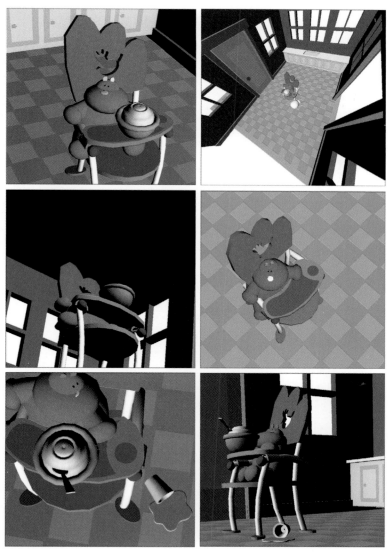

Figure 15

Another unique aspect, not found in many other children's books, is that events are also happening outside the page trim. For instance, Illustrations are cropped so that you get just a peek of the dad's and cat's heads, but you know that they're sliding on the kitchen floor just out of your view. To make the illustrations visually interesting and consistent, he wanted to get a firm grasp of how the room would look from all angles and from the perspectives of the various characters. To accomplish that feat, rather than starting with traditional pencil sketch thumbnails, he generated 12 digital comps using Adobe Dimensions (Adobe's 3D drawing program) and built what he calls his "set" to create his initial roughs.

Step 2: Trace individual characters from templates. Upon approval, Benfanti started by developing each of the characters in the scene. After making some rough pencil sketches of the characters, he scanned them and saved them as JPEGs. He then created a new 12-by-12-inch (final trim size was 10 by 10 inches), CMYK Illustrator file (he drew each character in a separate file), imported the scanned JPEG into Illustrator, and placed it on a separate locked layer. He used the sketches as reference for his illustration.

Step 3: Add fills and gradients to each character. Benfanti considers every element a character, whether it's animate or inanimate. He drew the bear first, then the chair, tray, bowl, oatmeal in the bowl, spoon in the oatmeal, cup, dog, and cat. He then drew the dad, mom, and

Figure 16

baby. In the drawings, he tried to develop the personality of each character. Benfanti began by working in Outline mode with a Wacom drawing tablet and stylus. Using the Pen tool, he drew the first shape of the character, using just a black stroke to ensure that the points and Bézier curves would be perfect. After refining the path, if needed, he then switched to Preview view and used the Gradient palette to mix the gradient he wanted to use for that particular shape. Because of the dimensionality of Benfanti's illustration, he fills almost every shape with a gradient of some kind. Although he does use blends, Benfanti prefers to use gradients because he can make global changes quickly. He reuses the same gradients, by creating swatches in the Swatches palette, and applying them throughout the set of illustrations. He adjusts the sliders and midpoints to get the correct shadowing and highlighting.

After the gradient was complete, he selected the shape and filled it with color, using the Gradient tool. In choosing a color palette, Benfanti says, "I chose a dominant color that each character could call their own. Color is extremely important to me." Benfanti achieves unusual vibrancy in his color palette. His says the secret is to use black rarely. "I feel that adding black dirties up the colors. I almost exclusively use cyan, magenta and yellow, even for the shadows." After drawing and coloring the basic shapes that comprise the character, Benfanti then adds the details (such as facial features) and finally any shadows, reflections, or ghosting. He drew each of the characters in what he calls the "classic view," the whole character viewed from the front. In addition to using these classic view characters in the main illustrations on each page, he also used them as icons in place of the words in the book (**Figure 17**). He completed each character, saved the files as PDFs, and emailed them to the client for approval.

Figure 17

Step 4: Add perspective in Adobe Dimensions, and mask objects. Upon approval and after making slight revisions, Benfanti launched Illustrator and opened the file he had saved as EPS from Adobe Dimensions. This file represented the perspective from a particular character's point of view. He positioned the Dimensions drawing as the bottom layer and used it as a template to redraw the shapes composing the room. Once the room was complete, Benfanti copied and pasted the character into the room. For the final step, Benfanti created a square, 10.643 by 10.643 inches, placed it on new layer and positioned it at the top of the Layers palette. He then selected all of his elements and chose Object > Clipping Mask > Make and masked all of the elements into the square.

Figure 18

The Steps (The Cat)

Step 1: Adding gradients and shadows to illustrate perspective. As described earlier, Benfanti created a new 12-by-12-inch CMYK file in Illustrator. He then placed the scanned rough sketch of the cat on the bottom layer to use for reference. Using his Wacom tablet and stylus, Benfanti drew the head of the cat with the Pen tool. Aside from the Ellipse and Rectangle tools, Benfanti almost exclusively uses the Pen as his weapon of choice, enjoying the precision and control it gives him in creating the shapes. Using the Color palette with CMYK sliders, he mixed three shades of orange, using various percentages of magenta and yellow, for the head and stored them in his Swatches palette. Then, in the Gradient palette, Benfanti used those same colors and created a radial gradient of light to dark orange. Next, he used the Gradient tool, dragging from the top of the head to the bottom, to fill the head with color. Benfanti achieves the feeling of dimension by being an expert "Mix Master" in creating gradients, from initially mixing just the right shades for his highlights, midtones, and shadows, to knowing where to adjust the midpoint sliders between these shades. He also drags the Gradient tool through an object and observes the effect. If the transition of color and blending isn't satisfactory, he redraws the gradient and examines the results. He continues to redraw gradients on an object until the blend and shade produce the effect he wants. Benfanti doesn't use a Pantone color chart. His experience and familiarity with his workflow and equipment have allowed him to view his color on the monitor and get satisfactory output.

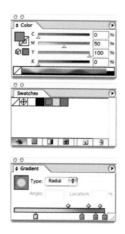

Figure 19

Step 2: Adding objects to separate layers. He created the outside left ear, mixed and created another gradient (with the same colors he used for the head), and filled the shape with color. He then copied and pasted the outside ear, scaled it slightly smaller with the Scale tool, and positioned it inside the outside ear. Again, Benfanti used the same colors and created the gradient for the inside ear and filled it. Benfanti then created a new layer for the right ear. Why does the right ear warrant its own layer? Because he wanted to later apply a Gaussian blur to the ear in order to create some additional depth. Benfanti repeated the same steps he used for the left ear.

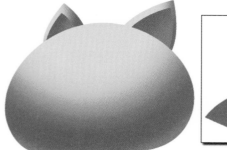

Figure 20

Step 3: Copying, pasting, and masking objects. Next Benfanti tackled the stripes on the face. First, he copied and pasted the head. He then created the actual stripes and placed them on top of the head. He selected both paths and then chose Object > Clipping Mask > Make. The mask allowed the stripes to match up perfectly with the edge of the head. Benfanti mixed a few additional shades of orange, stored those colors, created the gradient and filled the stripes.

Step 4: Adding detail to the face with strokes, shadows, and transparency. He then added the details to the face starting with the eyes, eyebrows, nose, and whiskers. Benfanti created the eyes with the Ellipse tool, and the eyebrows, nose, and whiskers with the Pen tool. He mixed new colors and stored them in the Swatches palette, and created new gradients for the eyes, nose, and whiskers. Next, Benfanti created the shadows behind the eyes and applied a solid medium orange. To create the transparent eyebrows and whiskers, he filled them with a solid light orange. He selected them all and in the Transparency palette, chose the Multiply blend mode. Says Benfanti, "I often use Multiply to create transparency. For the most part, I just like the look that the blend mode creates versus lowering the Opacity setting." He created the shadows for the whiskers and the nose, filled them with the same orange as the eyebrows, and also applied the Multiply blend mode.

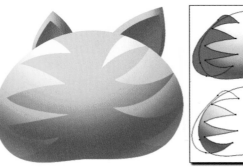
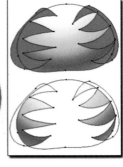

Figure 21

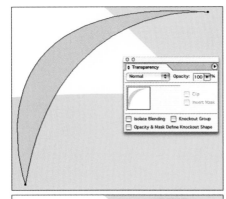

Figure 23

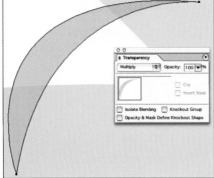

Figure 22

Step 5: Duplicating shapes. Next Benfanti moved on to the mouth. He first created a kidney bean shape for the outside shadow of the mouth. He mixed and stored a dark orange and filled the shadow with solid color. He then duplicated the shape and offset it to create the bottom highlight. Again, he mixed a light orange, stored it, and filled the highlight with solid color. Next, Benfanti duplicated the shape again, scaled it slightly smaller, and placed it inside the outer two mouths to create the inside mouth. He then mixed a dark, near black color in combinations with the same dark orange created earlier, made another gradient, and filled the inside of the mouth. With the Ellipse tool, he created the tongue. Benfanti mixed and stored shades of pink and purple, created the gradient, and then filled the tongue. Next, with the Pen tool, he created the teeth, mixed and stored a shade of blue, created a blue-to-white gradient, and filled the teeth. He copied the inside mouth shape and used it to mask the teeth and the tongue so that they would appear only inside the mouth. Finally, he created the shadow under the face and filled it with a solid dark orange.

Step 6: Creating the torso with strokes and gradients. After the face was complete, Benfanti created the torso and the tail. He mixed a few more shades of orange, stored them in the Swatches palette, and created the gradients. To create the stripes on both shapes, Benfanti used the same technique as the stripes on the face. He duplicated the shape, drew the stripes, and then created a mask, which allowed the edges to match up perfectly.

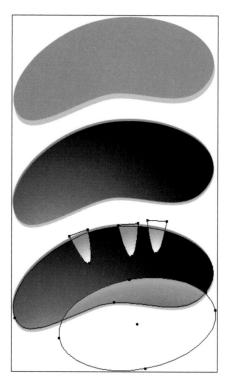

Figure 24

Figure 25

Figure 26

Step 7: Creating stripes and swirls. The final components to be drawn were the legs. Benfanti created the shapes, mixed and stored a couple additional shades of orange, created gradients, and filled the legs. He also used masks to create the left back paw and the stripes on the legs. Besides the use of gradients, another Benfanti signature style element is the use of stripes and swirls. In the final illustration (**Figure 30**), swirls appear on the bowl, the oatmeal, the dog's paw and in the spilled juice.

Step 8: Adding a shadow to the main figure. After the cat was complete, Benfanti duplicated it in its entirety, with the exception of the right ear. He put the duplicate cat on a new layer, offset it, and, in the Transparency palette, set the Opacity to 50% to create the ghosted shadow (**Figure 28**). He repeated the steps with just the right ear, again, isolating it so he could later apply a Gaussian Blur. He stacked the ghosted shadow layer underneath the cat layer. Next in the stacking order was the ear's ghosted shadow and then the ear layer (**Figure 29**).

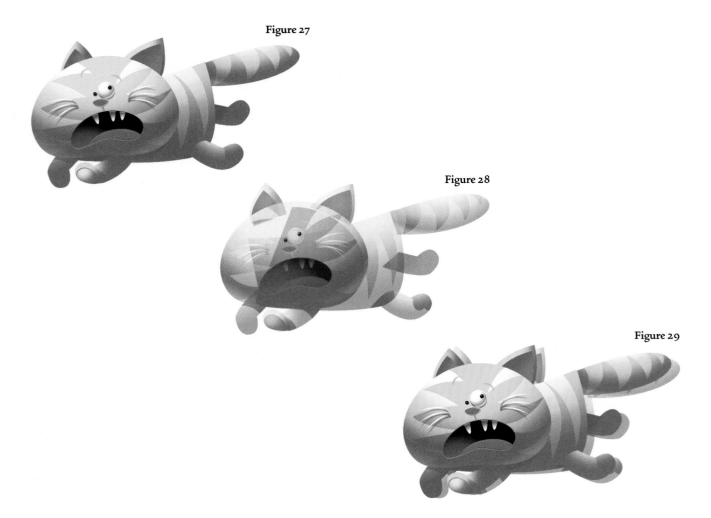

Figure 27

Figure 28

Figure 29

Step 9: Masking the illustration. Benfanti went on to finish the other elements in the illustration—the dog, the chair, the bear, and the background. He created a rectangle 10.643 by 10.643 inches on the topmost layer with the Rectangle tool. This dimension accommodated a sufficient bleed for the final trim size of 10 by 10 inches. He chose Select All and created a mask, which neatly framed the illustration and hid elements outside of the masking rectangle.

Step 10: Exporting to Adobe Photoshop. After the entire illustration was complete, Benfanti wanted to add a little more depth and dimension and to selectively focus on the actions of the cat and dog. Benfanti chose File > Export and selected the Photoshop (PSD) file format. In the Photoshop Options dialog box, Benfanti selected the High Resolution and Write Layers options. This allowed him to export the file while retaining the Illustrator layers. In Photoshop, Benfanti then applied progressive amounts of Gaussian Blur (Filter > Blur > Gaussian Blur) to various elements. The backmost layer of the room background has the most blur (a higher pixel radius), while the frontmost layer of the cat's ghosted image has the least. "I like using blur to create a greater depth of field. It also allows the commotion between the cat and dog to pop." And to further accentuate the action between the cat and dog, Benfanti added a slight motion blur (Filter > Blur > Motion Blur) to the cat's right ear and to the dog's ghosted leg.

Figure 30

Figure 31

Using Transparency in Illustrator

One of the truly great features of Adobe Illustrator 9 and 10 is the use of transparency—*real* transparency. Since version 9, Illustrator has been built on core PDF technology, which lets you save Illustrator files with true transparency. True transparency also means that the transparent objects are live and editable, giving you lots of flexibility and creative freedom. Unfortunately many artists avoid using transparency because of problems they've experienced at imaging centers. To help ensure success you must deal with two issues: first, the creation of transparent objects; and second, submitting proper files to imaging centers.

Transparency can be created in a few different ways in Illustrator 10. First, you can simply select your object and lower the Opacity percentage in the Transparency palette. The lower the opacity, the more transparent the object. This is the method Benfanti used to create the ghosted cat. You can also use the blend modes. Blend modes are algorithms that change how the colors of one object interact with the colors of the objects beneath them. While not officially a Transparency feature per se, artists such as Benfanti use blend modes in lieu of the Transparency slider to create a transparent feel. To test this out, select an object and choose your desired blend mode from the pop-up list in the Transparency palette. Benfanti used the Multiply blend mode on the cat's whiskers and eyebrows, which intensifies the darkness of the blended objects. Finally, you can use opacity masks. Opacity masks are similar in concept to layer masks in Photoshop. Opacity masks offer more flexibility in that they allow you to achieve different levels of transparency over an object or objects. To use an opacity mask, place a masking object over your artwork. Where you want your artwork to show fully opaque, you apply white to the mask. Where you want to completely hide your art, you apply black. And where you want art to show partially, you apply a percentage of gray—50% gray is the equivalent of 50% transparent. A great way to create a masking object is to use the Gradient Mesh tool. Once your masking object is complete, select it and your artwork, and choose Opacity Mask from the Transparency pop-up menu. Regardless of how you use transparency in Illustrator, it can be applied to fills, strokes, text, patterns, and even graphs.

The second issue related to properly producing transparent effects is considering the output and file format you use to submit the final artwork to imaging centers. If you save an Illustrator file in a format that doesn't support transparency, such as Illustrator 8, Illustrator 8 EPS, PDF 1.3 (Acrobat 4), PICT, or WMF, among others, the transparency is substituted with a simulated transparent effect. It's not the true

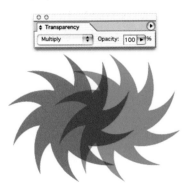

Original shapes

transparency that was created in Illustrator. What happens is that transparent objects go through a process called flattening and get broken into chunks consisting of both vector and raster objects. How the artwork gets divided into these two camps depends on the complexity of the artwork. You can also somewhat control how Illustrator makes this determination by adjusting the settings in the Transparency section of the Document Setup dialog box (File > Document Setup). The key to success in using this dialog box, if you must flatten an image, is to move the slider to the far right end. If the Resolution box is active, select 300 dpi. Now, while the flattened artwork may *look* transparent, it is really an illusion. All edibility is lost and results can include some less than crisp edges (due to rasterization) and slight color shifts. Saving the file as an Illustrator 10 EPS creates a hybrid file. The transparency data is saved, which keeps it intact and editable within Illustrator. However, the format also includes the EPS data, which is flattened. Therefore, if you import the EPS into QuarkXPress, for example, only the flattened EPS data is used.

If you wish to preserve transparency, stick with the native Illustrator 10.ai format or the PDF 1.4 (Acrobat 5) format which will honor the transparent objects as you designed them. Unfortunately, you may do all you need to preserve Illustrator transparency, but the imaging center where you send your artwork for color separations may turn your native Illustrator file into an EPS in order to print to their devices. More often than not, imaging centers and print shops avoid printing directly from Illustrator, because results may be unpredictable.

Before submitting Illustrator documents to imaging centers, be certain to discuss with the technicians how they will produce your color separations. Often you'll find saving Illustrator documents as PDFs the most desirable. PDFs retain transparency and preserve the type in your designs. In fact, what many people don't realize is that PDF is now Illustrator's native format, not EPS. Imaging professionals will be more likely to separate the PDFs rather than convert to EPS and print through a page layout program. However, even submitting PDF documents require you to have a discussion with the imaging people. When you know what they're doing on their end, you can rest assured that what you provide to your service center will be properly printed and retain the design attributes you expect.

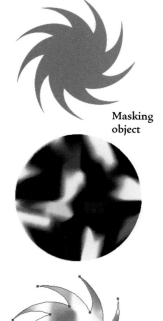

Masking object

Masked star

Chapter 4
Trade Show Displays

Artist

Martin French
Illustrator, Art Director, Designer
Sisters, Oregon
www. martinfrench.com

Project

U.S. Winter Olympics Murals

Client

Bank of America

Illustrator Tools and Techniques

Pen Tool, Layers

Opposite: Diver | *Physical Magazine*
Editorial illustration for an article on training
and nutrition

Martin French
A Touch of Gold

Martin French approaches design and illustration like Dustin Hoffman approaches a new film role. French gets intimate with his work, beginning with research, inspiration, and study while he's coming up with a new concept. He'll play music, study the masters, and read manuscripts and articles before he starts his sketches. By the time it comes to concept development, he understands thoroughly where his clients are and where he wants to take them.

If you've spent much time hitting buttons on a video game, you've probably come across some of French's illustrations. That's because after graduating from the Art Center College of Design in Pasadena (with a BFA in Illustration), his first job was with Atari in Silicon Valley. His designs of colorful video characters led to a job at Microsoft Corporation, where French

Peace | *Foreign Policy Magazine*
Editorial illustration for an article on conflict in the Middle East

spent eight years as an illustrator and design director for a kids' software division.

When French resigned from Microsoft in 1996 and went solo, he decided to move to an environment that was more inspiring than city life in Seattle, Washington. He moved to the rural town of Sisters, Oregon, nestled in the Cascade Mountains.

"Sometimes, deadlines don't allow me to step away from the project if it's just not happening. I have to be very aggressive and focused to make sure the image gets to that magic place that I know it's going to work. Then I can step back and take a breath."

"I had a clear vision of what I wanted my body of work to look like. So, I closed the door to pursue that. I don't know how long I will be this removed, but so far the change has been really positive. I have been able to let my work be mine and I have been true to what I want to do. If your work is good, people will notice you."

Drum | *Northwest Reach*
One of a series of posters dealing with kids, music, and cultures

Harp | Rockport Rythm and Blues Festival
Poster and clothing design

French opened his own studio in the wide-open spaces away from city influences and has been designing and illustrating as a freelance artist ever since. His client list includes a diverse group that ranges from corporations such as Bank of America and Honda to children's books and magazine publishers. In recent years he's acquired numerous awards, including a Gold Medal from the Society of Illustrators in New York. His work is consistently shown in art book annuals and feature articles.

Beginning a career with high-tech companies such as Atari and Microsoft introduced French to computers at the crest of the computer revolution. However, his introduction to Adobe Illustrator wasn't until version 5.0. Even though he worked at Microsoft for eight years, his platform preference was Macintosh. "I've always been on the Mac platform—even while working in the center of the Windows universe." Illustrator got off to a slow start

Fandango | Fandango restaurant, Seattle
Sign and logo

Native American | The History Center/
Smithsonian Institution
Part of a series of images on native tribes in the northeast.

under Windows, so it's not surprising that Microsoft didn't let it in the door until Adobe came out with version 4.0. Using a computer hasn't changed much about the way Martin French approaches a new design project, it just extends his traditional methods. Computer illustration offers him more flexibility. "When I begin a project, I have a clear vision for the art I want to create. From the start, the computer gave me the opportunity to put on paper what was in my head and my heart." Heart is exactly what's evident in French's style and method. He begins a new project with intensive research and tries to develop an emotional sense for the piece. "The process begins with getting as intimate with the subject matter as I can. I read articles, manuscripts, and background material, and listen to music to develop an understanding of the event or project. I then try to supplement this research with a broader look at the project, search for cultural symbols, historical references, attitudes, and issues surrounding the subject."

French gains his influences from painters such as Joan Miro, Richard Diebenkorn, and Jasper Johns, and art from posters and comic books. He merges his love of design and composition with dynamic drawings of human form—flat shapes and colors alongside aggressive lines and brush strokes are characteristic in his artwork. Using a computer gives him the freedom to explore the merging of design and composition with human forms.

Freestyle | Bank of America
Image from the Olympic set

Speed Skater | Bank of America
Image from the Olympic set

Snowboarder | Bank of America
Image from the Olympic set

Once he has the inspiration and an emotional sense for the project at hand, he starts rough-ing out traditional thumbnails on paper, sketching various small, gestural studies. "These sketches allow me to visualize how the symbols and the images interact on the page and how I can design with their respective characteristics. With the thumbnails I'm exploring angles, crops, and design elements that will interact with the main subject matter."

From a series of rough thumbnail sketches, he selects three to four concepts and takes these to a more finished pencil sketch. He then sends the rough sketches to the client for approval. Like many artists, French provides no color comps before the project is commis-sioned. He discusses color with clients over the phone and refers them to portfolio exam-ples for an overall color scheme and color applied to individual elements. The client signs off on a sketch and then the work begins.

After approval from his client, French schedules photo shoots. He gathers secondary design elements, such as symbols and inspiration from master painters, that he plans to use in the final image. He uses final drawings, brush strokes, and textures as separate elements that he'll integrate in the final design. "I'm creating and assembling these separate graphics with the final composition in mind, making sure that each separate element will enhance and support the overall concept and design of the final image."

French finds the most difficult part of the process to be the work in Illustrator. "This is the most intense part of the process. It's often like a marathon to get the image to that place where I know it's going to reach its full potential. Sometimes, deadlines don't allow me to

Hockey | Bank of America
Image from the Olympic set

Figure Skater | Bank of America
Image from the Olympic set

step away from the project if it's just not happening. I have to be very aggressive and focused at this stage to make sure the image gets to that magic place that I know it's going to work. Then I can step back from it and take a breath."

The most enjoyable part of using a program like Adobe Illustrator for French is the process of exploring, defining, and refining the overall composition of the art piece. "Even though the fundamental design has been formulated in my mind and put on paper for approval by the client, the true 'making' of the image, creating subtleties and nuances of line and color, happens at this stage. I've had the finished image in my head for days or even weeks in some cases, and when I finally see it and it matches my original vision, there is nothing better."

**Dance| Portal Publications Limited
Poster for sale**

Backpack | *Backpacker* **Magazine,
Image for anniversary issue**

The Project

An art buyer for Bank of America was researching artists for the project and was familiar with French's work from source books and illustration annuals. The buyer called his rep and told him about the project and that French was in the running with a few other artists. The buyer presented previous work from all of the artists in the running to a committee from Bank of America and the Olympic Committee. The committee chose French and met with him for a brainstorming session. French had worked with many big-name clients before, but this project had enormous scope and breadth. "Being chosen for the project was great, obviously, but I got the most fulfillment from knowing why I was chosen. When a talented art director like Michele Rosen at Bank of America connects with my art on an emotional level and really gets what my work is all about so much that they want to use it for such an important project, then you know you're doing something right."

The six athletes that French would showcase were a downhill skier, a freestyle skier, an ice skater, a speed skater, a snowboarder, and a hockey player. The secondary images included Olympic medals, ice skates, mountains, a hockey mask, a bobsled, a curling stone

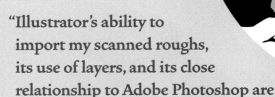

and four close-ups of athletes. French had created sports images in the past, so the subject matter was familiar. The art director was looking for images full of energy, passion, and movement, as if in pursuit of the win. The illustrations needed to have strong, dynamic visual impact, yet also attract a broad audience.

One of the most challenging aspects of the job for French was that he'd have to design images for a variety of formats—outdoor banners, the sides of trucks, posters and signage, and in interactive multimedia exhibits in the Olympic Village. The images had to be bold for large formats (up to 20 feet) and yet retain the subtleties and nuances of traditional brush and pencil strokes for smaller applications. He was given a deadline of one week for each illustration, from sketch to final. Because of the tight time constraint, he found that he couldn't spend an enormous amount of time thinking about the project, but instead had to derive the concept from the heart. He struggled with the fact that he had so many images (16 in all), so little time, and had to keep the bar of quality consistently high. But after he gave the client the first two illustrations, which they loved, he found the impetus to forge ahead.

"Illustrator's ability to import my scanned roughs, its use of layers, and its close relationship to Adobe Photoshop are what I enjoy most about the program. If I could ask Illustrator to do one more thing, it would be to automatically scan my artwork while I take a bike ride."

—MARTIN FRENCH

The Steps

Step 1: Creating a reference. French wanted to portray the skier "in the moment" to capture the movement and energy of a skier going into a hard turn. Because of the desire to catch that split-second in time, French did not have a formal photo shoot for the project. He also didn't want to draw from a photograph he didn't shoot. He felt looking at still photos, even if they portrayed a skier in a turn, didn't convey the motion he needed to capture. Instead, French watched videos of skiing. He wanted to get a sense of the movement of the athletes and also how their environment affected their bodies—how the snow flies off their poles and skis, how their bodies bend to hug the terrain. He posed a model only for the upper body positioning and used a Polaroid for reference in the sketch.

Step 2: Using sketches as templates. He started with six thumbnails of general poses, just small marker studies. He scanned them as EPS files and emailed them to the client. The client selected a pose that showed the skier coming towards the viewer. French tightened the thumbnail into two 14-by-17-inch graphite sketches on vellum. He scanned the two sketches, saved them as EPS files, and emailed them to the client (**Figure 15**). Upon approval, he placed the scanned sketches in Illustrator as templates, each one on a separate layer. Because he puts each element or set of similar elements on a separate layer, French typically uses several layers, between 10 and 15. The sketch on the top was the primary sketch, while he used the sketch on the bottom to render the right arm. Although French scanned the sketches and placed them into Illustrator, he didn't use them as an absolute blueprint. For example, he added the sun swirl which *wasn't* in the sketch, and he removed the pole, which *was* in the sketch.

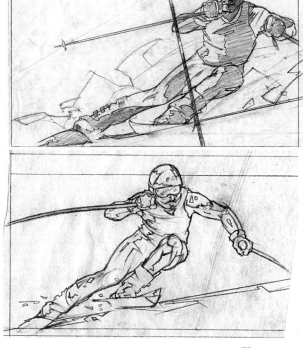

Step 3: Drawing the figure. Since French considered the figure to be the dominant element in the drawing, he started with the skier first. He also felt the placement of the figure within the frame of the illustration was an important reference to all of the other elements. French first created a layer for the skier. Using his template for reference, he drew the black portion of the figure with the Pen tool set to a 1-point black stroke and no fill. French spends a lot of time ensuring the line quality is true to his sketch—not true in the sense that it matches the template exactly, but true in that it doesn't lose that organic, loose feeling. He feels if you're not careful when using vector

Figure 15

paths, you can lose those subtle breaks and nuances of a pencil or paint stroke that make a hand drawing feel alive. "Sometimes I try to replicate the sketch template exactly, in other instances I veer off, but either way I try to make sure I don't lose that line quality, that I retain the broken edges. I am always balancing the two worlds between vector and sketch." (**Figures 16 and 17**)

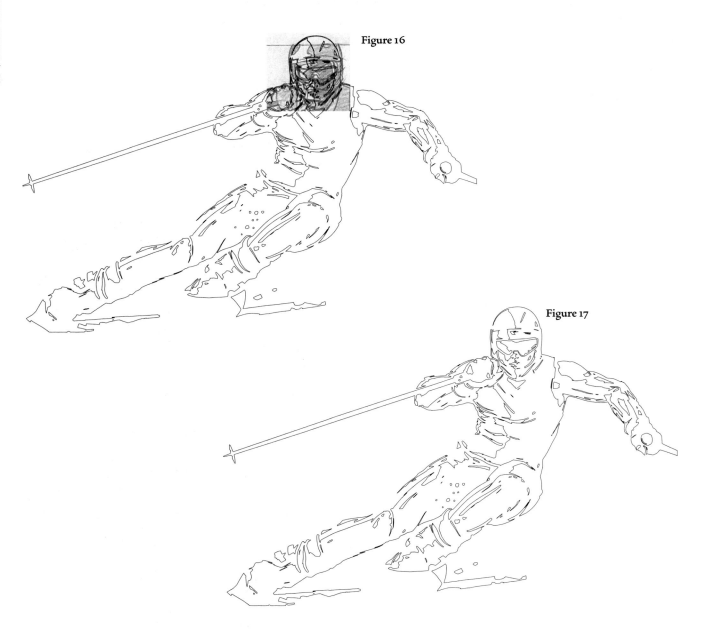

Figure 16

Figure 17

Step 4: Creating the background. Once he completed the figure, French moved on to the background shapes to show how they would play off the angles and lines of the skier. "I wanted to see how the background elements would break off the body." Because the background elements were either extremely loose in the sketch or not in the sketch at all, French created those shapes directly in Illustrator with no reference to the template. He created another layer and, again with the Pen tool, drew the first swoosh that would come across the left leg (**Figure 18**). He repeated the process, creating each swoosh or background element on a separate layer with the Pen tool.

He then created the swoosh that comes across the shoulder (**Figure 19**).

Next, he drew the swooshes behind the boots, off the right shoulder, and in the top left corner. He also added the spiral adjacent to the head (**Figure 20**).

French then moved on to the two background shapes on the left side of the illustration (**Figure 21**).

Figure 18

Figure 19

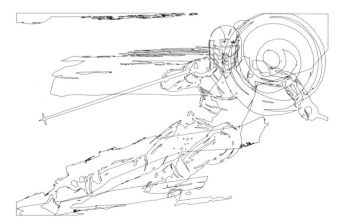

Figure 20

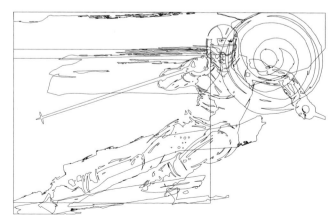

Figure 21

Then, he created the two background shapes in the bottom right (**Figure 22**). To finish the background elements, French added the snow swooshes and snow splats (**Figure 23**).

Step 5: Adding more shapes. With the background and most of the skier complete, French proceeded to create the shapes beneath and, in some cases, on top of the black portion of the skier. French created the shapes of the skier that would appear in white first. He then drew the shapes that would be colored blue, gray, and yellow, respectively, with the exception of the frame of the goggles (**Figure 24**).

French finished the illustration by creating the flesh colored areas of the face and the goggle lenses and frames (**Figure 25**).

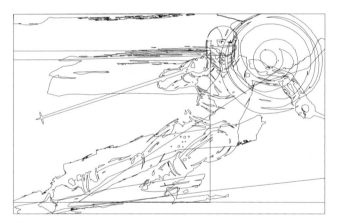

Figure 22

Figure 23

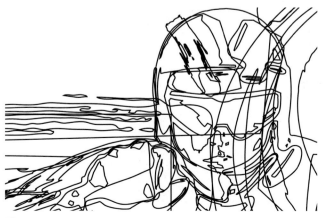

Figure 24

Figure 25

Step 6: Adding color. Finally, French applied color to all the elements, initially using spot colors in the Pantone Coated Swatch Library (**Figure 26**). He used Pantone colors so he and the client could discuss color options. Both French and the client agreed a cool color palette would work best. French decided to use teals, blues, and purples as his primary palette and then added two warm colors—red and yellow—as supplementary colors. After he decided on the spot colors, French then converted them to CMYK equivalents and played further with the CMYK sliders, shifting them cooler or warmer until they felt right, using his emotion as his guide. Although French usually flattens all his layers into one, he left the layers intact in the final file (**Figure 27**). The client wanted as much flexibility with the art as possible since it was being used in so many different applications. French deleted the sketch templates and emailed the file to the client. He also mailed a high-resolution print to allow the client to see the art exactly as he designed it with any color shifts that might occur between monitors and printers (**Figure 28**).

Figure 26

Figure 27

Figure 28

Spot Color Conversion to CMYK Color

In Illustrator, colors may be selected from a wide variety of color palettes, including Illustrator's vast number of spot color libraries. Like Martin French's illustration, the colors eventually need to be output to a CMYK device. You can make color conversion in several ways to produce process color separations.

If you wish to convert spot colors to CMYK equivalents in Adobe Illustrator, you can individually select objects in the Illustrator drawing and open the Color palette pop-up menu. From the menu choices, simply select CMYK. The spot color is then converted to its CMYK process equivalent (**Figure 29**). This technique works well when you have a few objects on the Illustrator page and wish to make color conversions. However, if you use a large assortment of spot colors, as French did, then you'll want to convert color globally for all objects in the illustration. To convert multiple spot colors to CMYK values, select all the objects by pressing Control-Command-A. Be sure to unlock any locked objects and layers before selecting all the objects. Select Filter > Colors > Convert to CMYK (**Figure 30**).

Be sure to save the file as an Illustrator EPS and check the CMYK PostScript option.

If you want to preserve all the spot colors and handle the CMYK color conversion at press time, you can elect to leave all the colors identified in their spot values. In a page

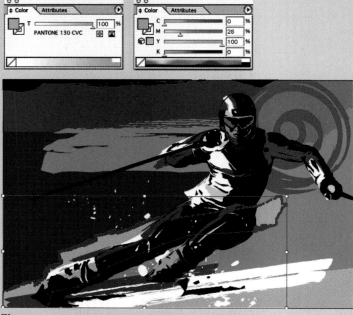

Figure 29

layout program such as QuarkXPress or Adobe InDesign (both great for outputting color separations), make a choice for color conversion from spot to process color at the time the file is printed. These choices appear in the respective print dialog boxes for the program your service center will use to print the separations.

Note: Few print shops and service centers print color separations directly from Adobe Illustrator. Service centers tend to use separating programs that offer a little more page and print attribute control than is provided in Illustrator itself. However, there's no limitation in using the program up to the print stage.

Another choice available to you is to save your Illustrator drawing as a PDF document. If colors are not converted to CMYK, you or your service center can use Adobe Acrobat to convert spot color to CMYK values at the time of printing. Unfortunately, printing separations and color conversion are not available within the core Acrobat features and require a third party utility to both print a color separation and instruct Acrobat to convert colors to CMYK values at the time the file is printed. For this activity, use a third party plug-in like Crackerjack (about $500) from Lantana (www.lantanarips.com). You can make color conversion via the Crackerjack dialog box much as you can with the separating programs mentioned above.

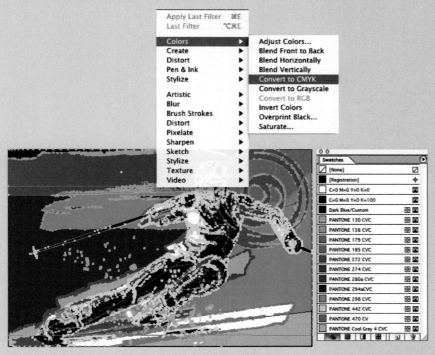

Figure 30

Chapter 5
Poster Design

Artist
Ellen Papciak-Rose
Illustrator, Designer
Johannesburg, South Africa
http://homepage.mac.com/inthestudio

Project
Poster

Client
Social Marketing Association (SMA), a non-governmental
organization that provides affordable health products and
education about HIV/AIDS and malaria
Windhoek, Namibia

Illustrator Tools and Techniques
Pen Tool, Brushes Palette, Pencil Tool

World Aids Day T-Shirt | Social Marketing Association

Ellen Papciak-Rose
Out of Africa

For Ellen Papciak-Rose, design inspiration comes from an intimate relationship with her audience—a relationship that has been developed through world travel and living among people in different countries. As a college student, she toured the U.S., Europe, and Asia. When she left the Southern Connecticut State University in New Haven, Connecticut with a degree in Art Studio, she signed up for a hitch in the U.S. Peace Corps, where she spent three years in Botswana, in Southern Africa.

The Peace Corps provides an individual experience in getting to the roots of a culture and viewing the world through the eyes of others. From "the toughest job you'll ever love," Papciak-Rose developed a style simple in design, yet strong in delivery. "I investigate the audience from as many angles as possible, such as how literate they are, their gender, and their age group. From this, I work on concepts or pretty much complete ideas and artwork, leaving nothing to client visualization." Her keen sense of culture and literacy, combined with the ability to deliver a clear message, are prominent in her work.

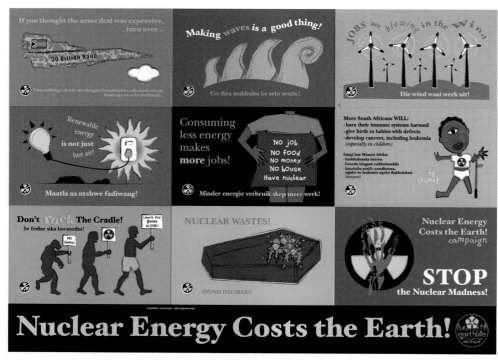

Earthlife Poster Expand | Anti-nuke campaign poster for Earthlife Africa. Each section was designed to be a postcard, printed separately, and sent to government officials.

After her Peace Corps tour she moved to Johannesburg, South Africa where she has garnered awards for designs dedicated primarily to social service and non-profit organizations. Her work can be seen in the Botswana National Gallery's yearly artists exhibition, South Africa's ABSA Atelier National Fine Art competition, and she has been a contributor to the *Illustrator WOW! Book* (Peachpit Press). She has illustrated art pieces for clients such as Unicef, *Newsweek* magazine, Americares/Homefront, the AIDS Law Project (ALP), Earthlife Africa, the Greenhouse Project, the Sustainable Energy and Climate Change Partnership (SECCP), Elance, the South African Department of Land Affairs, World Health Organization (WHO), South African Departments of Education and Health, and the National Association of People Living With AIDS (NAPWA).

> "My inspiration is based on my understanding of the audience. I act on particular cultural ideas and idioms. When I know as much as possible about the theme and who it's going to, then everything just sort of falls into place."

Mandela Haircut T-Shirt | Soweto Spaza; sold to tourists who visit Nelson Mandela's house in Soweto

Buskaid Poster | Buskaid, poster design for concert festival promotion

Computer illustration is relatively new to Papciak-Rose. "Up until the year of the iMac, I was still scraping away on my scratch boards and painting with gouache, having other people scan them and dropping them into their designed posters, booklets, and pamphlets. Upon purchasing an iMac and Illustrator 8, my life changed dramatically. I could not only illustrate on the spot but also design posters and have complete control over my work."

Untitled | T-shirt design for AmeriCares/Homefront

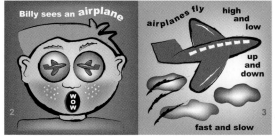

Children's Book samples | Book designs for Papciak-Rose

Ellen Promo Page | Self-promotion

CAA Front Cover | Book cover for Catholic AIDS Action (CAA)

Soweto ABC Poster | Poster for Soweto Spaza

When she begins a new project, she comments, "My inspiration is based on my under-standing of the audience. I act on particular cultural ideas and idioms. When I know as much as possible about the theme and who it's going to, then everything just sort of falls into place." She begins a new assignment with an in-depth conversation with an art direc-tor to clear up questions and understand precisely what the client wants, how the images should be portrayed, and details about the target audience. If a project is planned for a country she knows, and the content of the design—in terms of icons, symbols, and design elements—is within her frame of reference, she begins working in Illustrator. Papciak-Rose doesn't use sketches or templates. She starts her drawings in Illustrator immediately after formulating a concept and direction in her head.

Nelson Mandela House | T-shirt design for Soweto Spaza

Mandela House Postcard | Soweto Spaza

ALP Covers and Spots | Three booklet designs for the AIDS Law Project (ALP)

GTZ Relationship Cover | Booklet cover for German Technical Cooperation (GTZ)

For projects where the audience and culture are unfamiliar to her, she asks art directors for reference material, photos, and printed works related to the audience, demographics, and detail of the message to be delivered. After researching and reading material related to the audience and client, she develops a mental image of the piece and starts drawing in Illustrator. "When I have a vision in place, I get going. Feeling the emotions the overall illustrations are meant to portray helps set the scene for me. Once I have a mental visual of an art piece, I begin drawing in Illustrator."

Education Books Spots | Shuter and Shooter Publishing, Chapter Designs for Book Samples

The Project

"The project was to illustrate and design a calendar where the main image and message could be used as a standalone poster and also for a postcard for possible future use. The theme was malaria prevention, promoting the client's mosquito nets (Supanet), for a rural audience who lives near a large river in Namibia. I received the project because the client, Libet Maloney, of SMA (Social Marketing Association) in Windhoek, Namibia wanted something different and possibly funny that would grab people's attention long enough for them to read all the text. The SMA in Namibia produces materials and does education and training primarily about malaria and AIDS awareness. They distribute bright blue mosquito nets along with 'power' tablets—a repellant that you dissolve in water and use to soak the net. T-shirts went along with the calendar spreading another message concerning the mosquito nets—don't use them as 'drag nets' for fishing."

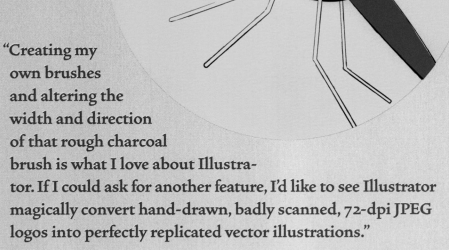

"Creating my own brushes and altering the width and direction of that rough charcoal brush is what I love about Illustrator. If I could ask for another feature, I'd like to see Illustrator magically convert hand-drawn, badly scanned, 72-dpi JPEG logos into perfectly replicated vector illustrations."

—ELLEN PAPCIAK-ROSE

The Steps

Step 1: Setting up the project. Papciak-Rose received an email from the client with a brief description of the job. "We then had a telephonic brainstorm session and she (Libet Maloney) emailed the final text to me and the two other logos that needed to be on the calendar. We also settled on the final size of the printed calendar as A1 (59.4 by 84cm)—a standard paper size here in Africa. As I have never physically seen one of these blue mosquito nets, I asked her for a photo and she faxed me a promotional flyer. We also discussed what the typical dwellings and environment looked like in her area." Consistent with her designs, Papciak-Rose wanted to know as much about the demographics and environment before she started her illustration. She asked about buildings and environmental icons and symbols to acquire a visual of the target environment.

Step 2: Creating the background. Papciak-Rose started the drawing by making a box, using the rectangle tool. She double-clicked the tool in the Illustrator toolbox and typed in the measurement for an A4 portrait (21 by 29.7 cm). The initial sketches fit within this size, so she could print them out on an inkjet printer. She found it easy to then scale up to A1, the final size, using the transform tool. To scale the drawing to final size, she selected all (including the A4 box) by pressing Control or Command-A, typed the new measurements, and clicked on the scale stroke weight checkbox in the Scale dialog box. She consistently toggled between the final size and a letter A4 size so she could judge how it would look at 100% and also print out a hard copy in the smaller size. To bring up the Scale dialog box, she double clicked the Scale tool in the Illustrator Toolbox (**Figure 16**). She clicked on the Preview button to view the scaled artwork before leaving the Scale dialog box and checked the boxes for Scale Strokes and Effects.

Step 3: Drawing the tent. She began with a couple sketches of the tent, using the Pen tool with a 1-point black stroke. Since this was to be the main feature, the proportions of the net and how it filled the poster size (A1), was important. Papciak-Rose needed to create the tent first in order to proportion all the other elements around this central object. She drew the tent freehand with the Pen tool and later applied brush strokes (see Step 10) to obtain a rugged edge on the lines (**Figure 17**).

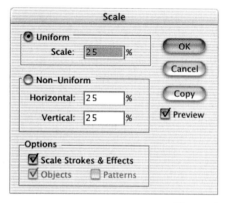

Figure 16

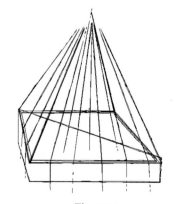

Figure 17

Step 4: Drawing the mosquito net objects. "I then drew the other elements in the calendar: cows, trees, houses. All these things were going to sit inside the net to assimilate a community being protected from malaria. I wanted them to be noticeable from a couple meters away so I made them quite graphic with minimal detail." She used the Pen tool to draw individual objects to capture the environment of the area where the poster would be displayed. She grouped each object and moved them to their positions. She could scale and move the grouped objects freely around the inside of the tent until she was satisfied with the design (**Figure 18**).

Step 5: Exporting to JPEG. "I then exported my sketches as 72-dpi JPEGs and emailed them to the client to make sure she was happy. She was pleased with the first round of illustrations I emailed to her." Papciak-Rose hid all objects, except the object she wanted to export as a JPEG file, by selecting the objects and choosing Object > Hide > Selection. She then selected File > Export to open the Export dialog box and chose JPEG from the Format pull down menu (**Figure 19**). After clicking Export, the JPEG Options dialog box opened and she selected 72 dpi for the resolution (**Figure 20**). By showing and hiding objects, she could quickly create multiple small JPEG files that were emailed to her client.

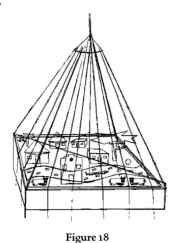

Figure 18

Figure 19

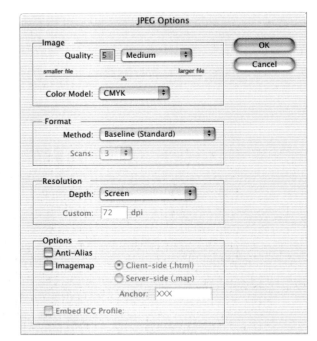

Figure 20

Step 6: Creating the calendar. After determining the space the net would occupy, she made the calendar, which occupied about 25% of the space. She left room on the left side for logos, which she would introduce later, and a few lines of text at the bottom of the poster. To create the calendar, she drew rectangles for each month, duplicated them, and created guidelines for the dimensions of each month. She added the text with tabs to provide equal spacing between the days of the month, and carriage returns for the vertical height between the lines of text. She exaggerated the divisions between the months with the same line styles she used for the tent (**Figure 21**).

Step 7: Illustrating icons. She wanted the illustration to be a scene at night—the time when the people of the area actually used the net—so she drew a bunch of stars and a moon with the Pen tool. Then she drew the mosquitoes. Again, she drew these objects freehand and shaped and rotated them with the transformation tools.

Step 8: Transforming objects. "I now had all the elements for the calendar and time to arrange everything. I wanted the mosquitoes to be exaggerated to show that even these huge mosquitoes couldn't get into a Supanet. The dead mosquitoes were killed by the repellant." She exaggerated the mosquito sizes using the transformation tools and moved the grouped objects to different positions until the design had the feel she wanted (**Figure 22**).

Step 9: Duplicating objects. She filled the box with black, sent it to the back, and played with the colors of the stars and mosquitoes. She drew a few stars and copied and pasted them, then reflected, rotated, and scaled them so they would all be slightly different. (In fact, since the deadline was so short, she drew only one cow and fish, and duplicated these as well.)

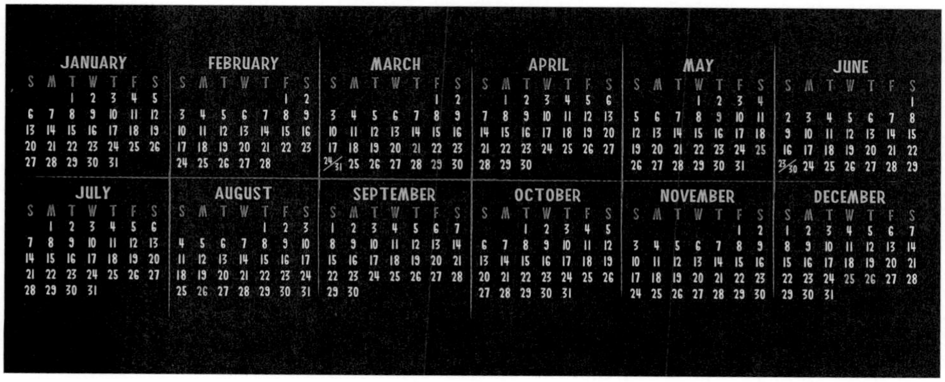

Figure 21

Figure 22

Step 10: Creating brush strokes. With the basic arrangement complete, she started with her favorite brush—the Charcoal brush. She double-clicked the brush in the Brushes palette and scaled the stroke weight to 50% to thin it out, made a copy, and flipped the copy so the brushstroke would go to the left and right. To apply the Charcoal brush to the strokes in the drawing, she selected the strokes and clicked on the Charcoal brush stroke in the Brushes palette (**Figure 23**).

Step 11: Color fills. "I applied the brush to all my outlines and filled illustrations with the swatch palette I made up. I wanted a sort of earthy brights look. I then made the stroke color on the illustrations to match their background colors. This gives a super scratch-boardy look. I love the organic nature of the overall feel."

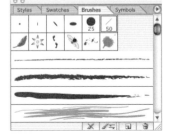

Figure 23

Figure 24

Step 12: Adding text. "Everything in the illustration is charcoal brushed except the text (**Figure 24**). I would have normally outlined the text (selected the text and converted to outline so it wasn't a font anymore) and brushed that as well, but since there was so much text, I needed to keep it clean and readable. That was especially important since English was a second language for the community." She added the text to the poster and eventually converted the text to outlines so that the printer didn't have to have the font used in the poster.

She copied and pasted the tent and some of the objects in the poster into a new document so that she could create T-shirts for the client (**Figure 25**). She used four spot colors in the T-shirt design for silk screening.

Figure 25

Creating Equidistant Spaces Between Objects

You may have a project like the calendar in Papciak-Rose's illustration with elements (such as the months) that must appear equidistant from each other and require precise placement on the drawing. Or, you might need to create a grid for a floor plan in which each square in the grid needs to be equidistant and set to a user-defined scale. In either case, Illustrator provides tools for easily establishing guides and grids with equidistant lines.

To create a grid, first draw a rectangle. If the center of the rectangle needs some guides, you can easily toggle to Outline view by selecting View > Outline or pressing Control or Command-Y. In Outline view, Illustrator shows the center point of all geometric objects with a small x, regardless of whether the object is selected. Drag guidelines to the center point to display a guide at the horizontal and vertical centers. Drag two additional guidelines to the top and bottom sides of the rectangle (**Figure 26**).

To create more guides for the divisions between elements—such as the months—spaced horizontally, first select the top side of the rectangle with the Direct Selection tool and press the Backspace or Delete key to delete the top line. Repeat the same steps to delete the bottom side (**Figure 27**).

Select the two remaining sides (vertical lines on the left and right side of the original rectangle). Select the Blend tool in the Illustrator Toolbox and click on one of the anchor points on one of the selected lines. Press the Option or Alt key and click on the same relative anchor point on the opposite line (for example, click on the top anchor point on the left line, Option or Alt-click on the top anchor point of the right line). The Blend Options dialog box opens after making the second click. In the case of Papciak-Rose's calendar, there are six columns. To create lines for six columns, enter 5 in the Blend options dialog box. Entering 5 creates the divisions but the total number of columns equals six.

At this point, you can create a template and move the lines you've drawn to a template layer or add more guidelines, using the blended lines as a template. If you choose the

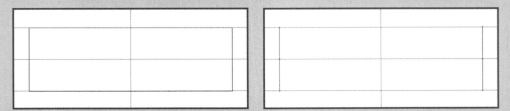

Figure 26   Figure 27

second route, delete the blend and all sides of the original rectangle. The result includes 12 evenly spaced squares (**Figure 29**). This method eliminates fumbling around with ruler divisions and trying to measure distances. If you want objects to snap to a grid, don't send the custom grid you make to a template layer. Select View > Guides > Make Guides and guidelines will be created by Illustrator that don't reside on a separate layer. All objects you draw will snap to the guidelines.

If you wish to create scaled drawings, follow similar steps to create a grid to scale. It's easy to create custom grids for any type of architectural design or illustration in Illustrator. Illustrator gives you a grid feature, but the grid lines are limited to horizontal and vertical. If you wish to draw isometric drawings or follow a rotated path, then custom grid lines might be helpful. By blending lines and using the rotation tool, you can create a grid at any angle (**Figure 30**).

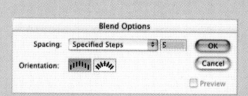

Figure 28

Figure 29

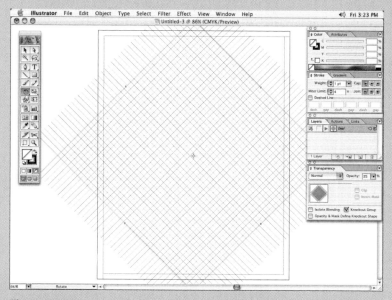

Figure 30

Chapter 6
Greeting Cards

Artist
Sarajo Frieden
Los Angeles, California
Designer, Illustrator, Fine Artist
www.sarajofrieden.com

Project
Birthday Greeting Cards

Client
UNICEF, Geneva, Switzerland

Illustrator Tools and Techniques
Pen Tool, Layers, Eyedropper Tool, Direct Selection
Tool, Pasteboard

**Opposite: ASTA Cover | Cover of a magazine for
American Society of Travel Agents**

Sarajo Frieden
Funky Bitmaps to Textural Designs

After graduating with a degree in fine arts from UCLA, Sarajo Frieden began her career serving beer in pizza parlors in Oakland, California, to support her work as an artist. She played the role of starving artist after college graduation, but soon returned to Los Angeles to work in graphic design with assorted design firms. After serving several years as professional designer she opened her own studio.

A self-taught graphic designer, Frieden has collected awards from the New York Type Designers Club, AIGA, Society of Illustrators in New York and Los Angeles, American Illustration, and

Portland Map | *Via* magazine

Communication Arts. Her work is also in the permanent collection of the Library of Congress. In addition to appearing regularly in publications such as *National Geographic World*, *Time Asia*, *QVC*, *Fortune Magazine*, *American Girl Magazine*, *Brown University*, *The New Yorker*, *Boston Globe*, *Pfizer Pharmaceuticals*, and *Doyle Partners*, her work has made its way into film titles, cookbooks, children's books, wallpaper designs, and more.

"When I first started getting commissioned illustration work, I had to work at not giving people what I thought they wanted. Whenever I did, the results, at least to me, seemed very uninspired."

Funny Transport | **Personal project for promotion**

No Ordinary Bird | **Personal picture book**

Hudson River Compilation | Individual spot illustrations for a brochure
and other marketing materials for a lower Manhattan music festival

Her introduction to a Macintosh computer began in the early days of the Mac with a Mac IIci and the first version of Adobe Illustrator. "The early Macs were like strange fashion accessories that hip studios just had to have, but weren't always quite sure what to do with. It was the era of funky bitmapped-looking print-outs." The funk was extended to sophistication when she grabbed a tablet, a light pen, and migrated to a more robust machine. For Frieden, working on a computer has been an on-again, off-again love affair. "Today, I would say it's very on."

Her background in fine art influences her current design style. "I love painting. I love the color and texture, and at the same time I like to be conversant in these different languages. They cross-pollinate and feed each other in surprising ways."

Adopt a Doodle | *American Girl* **magazine**

Hudson River Festival Bass and Woman | Poster and other
marketing materials for a lower Manhattan music festival

Hudson River Cover | Brochure cover and other marketing
materials for a lower Manhattan music festival

When she began her career as an independent illustrator and graphic designer, Frieden's first learning milestone was how to deliver an inspired illustration to her client.

"When I first started getting commissioned illustration work, I had to work at not giving people what I thought they wanted, because whenever I did, the results, at least to me, seemed very uninspired. So, I began trying to find a way to do the unexpected, to surprise myself, and ultimately the client." Inspiration and the unexpected is what she strives for in developing concepts for new projects.

Research for a new project may include studying theater, dance, music, cartoons, obscure Czech animation, art shows, and botanical gardens. "Sometimes research for a job is

Letters for Schurman | Custom type for a card company

the letter

Nº 5

FRESH ORANGES

EIGHTEEN-WHEELER

The letter "E" existed in the early Canaanite alphabet which developed around 1700 B.C.E. At the time, the letter was a consonant and it faced the opposite way. Within a thousand years, it had become a vowel. It's the most commonly used letter in the English alphabet.

EEL

ELEPHANT

ESCAPE

EYEGLASSES

The Letter E | Personal project for promotion

specific, as in hunting down the early versions of the *Jetson's* TV show, or looking at photographic references for a job on cadavers. It's best to possess a good sleuthing eye and know how to go about finding what you need. The Internet can be an amazing tool too." Design elements, textures, and colors from any one of these sources of inspiration may appear in a new illustration.

She further develops concepts from sources she may be exploring on her own and creates sketches that she ultimately shows to clients. Sketches may be in pencil or in Illustrator. "The advantage of using a program like Illustrator to create comps is the freedom of visualizing my ideas more quickly, especially in color, which means more time for exploring. With every design there are two objectives: Surprise myself and have fun. Without having fun, what's the point?"

Theolonius | Children's book

The Project

The United Nations Children's Fund (UNICEF) produces a full line of greeting cards and gifts that it sells through its Web site and catalogs. All proceeds from the sale of these items go toward improving the welfare of children worldwide. Elizabeth Gladstone, an art director for UNICEF, commissioned Frieden through her agent Lilla Rogers, to illustrate a single birthday card reflecting the themes of music, animals, and people. The card would also include the type Happy Birthday in various languages. Whenever she gets a job through her agent, the first thing Frieden does is contact the client and ask what they saw in her portfolio that they particularly liked. Because she has a number of different styles, she likes to narrow down the specific look that the client is after. In this case, Elizabeth did not indicate a specific piece or look, but instead liked the whole body of Frieden's work. They apparently liked what she did on this project as well because, when they saw Frieden's finished birthday card, they immediately asked for a second.

"I like to use Illustrator as a graphic design tool. It gives me freedom and flexibility in rendering many different shapes. If I could get it to clean and organize my studio and also provide me with a mix of Painter features for drawing textures, I'd have the perfect instrument."

—SARAJO FRIEDEN

The Steps

Step 1: Sketching on paper. To begin the project, Frieden spent a few days brainstorming and doodling. She finally settled on three preliminary pencil sketches and faxed them to Elizabeth Gladstone, an art director for UNICEF. Gladstone liked certain elements from the various sketches, so Frieden combined those elements, modified a few things, and created another sketch, which Gladstone approved.

Preliminary sketch

Step 2: Finishing the sketch. Frieden scanned the sketch in Photoshop at 150 dpi. She then used the Levels adjustment to increase the contrast of the image and saved it as a native Photoshop file. Next she created a new 8.5 by 11 inch CMYK file in Illustrator and placed the scanned sketch into the file on Layer 1. She didn't trace the scan exactly, but instead used it for reference and frequently hid it from view.

Final sketch

Step 3: Creating a color palette. Next, Frieden created her color palette. Using the paste-board next to her artboard as her digital desk, Frieden created a "color chip" by drawing a small square with the Rectangle tool. She then mixed her first color using the CMYK sliders and filled the chip. She repeated this process until she had her complete color palette (**Figure 14**). Frieden tries to limit the number of colors she uses, preferring to stick with a limited palette. "I feel it tends to negatively affect a piece if I use too many colors. I can make it stronger graphically if I work within a color family. I like using this chip technique because it allows me to see how colors interact in various arrangements, when they are apart, and when they overlap. It's also really fun for me to work with 'off' colors to see how I can get them to work together." In addition to color chips, Frieden uses the paste-board to store elements she has copied from other files or to try out different variations of elements she'll use in a piece. "Sometimes I even open up an entirely new file and play with a certain element. Then, when I like it, I'll copy and paste it into the final file."

Figure 14

Step 4: Creating the background. After she established the palette, Frieden created a new layer, grabbed the Rectangle tool, and clicked on the artboard. She entered 4.778 for the width and 6.778 for the height to create a background rectangle the size of the card, and clicked OK. She then selected the rectangle, selected the Eyedropper tool, and clicked on the brownish red color chip to fill the rectangle (**Figure 15**). Rather than use the Swatches palette, Frieden tends to use the Eyedropper tool to sample color to fill her elements. "I created the background rectangle first because I wanted to make sure the colors would work well against it." Depending on the project, Frieden will either fill her elements as she draws them or draw them with just a black stroke and fill them after the paths are complete. In this piece, she needed to see the elements filled as she designed her illustration. "I find that it's actually a good thing to fill my shapes as I draw them. That way the filled shapes cover the scanned sketch and I challenge myself when I draw the shape. If I happen to get a better idea for the element at that moment, then I will draw it that way instead of using exactly what I had on the sketch. Tracing is the death of a fresh-looking drawing."

Figure 15

Step 5: Adding the first elements. She created another layer and with her Wacom tablet and the Illustrator Pencil tool, she drew the top flower, bird, and the Happy Birthday type. Frieden created each shape as a separate closed path and then rearranged the shapes, using the Object > Arrange menu until she got the correct stacking order. "I use the Pencil tool a lot now. When I first started using Illustrator, I used the Pen tool almost exclusively. I was doing a lot of graphic design at the time, logos and things that required more precision. I find the Pen tool too rigid for me now. I am looking for the not-too-perfect line. I want it to be off a bit, so that it looks more hand drawn." When queried as to why she combined those elements on a single layer, Frieden responds, "Sometimes I work logically and sometimes I don't. I often create my piece intuitively, rather than in a really specific logical order. In this particular case, I drew these three pieces together because they were a similar color."

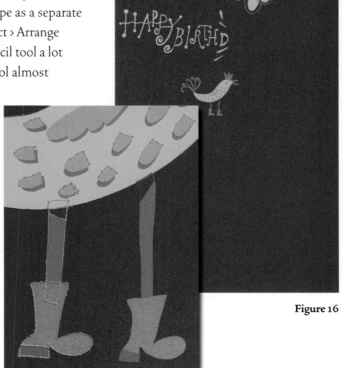

Figure 16

Step 6: **Getting shapes just right**. She created another layer for the trumpet player, the trumpet, three of the pink flowers, and the bar of the bicycle. While the light pink outline of the flower is a 1-point stroke, the stems and viney tendrils on the flowers are not strokes, but filled shapes. Frieden prefers using shapes, rather than strokes, even on thin elements because she can control the contours better, making the lines thick and thin where she wants. After drawing the stem or tendril, she zoomed into the element at a high magnification and used the Direct Selection tool to adjust the shape to her liking. "If I had to define my signature style, I guess it would be that I like decorative elements and I have a love of pattern. When left to my own devices, those elements will usually come through."

Frieden created another new layer and drew the bicycle for the trumpet player. Once again, all of the line details, including the spokes on the wheels, were created as shapes and not strokes, in order to retain a loose, organic appearance. "I like working with layers because I can build with my background and play by rearranging elements. Because my work is flat—there's not much shading or modeling—I try to add depth using layers and pattern."

Figure 17

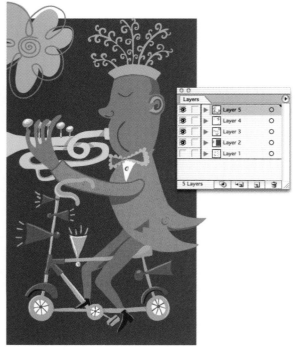

Figure 18

Step 7: Hand crafting type. She created yet another layer and drew the tuba player, the tuba, and the Feliz Cumpleaños type. All of Frieden's type was created with the Pencil tool. The hand crafted look of the type, with the same thin and thick strokes and curly embellishments as illustrations, lets her seamlessly integrate the type with the drawings. "Typography comes easy to me," she says. "I worked with type as a graphic designer, but when I started illustrating, I really shied away from using any type at all. I wanted to separate myself from that other world. But over the years, I have learned to play with type, and now type and illustration are completely merged."

Step 8: Creating the final layer. On the final layer she drew the girl, the saxophone, the flowers in the bottom left corner, and the Buon Compleanno and Feliz Anniversario type. She also added her signature in the bottom right corner. "When they gave me the specs for the job, there were a lot more languages, such as German and Japanese, that they wanted on the card. But the layout was already so dense. I talked it over with the art director and we decided to leave them off. The piece is stronger without them."

Figure 19

Figure 20

Step 9: Finishing up. Frieden cleaned off her artboard, what she refers to as her "messy desk," by deleting all the color chips and other elements. She deleted the scanned sketch, but left the layers intact and emailed the file to her client. She didn't worry about setting up the project for print. UNICEF handled the trapping and other prepress issues. The client had no changes to the design or to the colors. Even though it didn't turn out to be an issue, at the beginning of the project, the art director made it quite clear that she would consult Frieden about any color changes. "One color may look very different juxtaposed with another. In an illustration, colors don't exist separately, they exist within a world of other colors. As an artist, you have to look at it as a total piece. Elizabeth was sophisticated enough to realize the complexity of color dynamics. I am very fond of art directors and designers who realize that." Producing the card in Illustrator took her around seven hours.

Figure 21

Step 10: Creating a second project. Frieden was able to create the second card that UNICEF commissioned without a concept sketch since the organization loved the first card so much and since Frieden knew what they liked. She printed out a preliminary comp halfway through the illustration process, which she faxed just to double-check that she was on track. When Frieden emailed the final second card, again the client requested no changes, not that making changes is something that Frieden stresses about. "The great thing about digital art versus painting is that it is so easy to alter things. It makes me feel incredibly free and flexible. The idea of repainting something that I have done in gouache...well, it just doesn't happen. I mean it's not something that can be done without wrecking the entire job. Illustrator is much more forgiving."

Figure 22

Overcoming Printing Problems with Excessive Points on Paths

If you elect to use the Pencil tool or the Auto Trace tool or even another application, (such as Adobe Streamline) for auto traces, you run the risk of creating printing problems. In many cases, imaging centers with fast, powerful RIPs will be able to RIP and print your files. However, that one time when you need a file printed and express mailed to your client, you may find a PostScript error that rears its ugly head. At times your files can print fine on your laser printer, yet the imaging center will struggle to print your Illustrator files. To improve your chances, exercise care in the use of tools, such as the Pencil tool and auto traces.

Use of these tools produces an extraordinary amount of anchor points on paths. In Illustrator 10, the Pencil tool performs much better than in previous versions, however, you may occasionally find some problems with excessive use. Too many points on a path can overburden a PostScript RIP and render a file unprintable on many devices. There are some workarounds that you can use to improve your chances of successful output. After auto tracing a file or using the Pencil tool, select Object > Path > Simplify. This opens the Simplify dialog box, which lets you make the necessary changes regarding path attributes.

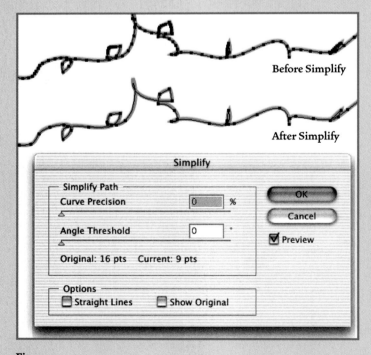

Figure 23

While in the Simplify dialog box, check the box for Show Original. The original drawing will be displayed in red while the changes you make to the path will be displayed in blue. Move the Curve Precision slider to the far right and you'll see the maximum points you can add to the paths. As you move the slider to the left, points are removed from the paths. Try to move the slider as far to the left as possible without altering your shapes to get the minimum number of points.

The Angle Threshold can change the shapes of arcs and curves. Try moving the slider back and forth to recapture any curves in the objects that you may have disturbed by moving the Curve Precision slider. By enabling the Preview check box, you can see the changes dynamically as you move the sliders. When finished with the edits, click OK and you are returned to the Document window. You can also simplify complex paths in Illustrator by selecting File > Document Setup and selecting the Printing and Export command from the pull down menu. Check the box for Split Long Paths. The resolution of the file won't change and the output results won't be affected. The paths will be split into sections so that a portion of the objects is sent to the RIP, processed, and the next portion subsequently delivered to the RIP, and so on.

When converting type to outlines, you'll run into the same problems with the auto trace feature. However, using the Simplify dialog box with type will cause display problems since our perception of type is much more precise than it is of objects. If designs require a large amount of points on paths or need the conversion of fonts to outlines, then save your Illustrator files as PDF documents. PDF files can reduce the complexity of a vector drawing and reduce some of the redundancy often found in PostScript. More often than not, you'll find PDF files are easier to image than EPS files.

When you save an Illustrator file as a PDF, be certain to include Preserve Illustrator Editing Capabilities. You can then return to the Illustrator file for editing by opening the PDF document in Illustrator.

Chapter 7
Advertisement

Artist
Amore Hirosuke
Tokyo, Japan
Designer, Illustrator
www.monster-mix.com

Project
Advertisement

Client
Screaming Mimi's—a vintage clothing store in New York City

Illustrator Tools and Techniques
Pen Tool, Pathfinder commands, Patterns, Align Palette

Opposite: Untitled | Editorial illustration for *Co's Magazine*, Human Planning

Amore Hirosuke
Illustrations from Japan

After graduating from Doshisha University in Kyoto, Amore Hirosuke became a freelance illustrator in 1986. His creative work is wide-ranging—illustration and graphic design for Web sites, advertising, magazine illustration, and store displays. Being a creative type, his talents are also extended to music. If you tour around the city of Tokyo, you might find Amore standing on a stage where he performs as a club DJ.

The name Amore was something he added after starting a band that played Boogaloo music over ten years ago. At that time, it was popular for artists to take on a another name,

Untitled | Poster, Aoi-Heya (nightclub)

although it was not common in Japanese culture. He is fond of the Italian language and thought "Amore" was apropos for a professional name in the music business.

Hirosuke has had seven solo exhibitions at such popular venues as Art Wad's in Shibuya, and Rocket Gallery, Key West Studio, and Space AD 2000 in Harajuku.

"The first step for me is to focus on the 'grooviness' of the subjects I want to illustrate, such as a female dancer in a funky outfit. Then I visualize the overall atmosphere and the color combinations before sketching on paper."

Untitled | Poster, Aoi-Heya

Untitled | Poster, Aoi-Heya

Untitled | Poster, Aoi-Heya

Among Hirosuke's many clients are Blue Note Label, *Seventeen* Magazine, Screaming Mimi's, *Nickelodeon* Magazine, Microsoft (Japan), NTT (Japan), FM Fukuoka (Japan), Vivid Sound (record label).

Both Apple Computer and Adobe Systems have been as active in Japan as they have in the United States for more than a decade. So, it's not coincidental that Hirosuke picked up a computer early in his illustration career. He's been working with Adobe Illustrator, starting with version 3.2, on a Macintosh computer since the early 90s.

"Using a computer made it much easier to create graphic and mechanical drawings without utilizing manual devices, such as rulers. This changed my approach to illustration, bringing it aesthetically closer to graphic design than if I were to use the traditional illustrator's technique of drawing on paper."

Untitled | Direct mail, Junowa

Untitled | Postcard, Club Jamaica

When Hirosuke begins a new project, it's creativity and fun wrapped up in a single package. "I personally enjoy illustrating figures, especially female figures. The first step for me is to focus on the 'grooviness' of the subjects I want to illustrate. For example, I'll create a theme, such as a female dancer in a funky outfit. Then I will visualize the overall atmosphere and the color combinations in my mind before sketching the ideas on paper. Once I have the idea formulated, I sketch the figure and the various possible backgrounds separately, using pencil and paper until I am satisfied."

"I scan in the sketches and add final touch ups, using Bézier curves. Then, I try different backgrounds in various compositions in different colors until the whole image settles in. The most important thing for me when working with clients with specific instructions is to enjoy drawing in and of itself. Instead of appealing to the clients by following their instructions exactly, I find a way to illustrate using my own sense of style."

Untitled | Direct mail, Junowa

Untitled | Poster, Aoi-Heya

Untitled | Poster, Aoi-Heya

"I enjoy the process of using Bézier curves the most because when I finalize touch-ups, the illustration begins to look more and more like the final printed work. This quick change can only be done on the computer and is one of the fun advantages of combining the computer and illustration."

Hirosuke finds the most difficult part of the process to be the color discrepancies between the computer image, his personal inkjet printer, and the offset printing, with the offset printing creating the most difficulty. Due to color variances among devices, he specifies color based on the final output device—in most cases offset printing. The colors printed from inkjets give an estimate of the final color, but he relies more on the color charts that he uses when he originally designs a piece.

Untitled | Editorial illustration, *Cancam Magazine,* **Shogakuan (publishing company)**

Untitled | Poster, Aoi-Heya

The Project

Amore acquired this job, the second illustration for his client Screaming Mimi's, from his agent Koko Nakano of CWC International in New York City. The client requested an illustration for a magazine print ad that would show a hip, young couple wearing the kind of retro clothing sold in the store. Screaming Mimi's emailed numerous digital photos of actual clothing and accessories from the store to Amore. Amore then sorted through the photos and mentally visualized the overall illustration with the goal of making the image look "groovy".

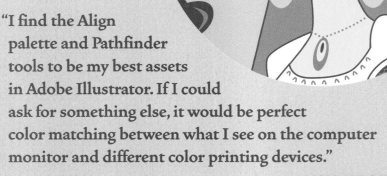

"I find the Align palette and Pathfinder tools to be my best assets in Adobe Illustrator. If I could ask for something else, it would be perfect color matching between what I see on the computer monitor and different color printing devices."

—AMORE HIROSUKE

The Steps

Step 1: Creating the sketch. Amore began the illustration by studying his chosen photos. He then sketched out a conceptual rough. "Based on the photographs, I drew the figures, trying to be aware of integrating a whole image and making it reminiscent of the mid-70's." Amore faxed the initial pencil sketch (**Figure 15**) to the client, who requested a couple minor revisions. They then approved the final sketch.

Step 2: Scanning the sketch. He scanned the sketch into Adobe Photoshop, saved it as a Photoshop file, and placed it into a new A4-size, CMYK Illustrator file. He created a layer with guidelines to use as a framing reference. With the rectangle tool, he drew two rectangles and then chose View > Guides > Make Guides.

Step 3: Drawing the woman. Using the sketch as a reference, Amore started the illustration by drawing the woman—the focal point of the composition—on a separate layer.

Figure 15

Figure 14

Figure 16

He began with her face (**Figure 16**), then moved on to her body and, finally, to the details, such as the jewelry. His tool of choice for almost 100% of his illustration work is the ever popular Pen tool. Amore usually uses either dark brown or dark blue for his vector paths. For this illustration, he mixed a dark process brown, using the CMYK sliders in the Color palette. He set his stroke to this color, leaving the fill with no color. "I started out by doing all of the vector line work first. Then, I went back and added color little by little."

Step 4: Drawing the man. Again, using the sketch as a reference, Amore drew the paths comprising the man on a separate layer. As with the woman, he started with the face, then moved on to his body, and then to the details. Amore uses layers for the major elements of his illustrations. That way, besides having the benefit of organization, he can lock the layers once he has completed the elements. This allows him to use the Select › Same command and choose elements based on similar stroke widths and other attributes, without affecting the completed portions of the drawing (**Figure 18**).

Figure 17

Figure 18

Step 5: Drawing the background. Amore decided on different size circles as the dominant element for the background. He created the circles with the Ellipse tool. "I wanted to create something geometric and kinetic for the background," he said. "I feel it turned out successfully and added some dynamism." Once he drew the circles , he then created a rectangle the same size as the inner guideline frame. Amore selected the rectangle and all of the circles that overlapped the frame and then clicked the Divide button in the Pathfinder palette. The Divide command created separate, closed shapes wherever the paths overlapped, allowing Amore to delete portions of the circles that lay outside the frame (**Figure 19**).

Step 6: Creating designs and patterns for the woman's clothes. Amore makes great use of the Pathfinder palette, using the Divide and Outline buttons when creating designs and patterns. Amore simplified the patterns of the woman's skirt and the man's shirt from his original sketch, wanting to stay closer to the actual photos of the clothing. To create the design of the woman's skirt, Amore first drew a gray circle on the pasteboard. He often creates detail elements and patterns in grayscale first, not worrying about applying the color until after he draws the elements. Amore leaves the original artwork for the pattern on the pasteboard so he can access it for modifications later.

With the Pen tool he created lines representing the petals of the rose. He selected the circle and paths and selected the Divide button in the Pathfinder palette, which cut the rose into separate shapes. He then pulled the petals apart leaving white spaces in between. For the stems, he drew a stroke of .7 points with the Pen. He used the Ellipse tool to create the leaves (**Figure 20 inset**). He clicked on the end of the oval with the Convert Anchor Point tool to give it a point. Amore created two variations of the rose design, selected and grouped the elements, and then scaled and positioned them on the woman's skirt. He selected the skirt and the elements of the design that overlapped the edge of the skirt and applied the Divide command again. He then deleted any portions of the design that protruded outside of the skirt (**Figure 20**).

Amore created the patterns, again initially in grayscale, of the woman's shirt by creating an oval with the Ellipse tool. He then duplicated the shape and rotated it to create a flower shape. He then duplicated the flower and placed it

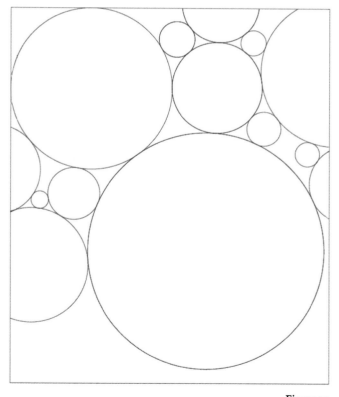

Figure 19

above the original. He duplicated the flower twice more, rotated the copies 45 degrees, and placed them to the right and left of the original, using a rectangle as a positioning guide (**Figure 20 inset**). He then selected all four flowers and chose Edit > Define Pattern. He created the second pattern for the shirt by creating a simple crosshatch using the Pen tool.

Finally, Amore used the rectangle tool to create a simple checkerboard pattern for the sandals. Once he created the patterns, Amore selected the shirt and sandals and filled them with their respective patterns.

Step 7: Creating the design for the man's shirt. For the man's shirt, Amore created one heart-shaped petal, again in the color gray. He then duplicated the shape and rotated it to create a flower. The stem is a path that he created with the Pen. To create the leaves, Amore created ovals with the Ellipse tool. He rotated and positioned them along the stem and then selected all of the elements and grouped them (**Figure 21 inset**). Next, Amore created several duplicates of the flower design, scaled and rotated them, and positioned them on the man's shirt. He then selected the man's shirt and the flower design on the top left, chose the Divide command, and deleted any portions of the flower design that lay outside of the edge of the man's shirt (**Figure 20**).

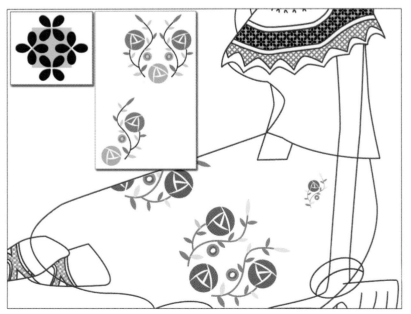

Figure 20

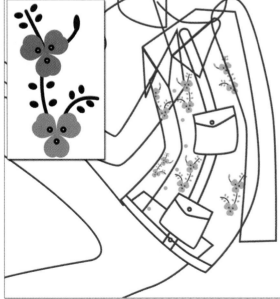

Figure 21

Step 8: Adding color. Amore mixed his colors using the CMYK sliders in the Color palette and saved them in the Swatches palette (**Figure 22**).

Step 9: Adding pattern and color to the background. To create the striped background rectangle, Amore created a pattern. He first drew a rectangle and filled it with white. Then, he created a single gray stroke from the top of the rectangle to the bottom, using the Pen. He Alt/Option-Shift-dragged the stroke to create the second stroke. From there, he used Object > Transform > Transform Again, which added copies of the stroke evenly spaced. He copied this design to two new layers, where he experimented with different color combinations, ultimately settling on two versions. He selected the striped rectangles on each layer and chose Edit > Define Pattern, creating three different stripe patterns (**Figure 23**). Adding color to the background elements was the hardest part for Amore. "It was difficult to create the best color combination for the background. I needed to have a color combination that made the figures stand out and, at the same time, look kinetic as a graphic element in and of itself."

Step 10: Adding the logo. On a separate layer, in the top left of the illustration, Amore added the store logo, which the client provided. He also drew a couple of flower graphics

Figure 22

Figure 23

with the Pen tool to frame the logo. He then applied color to the flowers. Finally, Amore added his credit line under the man's shoe (**Figure 24**).

Step 11: Creating a mask. Amore drew a rectangle the same size as the inside rectangle of the guideline frame. He selected the rectangle and his entire illustration and chose Object › Clipping Mask › Make. Being the perfectionist that he is, Amore created and saved a total grayscale version of the illustration on a separate layer, which contained the client's address and phone number (**Figure 25**). This grayscale version could be used for newspaper ads or other applications that don't require the color version. Amore finally locked all of his layers, saved the file (**Figure 26**), and emailed it to his client in New York City.

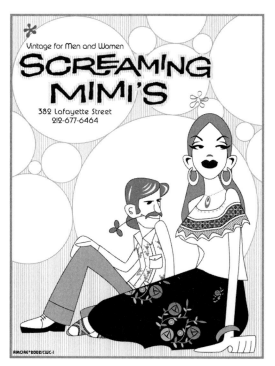

Figure 24

Figure 25

Figure 26

Using Illustrator Patterns

Hirosuke is a great fan of Illustrator's Define Pattern command. Using patterns can help you create the look you want with backgrounds, textures, and filled objects. Rather than recreate and duplicate objects, you can create an Illustrator pattern and fill any closed path with the pattern, much as you would fill an object with color.

Patterns you create with the Define Pattern command can't contain gradient objects, even if they're rasterized. However, you can get around these limitations by using blends that look like gradients.

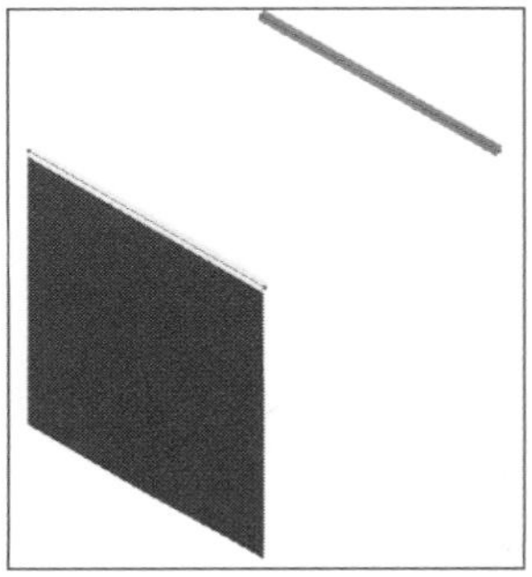

Your first step is to create the objects to use in the pattern (**Figure 27**). If you need to have a square or rectangle shape, draw the shape, transform the object as needed, and delete two sides by clicking with the Direct Selection tool. The deleted sides should be opposite the direction of the blend. For example, if the blend is vertical, delete the vertical lines in the square or rectangle so the horizontal lines remain. When you create the blend, it will be vertical, going from the top horizontal line to the bottom.

Assign a small stroke weight, such as .25, and apply a color to the stroke where you want the darkest area of the gradient to appear. Select the second stroke and apply a lighter value or a different color. Select the Blend tool in the Illustrator toolbox. To blend a user-specified number of steps, click an anchor point on one line with the Blend tool and Option or Alt-Click on the corresponding anchor point in the second line. In the Blend Options dialog box, choose Specified Steps from the Spacing pop-up menu and enter the number of steps you want to use (**Figure 28**). Be sure you enter enough steps so that the gradient appears smooth, but not so many that it will take a long time to print.

After you've drawn all the objects, create a rectangle around the objects to form a bounding box. Note that the pattern is defined by the size of the bounding box. If you wish to leave no space in the pattern outside the objects, be certain that the bounding

Figure 27

Figure 28

box fits tightly around the edge of the elements. Zooming in on the artwork can help you precisely position the edge of the bounding box rectangle.

Select the bounding box and select Object > Arrange > Send to Back. This is a very important step—the bounding box must be behind all the objects in the pattern.

With the Selection tool, drag a marquee around all objects, including the bounding box (**Figure 29**). Click and drag the selected objects to the Swatches palette. You can alternately select Edit > Define Pattern, but Illustrator's drag and drop is faster and easier.

Resist the temptation to shape the blend by masking it to a rectangle or other shape, since patterns can't include masked objects.

Illustrator automatically names the pattern, but you can change the pattern name by double clicking the pattern in the Swatches palette. When the Swatch Options dialog box opens (**Figure 30**), enter a name and click OK.

To apply the pattern, draw a shape and select it. Click on the pattern in the Swatches palette and the object will be filled with your new pattern (**Figure 31**).

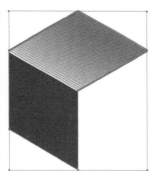

Figure 29

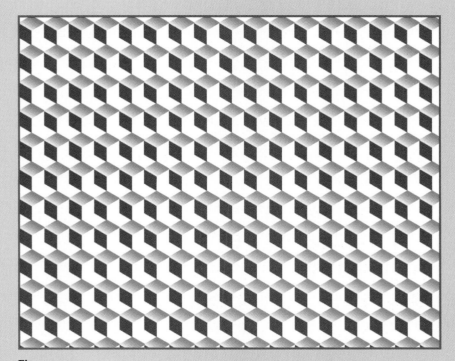

Figure 31

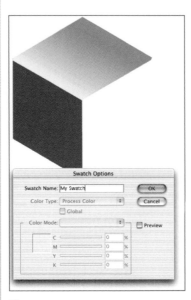

Figure 30

Chapter 8
Typography

Artist
Daniel Pelavin
New York, New York
Designer, Illustrator, Typographer, Educator
www.pelavin.com

Project
Magazine Cover—Special Issue

Client
TAM Publications

Illustrator Tools and Techniques
Pen Tool, Free Transform tool, Pathfinder commands,
Patterns, Masks, Adobe Streamline

Opposite: Canton Market | Identity for DFS Canton Market store, Hong Kong

Daniel Pelavin
Type with Style

If you had the chance to stop into a little New York cafe and sit, espresso in hand, across the table from Daniel Pelavin, you might wonder whether you were talking to one of the America's premier artist-typographers or an upstart for the Comedy Club. With Pelavin, you can get a flavor of both artistic genius and a conversation that keeps you wondering, "Did that really happen?"

Pelavin laments, "I'm the creator of the popular typeface ITC Anna and I'm President of the Type Directors Club, owing to the fortunate positioning of my name on the ballot. I was the designer for the 38th competition of the Type Directors Club, chairman of the 42nd, and will be getting sandwiches for the judges during the current competition."

To get a true flavor for Pelavin's work, you can look at featured articles in magazines, such as *Print*, *Art & Design News*, *Idea* (Japan), *U&lc*, *How*, *Step-by-Step*, *Baseline* (UK), *Grafica* (Brazil), *Macworld*, *MacUser*, *MdN* (Japan), and *Computer Artist*. Or look at some of the many books that carry his work, such as *Designing with Illustration* by Steven Heller, *Contemporary Graphic Designers* by Ronald Labuz, *A History of Graphic Design* by Philip B. Meggs, *One Hundred Years of Line Art* by Leslie Cabarga, *The Digital Designer* by Steven Heller & Daniel Drennan, and *Typology* by Steven Heller and Louise Fili to name but a few.

"Usually clients want something striking and bold, yet they also want the illustration to be recognizable. It's like something hot and cold at the same time—like a scoop of ice cream with hot chocolate sauce."

BEA | **Program guide to an annual publishers conference**

CEO | *IndustryWeek* **magazine, cover for a special issue**

Pelavin was born in Detroit, Michigan and began his training as an artist in 1948. In 1979, he moved to New York City, the same year he started digital work with an Apple II computer. In 1991 he found Illustrator 88, loaded it on his Macintosh IIcx and since then has used the program in every version to date. "The computer offers me the opportunity to do more variations, it's easier to store my illustrations, and I can quickly correct advertising mistakes."

When he began illustrating, he quickly earned recognition nationally in the U.S. and internationally for his precisely drafted shapes, unique color palette, and original typography.

Pelavin has also created a large number of stock illustrations. "I have illustrated *Stock Cuts for Art Directors*, now in its third edition, which represents my extensive catalog of stock illustration and is used in 45 states, five Canadian Provinces, a dozen foreign countries, and several planets in nearby galaxies." The archive, consisting of over 1000 images, is entirely in Illustrator EPS format.

Wall Street Journal Icons | Column heading icons for the "Money and Investing" section of *The Wall Street Journal*

Night Men | Cover of a book published by Walker and Co.

Pelavin earned a BA in advertising and an MFA in Graphic Design, "but I credit my high school industrial arts classes and apprenticeship in Detroit art studios as my most valuable source of training and inspiration." It was the high school classes that taught him how to use drafting tools to draw perfect lines and it was the Detroit ad agencies where he began his study and work in typography.

"When I moved to New York, I worked in a low-end commercial studio as a freelance artist on call. This lasted only six months, during which time I continually brought my portfolio to prospective new clients. The turning point in my career happened when I rented my first apartment in New York City. I set up a studio in my apartment and have worked as an independent freelance artist since then."

For Pelavin, new projects are client-initiated and requested. Most often his work with a client begins with a telephone inquiry. "When I started freelancing, I usually had my first contacts with clients face-to-face. Now, it seems as though everyone is too busy to sit down in a meeting to discuss a new project."

"From the initial meeting I try to get the client to tell a story in regard to what they want. I sit down with a note pad and take notes. If it's an editorial assignment, I ask for the copy and read over the text to get an idea for what will be communicated to the reader. The challenge is to deliver the unexpected in an illustration while still displaying a recognizable product. Usually I find clients want something striking and bold, yet they also want the illustration to be recognizable. It's like something hot and cold at the same time — something like a scoop of ice cream with hot chocolate sauce."

One of the most important aspects of the process is the creative thinking stage. Pelavin calls this his procrastination period. "Procrastination only works if you set a deadline. I intentionally procrastinate until the night before a project is due." During this time he keeps the project at the back of his mind and does not consciously struggle with a new concept. "The period lasts from four days to several weeks. At 10:30 PM the night before a project is due, I begin to develop rough thumbnails. I create thumbnail sketches in an Aquabee super-deluxe sketchbook with Pilot Precise V rolling ball." In a one-and-a-half to two-hour time frame, he may create as many as 40 to 50 different

Hi Test | *Data Communications*, illustration for an article on Internet providers

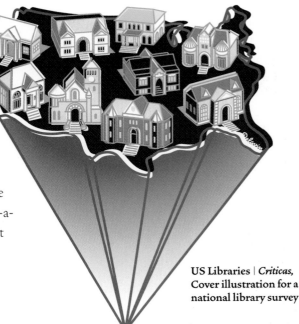

US Libraries | *Criticas*, Cover illustration for a national library survey

Mumfest | Poster for annual chrysanthemum festival

Taste of Tribeca | Poster for a NY restaurant

thumbnail sketches. "At the end of the drafting stage, I hate everything I've created, go to bed, then look over the sketches the next morning. Everything looks better the next day and I pick four to five illustrations that I believe will work for the project."

The morning after, Pelavin scans four to five or sometimes as many as a dozen of his thumbnail drawings and opens them in Adobe Streamline. He sizes the Streamline traces to proportion, prints the drawings, and either faxes them or emails EPS files to the client for review. They discuss the drawings and select a single thumbnail .

Once they've determined the direction for the new project, he begins his work in Illustrator. "When I begin a new drawing, I like to experiment and alter shapes. The flexibility of reshaping objects and applying features—such as the Pathfinder tools, Expand and Outline paths, and the Free Transform tool—offer methods for type design unparalleled by analog methods. What's most difficult for me in the process is remembering to save files frequently before my computer crashes again—what do you expect? I use a Mac."

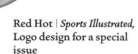

Red Hot | *Sports Illustrated,* **Logo design for a special issue**

Puzzle | **Ronn Campisi Design , illustration for a magazine article titled "The Hazards of Object-Oriented Programming"**

The Project

Daniel Pelavin received a call in his New York studio from former client TAM Publications, publisher of magazines for owners of Harley-Davidson Motorcycles. The readership is loyal to the brand even though they create many different and sometimes unusual modifications of the original Harley-Davidson design. In the year 2003, Harley is celebrating its 100th anniversary. TAM decided to publish a special issue—a one-off publication that's not part of the regular edition. They anticipated the special issue would have more shelf life than monthly or bi-monthly publications.

TAM wanted Pelavin to design the cover. They had some wording in mind , but left developing the design up to Pelavin.

"The ability to easily create design variations is what I like about Adobe Illustrator. What I'd like to see in the next release is for Illustrator to detect when the program is being used by an amateur and quit unexpectedly."

—DANIEL PELAVIN

The Steps

Step 1: Converting rough sketches to vector art. True
to Pelavin's style, and a step he insists is very important, he
postponed the project until the eleventh hour. As a matter
of fact, Pelavin asked us not to leave this step out. "It's
important for me to put as much pressure on myself as
possible. Working under pressure is very important in this
business." After his discussion with the art director, he had
a feel for what TAM wanted, then put the project aside until
the night before the sketches were due. "I like to discourage
people from planning ahead in this business—it's point-
less." The night before the roughs were due, Pelavin spent
about one and a half hours sketching between 40 to 50
drawings. He went to bed hating them, then took a second
look in the morning. "This little Rumplestiltskin magically
appears over my shoulder, whispers in my ear, and the
drawings somehow look a little better," he says. From
the roughs drawn the night before, he picked out twelve
"incomprehensible sketches" and scanned them. After
scanning, he opened each file in Adobe Streamline and
auto traced the artwork so that he could scale and proportion each thumbnail to the same proportions of the final
design. He copied and pasted the sketches into a single
page and numbered them for reference (**Figure 14**). He
saved each drawing as an Illustrator file and emailed them
to the art director.

Figure 14

Step 2: Approving the concept. The art director chose
sketch number 9 (**Figure 15**) from the roughs, but wanted
a few changes. The client liked the design, but wanted the
words Harley-Davidson above the engine. The client also
asked that he draw the engine precisely like the logo in
their regular publication (see Step 11 for the engine figure
description).

Figure 15

Step 3: Setting up the page. Pelavin went to work on the project and first set up the page attributes in Illustrator by selecting File > New. He created a 10-by-12 inch page, set for CMYK color. He wanted the page size to be large enough to create his own bleed and trim marks within the Illustrator page. He verified the Document Setup Output Resolution by selecting File > Document Setup and selecting Printing and Export from the pull-down menu in the top left corner. Pelavin double-checked to be certain the Output Resolution was set to 800 dpi to avoid any banding problems when the file went to print (**Figure 16**).

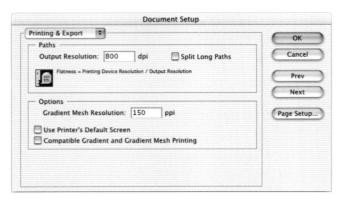

Figure 16

Step 4: Creating a template from vector objects. He opened the Streamline file and dimmed the artwork to 35 percent. The Streamline drawing had fills, strokes, and compound paths. The streamlined art was composed of black or white shapes, so Pelavin selected all the black shapes using 'select same fill' and changed the color to 35 percent.

He double-clicked on the Layer, selected Template, and clicked OK in the Layers palette (**Figure 18**). Pelavin preferred using the traced thumbnail as a template so he could easily toggle views between showing and hiding the Template (Command or Control-Shift-W). If he had left the artwork on a separate layer without making the layer a template, he would have had to use the mouse to click on the Toggles Visibility button in the Layers palette.

Figure 17

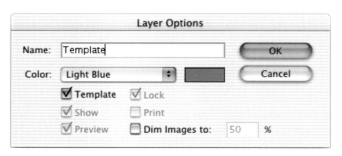

Figure 18

Step 5: Creating the line art. He first created the overall look of the design in line art without any fills. Pelavin went to work on the line art (shown in completion in **Figure 19**), focusing on several tasks, such as adding text without stylizing the font (as shown in the title at the top of the drawing), the words Harley-Davidson (middle), and the words The First (below Harley-Davidson). He also stylized the type to fit the banner at the bottom of the drawing and the words American Glory at the top, created type from scratch without using a font for the number 100, created the ribbon at the bottom of the drawing, and created the shield and engine. He reserved the last step for creating the background and border.

Step 6: Setting type. For the words American and Glory, he used a typeface he had created himself. He converted the type to outlines by selecting the type and then selecting Type › Create Outlines.

"I drew a typeface I named Bokar, which was originally inspired by A&P coffee packaging. I drew the letterforms by hand, scanned them, traced them in Illustrator, and finally con-
verted them to a font in Fontographer. I liked that style of lettering, so I keyboarded it in and used it for all the type in the design except for the type for Harley-Davidson and the 100 number above the engine. The type for Harley-David-son was a font called Knockout, designed by Jonathan Hoe-fler for Sports Illustrated." Pelavin used that font inside the shield. However after the client saw the first drawing, he wanted the Harley-Davidson words to be more obvious. Pelavin accommodated them by choosing a different weight of the same font and set the type across the middle of the illustration. He converted the Bocar and Knockout fonts to outlines so the print shop wouldn't need the fonts to print the file. "The Knockout font offers an incredible range of weights. The font sets use names derived from wrestling, such as Sumo, Fly-Weight, and Middle-Weight, but this is for another story."

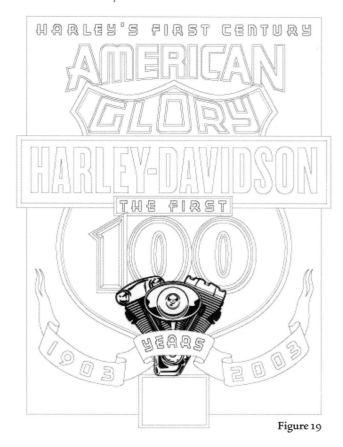

Figure 19

Step 7: Stylizing type. "When I set the type for American Glory, I didn't like the way it sat in there. It started out as Bokar and it didn't fit the look I wanted. So, I reshaped all the points and completely redrew the type." Notice the type in the final illustration. The American Glory typeface started out as the same type he used for the headline and the type inside the ribbon. Pelavin converted the type to outlines and individually selected points on the paths. He used the Direct Selection tool to move points to reshape the characters. He fit the characters to baselines drawn as ellipses converted to guides (**Figure 20**).

Step 8: Creating type. Sometimes you can't find a type font for a design piece. If you're Daniel Pelavin, you create your own type to fit the drawing. He drew the 100, appearing at the bottom of the shield, from geometric objects. Pelavin drew a rectangle and reshaped it to the number 1. He used the Direct Selection tool to drag points and used the Add Anchor Point tool to add points on the path. He drew the zeros from ellipses first and later modified the shapes with the Transformation and Direct Selection tools (**Figure 21**). He used Expand and Outline Strokes (described in step 10) and transformed them to create the multiple strokes for each type character. He would later fill these strokes with gradients and stroke colors to add dimension to the type.

Step 9: Creating the ribbon. The ribbon was a freehand illustration that he drew with the Pen tool. Without a template, the ribbon illustration presented a challenge. "At one point I didn't like the ribbon," says Pelavin. "I didn't like the way it appeared on either side of Years. It seemed awkward to me. It wasn't candid enough. If something is supposed to be vertical,

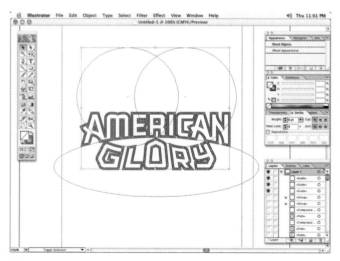

Figure 20

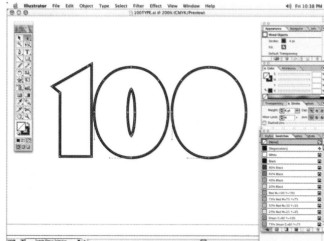

Figure 21

it should be vertical. If it's not, people think it's a mistake." Pelavin adjusted points and kept reworking the ribbon, creating several versions until it appeared right to him (**Figures 22, 23, and 24**).

Step 10: Creating the shield. "I took a shield from somewhere, put it in, sized it, and traced the shape." He drew the shield with the Pen tool and used Object > Expand to expand the stroke. He then chose Object > Paths > Outline Stroke. By Option-Control clicking with the Scale tool, he selected a scale size and clicked OK (**Figure 25**). He repeated the process to create the third stroke. He moved the points on the new objects individually to the position he wanted. According to Pelavin, "It's a morphing process. You can't just take something, trace it, and drop it in your drawing. You have to play with it and rework the shape until it fits your design."

Step 11: Creating the engine. The one element the client insisted on controlling was the engine. The Harley-Davidson engine shown in the drawing is a logo used by the publisher. The engine is a combination of the original Harley engine appearing on the left side and the contemporary engine on the right. (Notice the difference between the shapes on the top of each side and the differences in the positions of the engine bolts). Pelavin received a scan of the engine in a PICT format and used the scan as a template in a separate Illustrator document. "You can call the engine a 'trace,' but I had to decide how to threshold the strokes. Since it was the only black-and-white object in the design, I had to use solid black fills to create shadows and dimension."

Pelavin used the Pen tool to draw the engine and reworked strokes and fills to add dimension to it. "It didn't happen automatically. I had to play with the strokes and fills a little

Figure 22

Figure 23

Figure 24

Figure 25

to create the view I wanted." (**Figure 26**) He copied the engine from the separate document, pasted it into the final illustration, and scaled to size.

Step 12: Saving the composite drawing. When the final line art was complete, Pelavin saved this file and put it aside. He handled the actual artwork for detail in all the different elements in separate files, where he copied the line art forms, pasted them into a new document, and applied the color and fills. As he completed each part of the design, he copied and pasted them into the composite design. Pelavin works in a nonlinear fashion by working on one file until he gets tired or bored, then jumping to another file and working on a completely different part of the design. "I separate different pieces and begin to work on them without any particular plan in mind."

Step 13: Adding fills to type outlines. The filled type characters for the American Glory type had a combination of different fills for each type outline. After Expanding, Outlining Strokes, and creating two copies, Pelavin had three sets of type characters. He set the outside stroke weight to 8 points with no fill (**Figure 27**). Pelavin grouped the type characters so he could easily select them again if he needed a change in color or fill.

He filled the next inside outline text with orange and no stroke. Pelavin intentionally limits the number of color hues and color brightness in his designs. He chose orange for one color and the complement of orange (blue) for another. He reused these colors several times on different objects to add the contrast he wanted in the design. "I consistently limit my color palette. If I want one element to contrast with another, I can easily select a contrasting value from a limited color palette."

Figure 26   Figure 27

The third outline for the type characters carried a gradient fill with no stroke (**Figure 28**). Pelavin created the gradient in the Gradient palette, choosing different CMYK colors. He grouped the characters and applied the gradient to the grouped object.

To simulate a reflector look on the hand drawn type characters, Pelavin created a crosshatch with different strokes at 45 degree angles and masked the strokes to the type outlines (**Figure 29**).

Step 14: Creating a pattern for the shield. Pelavin wanted to simulate a taillight reflector on Harley-Davidson motorcycles in his drawing. After drawing the shield and creating copies of the outline shape, as he did with the type characters, he created another copy and cut the top of the outline. Then he joined the two sides so the shield with the reflector fell midway within the Harley-Davidson banner across the design. He created a pattern with several objects using the transformation tools to shear the angles and assembled them in an isometric view (**Figure 30**).

Normally Pelavin would create an Illustrator pattern and fill the shield outline with the pattern. Since one of the objects had a gradient, he couldn't use the Pattern tool. As an alternative, he created a pattern manually. He duplicated the object by holding down the Option or Alt key and the Shift key and dragged away a copy. He used Transform Again (Command or Control-D) and replicated the copy horizontally across a distance to accommodate the width of the

Figure 28

Figure 29

Figure 30

shield. He then selected the row, and Option- or Alt-dragged down to create additional copies vertically. He repeated the steps to create enough rows to fit the half-shield shape. He then selected the shield outline, brought it to the front of the objects, and created a mask by selecting Object > Clipping Mask > Make (**Figure 31**).

Step 15: Creating lighting and shading for the shield. The reflector shield needed some lighting detail to appear more realistic. When Pelavin created the objects for the pattern, two squares contained a fill and a gradient. The third side of the view contained no square —yet when duplicated like a pattern, it appeared as though there was a white rectangle on the shape. When he assembled it in an isometric view, the front side of the cube was empty (or contained no object with a fill to prevent the background from showing). Pelavin avoided creating a square for the face of the cube, so all the shadowing behind the face would show from shaded background objects.

Pelavin added a gradient for the background on the inside copy of the original shield outline (**Figure 33**). He copied the partial shield that he had created earlier and pasted in front (Edit > Paste in Front). He created a duplicate copy of the partial shield by again pasting in front. He scaled this object down, using the Transformation tool. He filled the front copy with a radial gradient, using white, the same red color as the pattern objects, and black

Artwork mode   **Preview mode**

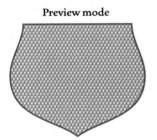

Figure 31

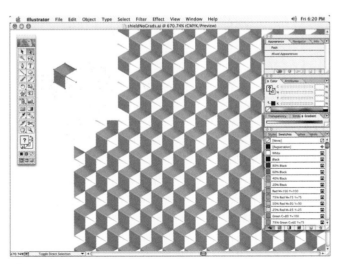

Figure 32

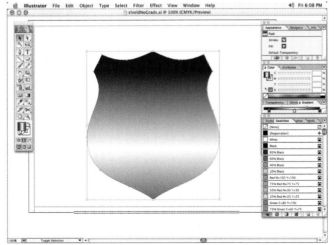

Figure 33

(**Figure 34**). He filled the rear partial shield with a linear gradient, graduating from light red, to medium red, and finally to black (**Figure 35**). He hid the pattern and shield that he used for the mask by selecting the objects, then selecting Object > Hide > Selection.

Pelavin drew a rectangle at the top of the shield and filled it black to create a shadow behind the elements. He made copies of the type he created, selected the type characters, then selected Edit > Paste in Back (**Figure 36** with foreground objects hidden from view).

Pelavin then created the edges of both the background object and the partial shield. He created a beveled effect by taking a one-dimensional stroke and expanded it into two-dimensional shapes in order to create a three-dimensional effect. He duplicated the strokes and joined paths by selecting points to be joined and then selecting Object > Path > Join (**Figure 37**).

He created beveled edges using several different paths with gradients flowing in different directions. The edges of the type characters and the shield edges contained several different objects, each with a gradient in directions to provide the illusion of reflection (**Figure 38**).

He made the type fills visible again by selecting Object > Show All. When he created separate elements, he grouped objects together. Pelavin worked on a single layer. He could easily show and hide grouped objects by expanding the Layers palette and selecting a group for hiding and showing (**Figure 39**). He grouped the final image, then copied and pasted it into the composite drawing.

Step 16: Adding the border and background. He created the background behind the individual objects with a rectangle and a black fill. He added freehand objects to mimic pinstripes along the edge of the background and the illustrated artwork for the border. "It was my intention to create the

Figure 34

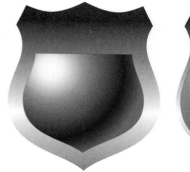

Figure 35

Figure 36

Figure 37

Figure 38

Figure 39

pinstripe effect you often see on custom Harley-Davidson motorcycles. I studied pinstripe illustrations on the Web. I then hand drew the artwork from a recollection of how pinstripe designs appear. I didn't trace any existing artwork. I'm morally opposed to tracing someone else's art and reshaping it. This belief is a handicap in my work, and I know I'll never get rich, but it's the way I approach all my artwork." Sometimes Pelavin finds a piece that's a source of reference. He prints the artwork and refers to it while he creates his own illustration. In the case of pinstripes, he didn't find anything worth using as a reference, so he began to draw lines with the Pen tool and reworked the shapes, moving direction lines and anchor points with the Direct Selection tool.

"I created a point with the Pen tool, then clicked and dragged to form a Bezier curve. I switched to the Pen too and then pressed the Option key down and click and dragged the line to duplicate it and joined the endpoints. I went through several iterations until I found the right shape and color fill."

Throughout his design process, Pelavin plays, experiments, and reworks shapes and colors. He starts with a line art drawing as he develops a clear vision for the end product. However, during development, he frees himself of a rigid sequence of steps and moves back and forth between different phases of the design. He often changes the completed drawing through further experimentation using his limited color palette. With the TAM Publication magazine cover, he created several different looks (**Figures 40, 41 and 42**) until he settled on the final design (**Figure 43**) and sent that to his client.

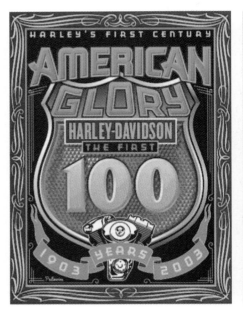

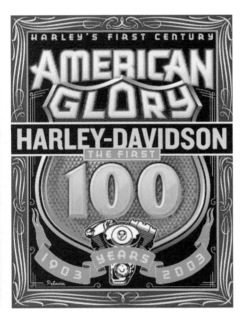

Figure 40

Figure 41

Figure 42

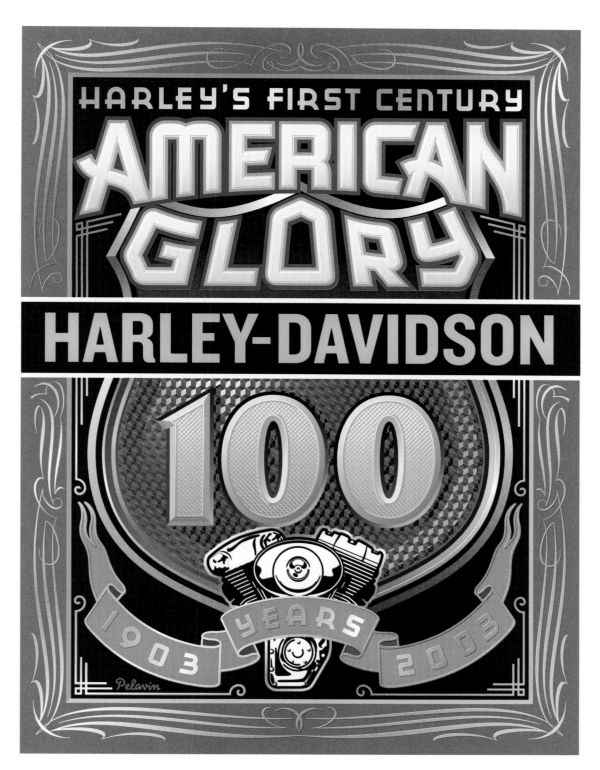

Figure 43

Using Vector Art Templates

Rather than using raster art for templates in Adobe Illustrator, Pelavin prefers to convert his scanned sketches to vector art. As vector art he can manipulate paths with transformation tools and modify the template to suite a particular size and perspective of the rough sketch. Although Adobe Illustrator provides you with an Auto Trace tool for converting scans to vector art, the tool is limited in performance and doesn't work well with complex drawings. For a superb job in converting scans to vector objects, Pelavin uses Adobe Streamline. With just a few menu selections in Streamline you can convert any kind of scan to vector art.

If you haven't used Adobe Streamline and want to experiment with the program, you can download a trial version from Adobe's Web site at: http://www.adobe.com/products/streamline. The trial version enables you to convert any scanned image to vector art. You can't copy or save the artwork after conversion, but you can get a good idea of how well the program works.

Streamline works with any kind of scanned image —even continuous-tone scanned photographs. Scan your artwork and save the file as a TIFF image, then open the file in Adobe Streamline (**Figure 44**).

Streamline offers you various menu selections for how the artwork is converted. If you wish to retain color fills from color photo scans, Streamline gives you several choices in the Settings menu (**Figure 45**).

Figure 44

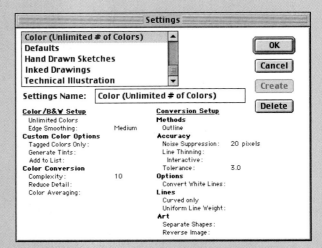

Figure 45

Figure 46

After making selections for the conversion, type Control (or Command) + R and Streamline works through the scan, creating paths and fills. After a few minutes, the conversion is completed and you can save the drawing as an Illustrator .ai or Illustrator EPS file (**Figure 46**).

You can open the converted file in Illustrator and modify paths, strokes, and fills. If the artwork is to be used as a template and you wish to dim the artwork, you can select the vector objects by selecting Select Same and fill them with a percentage of gray as Pelavin recommends. Creating a template and selecting Dim in the Layer Options palette won't dim vector art. Rather, select all the objects by striking Control or Command + A. Open the Transparency palette and adjust the transparency by moving the slider left or enter a percentage value in the palette (**Figure 47**).

If you need to size or shape the template, you can use Illustrator's transformation tools. Move the artwork to position and double click on the layer in the Layers palette. Select Template from the Layer Options and lock the layer. All artwork on new layers appear above the template layer. To toggle views for showing and hiding the layer, strike Control (or Command) + W (**Figure 48**).

Figure 47

Figure 48

Chapter 9
Billboard/Large Format Designs

Artist

Michael Bartalos
Illustrator
San Francisco, California
www.bartalos.com

Project

Microsoft Discovery Bus

Client

Sandstrom Design, Portland, Oregon; for Microsoft/NEC

Illustrator Tools and Techniques

Pen Tool, Layers, Pathfinder commands

**Opposite: City Livability Awards | U.S. Conference of Mayors,
poster and brochure cover**

Michael Bartalos
Bigger Is Better

If you want a wall mural, trade floor design, or a bus completely covered with an illustration, then Michael Bartalos is your illustrator. With awards and citations that would fill this book from cover to cover, Bartalos has impressive credits extending over two decades. He's been consistently winning awards of excellence since the 1980s and his client list spans three continents , some of whom include Apple Computer, Microsoft, Adobe Systems, Japan Airlines, AT&T, British Telecom, Nickelodeon, and the U.S. Postal Service.

Bartalos began his education and training with a Bachelor of Fine Arts degree from Pratt Institute in Brooklyn, New York, and then attended the School of the Art Institute in Chicago. Since graduating from college over 20 years ago, he has designed illustrations for print, packaging, broadcast, and window displays.

Happy Home Office | Sierra Club, *Sierra* magazine

Bartalos discovered the Macintosh IIci back in 1991. He couldn't wait to get his hands on this Mac, considered a screamer at the time. With a IIci and the power of Adobe Illustrator 1.9.3, he became hooked on digital methods.

Before computer illustration, Bartalos hand cut graphic shapes to formulate his design concepts. Illustrator replaced the tedious task of cutting shapes and arranging them on a background and offered instead bezier curves, objects, and transformations. The result is a more spontaneous response when conceptualizing a design and more flexibility in altering shapes. With a few mouse clicks, some transformations, and a few point conversions, designers can develop alternatives in a

"I try to introduce humor, allegory, and a flair for the unexpected into the design concept. My objective is to produce an illustration that's light and interesting, but also sophisticated and intelligent."

**Harvard Discovery |
Harvard Medical School,
Dean's report**

Year of the Dragon (Red and Black) | Interform Japan, postcards

Year of the Dragon 2000 | Interform Japan, postcards

Year of the Dragon (Green) | Interform Japan, postcards

Japanese New Year Kite | Interform Japan, postcards

fraction of the time that traditional methods required. Bartalos is also particularly fond of the Multiple Undo feature that lets him change concepts without completely redesigning shapes.

He developed his style from influences in his culture (both parents are from Hungary), his background, and a love of exploring new cultures. He felt particularly at home in Europe and traveled extensively, with portfolio in hand, to places like Paris and London. He found the market there to be dry and unapproachable, so he switched gears and countries and headed to Japan. The reception he received there was warm and open. The environment gave him an opportunity for new vistas in illustration.

Opera 101 | Hyperion Publishing, book cover

Heart Quiz | *Reader's Digest*

opening friday
8 june · 6 to 8 PM
Reading
the
cards
in exhibition
june 8 – August 24

the San Francisco CENTER for the BOOK

300
De Haro
94103
415.
565.
0545
www.
sfcb.
org

Reading the Cards |
San Francisco
Center for the Book,
exhibition poster

During his first half dozen trips to Japan, Bartalos traveled from the northern island of Hokkaido to the southern island of Okinawa, subletting apartments and staying for at least six months each visit. He spent time scouting work by knocking on doors. In short order he commissioned work with high-profile clients, including Asahi Bank, Japan Airlines, and Sony Corp. His work increased through referrals from satisfied clients. "In a country like Japan, word of mouth and referrals are extremely important. Once you get known and your clients like your work, they liberally share their experiences with colleagues and associates."

San Francisco Swatch store mural comp | Swatch

Exposure to Japanese culture—including the trips to Japan as an adult and watching Japanese animated cartoons (such as Astro Boy and Speed Racer) as a child—has helped Bartalos develop an interesting and unique style. He integrates Japanese icons, symbols, and characters into many of his designs. Some projects contain a central theme rooted in Asian design, while others include subtle introduction of icons and shapes in an obvious Western theme.

Bartalos begins a new project with a client interview, then immediately begins to think about the general concept of the design and what he wishes to communicate in the illustration that meets his client needs. The first point of illustration is pencil to paper, not pen to document window. "I sketch out a variety of compositional possibilities to begin a project."

Multiplex | *Inc.* magazine

Eventually he produces one or two acceptable black and white sketches. "I try to introduce in the design concept humor, allegory, and a flair for the unexpected. The objective is to produce an illustration that is light and interesting, but also sophisticated and intelligent."

After he's created the pencil comps, he scans them as line art into Adobe Photoshop. He saves the two Photoshop files, one as a .psd file and the other as a PDF, and emails the PDF to the client for approval before he performs any work in Illustrator. Once he gets approval, he saves a second file in TIFF format and places that file in Adobe Illustrator to use as the template. You'll notice many illustrators in this book work similarly. They typically acquire client approvals from roughs before the illustration work begins. This is a worthy method that will save time, money, and potential misunderstandings between artist and client.

Capital Research | Capital Research and Management Company, annual report

Investing in China | Time Inc.,
Time magazine

Sober CRM | International Data Group,
Computer World magazine

The Project

George Vogt, art director of Sandstrom Design in Portland, Oregon, asked Bartalos to design the exterior of a refurbished school bus that would serve as an educational and entertainment attraction, a kind of mobile learning center, that would travel across the United States touring schools , libraries, and museums. The Microsoft Discovery Bus would be furnished with eight state-of-the-art NEC computer workstations, Microsoft software, and a wireless Internet connection. The interior of the bus would be converted by Standby Power of Detroit, Michigan. The illustration on the exterior would wrap over the entire external surface of a bus (including the roof and windows). Vogt requested a colorful, engaging design that appealed to adults and children alike. The illustration of the Microsoft Discovery Bus is an interesting example of an Illustrator-created project reproduced on a large three-dimensional scale.

"I love Illustrator's Pathfinder filters, especially Intersect and Divide. High on my wish list for a new feature is the ability to select multiple objects and use the Pathfinder > Intersect filter."

—MICHAEL BARTALOS

The Steps

Step 1: Preparing a Comp. Vogt had seen Bartalos' work before—"Nocturne," a box set of 50 postcards for Gulliver Book in Japan—and wanted similar artwork for the bus design. Vogt asked for Bartalos' input for an initial presentation to Microsoft and Bartalos suggested using rectangular color fields, containing iconic vignettes for the bus design. Vogt then worked up a comp using Bartalos' "Nocturne" postcard images, which included a flying fish, winged robot, and a man-shaped building. He separated the elements using heavy black strokes.

Step 2: Creating the first design. Microsoft approved the general direction of the design and Bartalos developed some sketches. At this point, the exact specifications of the bus were unknown, so he worked from the client's temporary template—the outline of the bus

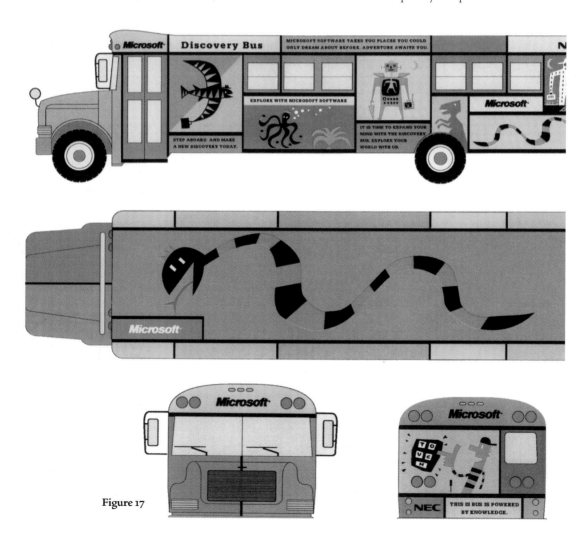

Figure 17

drawn with a black stroke and no fills. This approximated the shape and proportion of the bus (**Figure 18**). He printed out several copies of this bus template and used them as a basis for his sketches. He replaced the "Nocturne" images with original images. He rendered all graphics in black and white so that he could establish the subject matter before moving on to color. Bartalos also eliminated the heavy black strokes which he found to be unnecessary and too similar to the Partridge Family bus. He wanted the design to reflect the educational aspect of the Bus project, yet also wanted it to be fun and light (**Figure 19**). He scanned the sketch and saved it as a PDF that he then emailed to Vogt.

Step 3: Refining the design. Not yet satisfied, Bartalos created an alternate set of sketches, which also included a rear view (**Figure 20**). Again he scanned the sketch, saved it as a PDF that he emailed to the client. Everyone felt that this set of sketches was an overall improvement on the first set. Ultimately, however, Bartalos combined the best elements of both sketches for his final design. Of course, any project is not without its snafus, and he discovered that the bus would have a series of vents

Figure 18

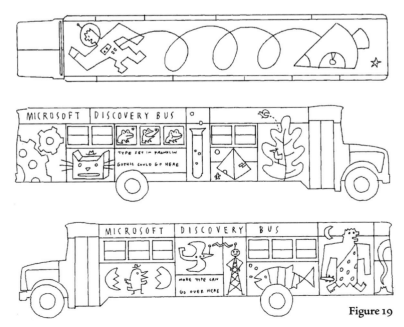

Figure 19

Figure 20

along the roof. The complexity of the vents made applying a graphic impractical, so the roof image was scrapped (**Figure 21**).

Step 4: Getting composition right. Bartalos rearranged the elements to improve the composition. He used a dinosaur to illustrate history and the past; robots, an airplane, a submarine , gears, and space to represent technology and the future; animals, a leaf, and a volcano to represent science, nature, and the present. A hip student computer user added the human element. At this point, the client still planned to place large fields of type under the frog sequence and under the airplane (**Figure 22**). Bartalos finalized the sketch and both Vogt and Microsoft signed off on the PDF document.

Step 5: Organizing in Illustrator. It was only after he finalized the pencil sketch that Bartalos began working in Illustrator. He opened the temporary bus outline file, saved the sketch as a bitmap TIFF file, and placed it into Illustrator as a template. Bartalos used the Layers palette to organize his illustrations. He put the sketch template (called art template) on layer 1 and the bus outline (called bus template) on layer 2 (**Figure 23**). *Note: The template is colored and offset to show separate layers.*

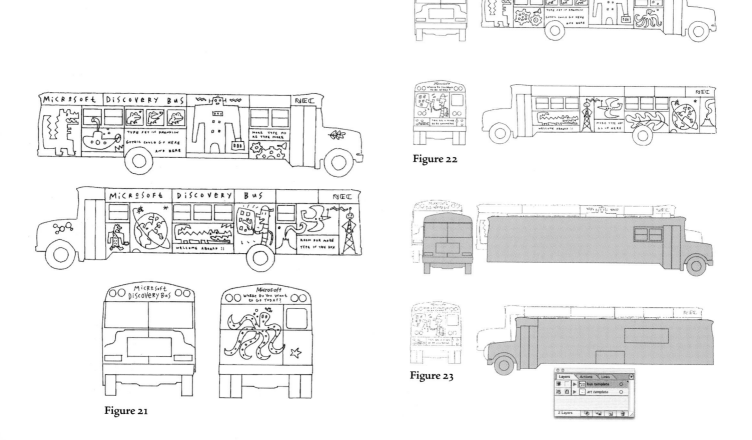

Figure 22

Figure 23

Figure 21

Step 6: Creating background color. With his artboard and preliminary layers organized, Bartalos was ready to begin drawing in Illustrator. Because he likes to use layers while the artwork is in progress, he first created a third layer (called background colors) for his larger background elements. Bartalos usually prefers to draw the entire illustration with a thin 1-point black stroke and no fill and apply color at the end. But in this project, due to the number of interacting elements, he applied color to each shape with the Color palette as he drew. He toggled back and forth between Outline and Preview views, checking color as he applied it. Bartalos began by grabbing the Rectangle tool and, starting on the right side of the bus, he drew the rectangles behind and above the octopus (**Figure 24**).

Continuing right to left, Bartalos drew all of the background shapes using the Rectangle tool. In the case of the rounded rectangles of the bus corners, he used the shapes provided on the bus template (**Figure 25**).

Bartalos is a huge fan of the Pathfinder filters, finding them a tremendous time saver. To create the two-colored square behind the robot, Bartalos drew a square with the Rectangle tool. He then created a diagonal line, starting from just outside the top right corner to just outside the bottom left corner. He selected both elements and used the Divide filter in the Pathfinder palette, thereby creating two triangles, which he could later color separately (**Figure 26**).

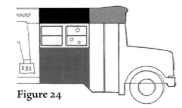

Figure 24

He repeated the process of drawing background elements for the opposite side of the bus, as well as, the front, back, and top (**Figure 27**).

Figure 25

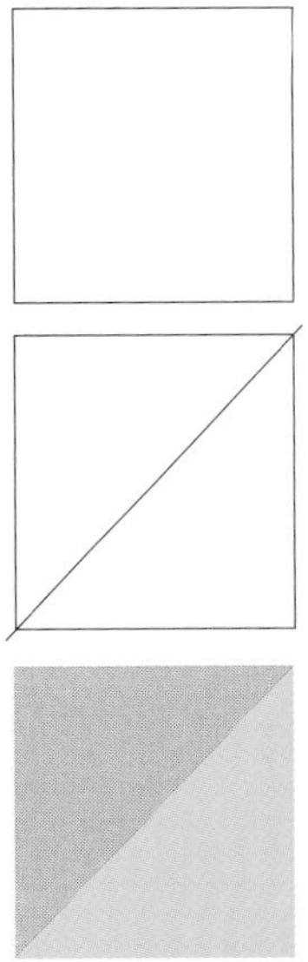

Figure 26

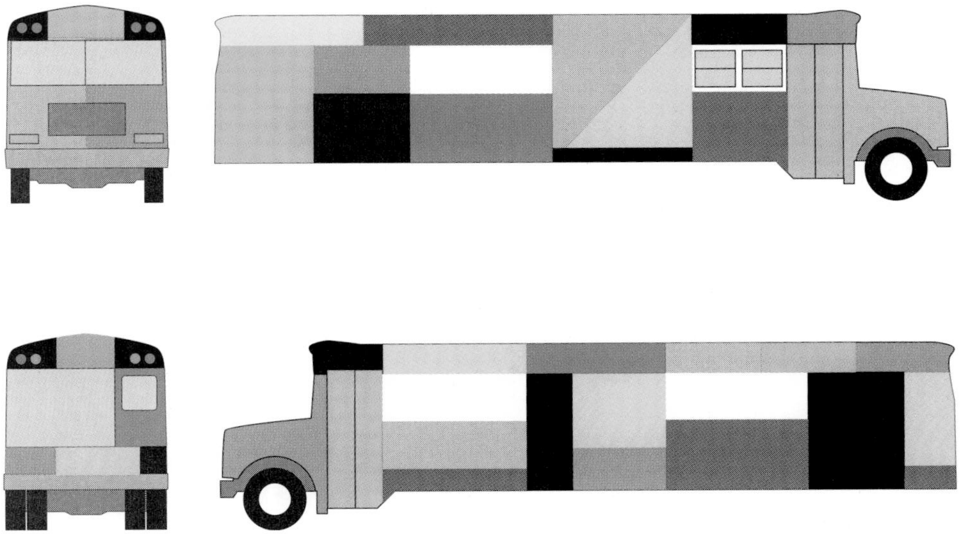

Figure 27

Step 7: Drawing the shapes. Next Bartalos created another layer for his foreground elements. He randomly chose which shapes to draw, but usually started with the larger elements first. Besides the Rectangle and Ellipse tools, Bartalos relied heavily on the Pen tool to create his shapes. In this case, he first drew the robot, and then the dinosaur. To create the open mouth on the dinosaur, he once again relied on the Pathfinder filters. Bartalos drew the dinosaur without the mouth. He then created a separate shape for the mouth, positioned it on the dinosaur, selected both shapes, and chose the Subtract from shape area Shape Mode in the Pathfinder palette (**Figure 28**).

Step 8: The octopus. Bartalos drew the octopus' head and then the legs, each as separate shapes. He overlapped the legs and the head and chose the Add to shape area Shape Mode in the Pathfinder palette, which combined his separate shapes into one single path.

Step 9: Smaller elements. He drew the gears next and then the frogs. Bartalos used the same technique to create the frog's open mouth as he did with the dinosaur. He utilized the windows as frames for a kind of simple, animated story. Finally, he added small details, such as the bubbles, the fly, the oil can drip, and the electric waves of the robot (**Figure 29**).

Step 10: The crocodile and leaf. Bartalos created the foreground elements of the opposite side of the bus, starting with the crocodile. Again, he created the mouth of the croc just as he did for the dinosaur, by using the Subtract from shape area Shape Mode.

He drew the leaf by first creating the basic shape. He then drew a curve down the center of the leaf. Using the same technique as the two-colored square behind the robot, he selected

Figure 28

Figure 29

the leaf and the stroke, and chose Divide in the Pathfinder palette. That created two halves that he later colored separately. He used a 13-point black stroke with the Pen tool to make the veins and stem.

Step 11: The earth element. Next, Bartalos created the airplane and the earth. The earth started as a circle, which he created with the Ellipse tool. With the Pen tool, he created the two land masses that overlap the earth, with no regard to matching them up to the edges of the earth. He selected the earth, copied it, and pasted it in front (Edit > Paste in Front). Bartalos then selected both the copy of the earth and the landmass on the right and selected the Intersect shape areas Shape Mode from the Pathfinder palette. By using the Intersect mode, only the landmass that overlapped the earth remained. Bartalos repeated the process with the landmass on the left. To finish the earth, he created shapes representing Greenland, Cuba, and the Mediterranean Sea with the Pen tool (**Figure 30**). Finally, he drew the orbit and the satellite with the Pen tool.

Step 12: Final images for the second side. The volcano and the robot tower man were the last large foreground objects to be created. As he often does with symmetrical elements, Bartalos drew only half of the face of the robot tower man. He then copied the elements and then pasted them in front. After flipping the copied half, he slightly overlapped the two sides and chose the Add Shape Mode from the Pathfinder palette. This created a perfectly symmetrical face. The body of the robot tower man consists of 7-point Strokes created with the Pen tool.

He added detail elements, such as the stars, after completing the foreground elements (**Figure 31**).

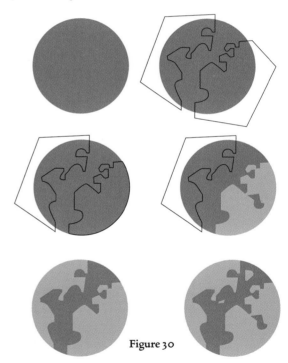

Figure 30

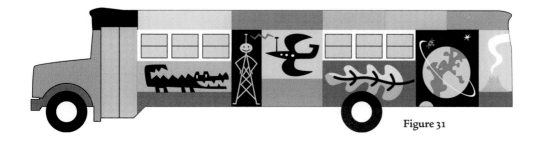

Figure 31

Step 13: Adding the type. Bartalos created the student image on the back of the bus and then created one more layer for the custom type, which would include the word "click" on the computer panel and "Microsoft Discovery Bus" on the side of the bus (**Figure 32**) Bartalos felt strongly about creating this type by hand rather than using a typeface because he wanted to retain an organic and loose feeling that would complement the fun and light-hearted illustrations. He again used the Pen tool to trace the letters, creating separate shapes (**Figure 33**).

Step 14: Pasting in the final elements. Finally, he copied, pasted, and scaled to fit the NEC and Microsoft logos (which were provided as Illustrator files with type outlines) in their respective locations. Sandstrom Design added the tag lines, such as "All aboard for fun" and "Explore the world" in Franklin Gothic Demi font.

Step 15: Reviewing color. Bartalos did a final review of the colors (**Figure 34**), referring to Vogt's comp. Both Vogt and Bartalos agreed to choose colors that were slightly off the traditional primary children's spectrum, for example, substituting terra cotta for red and olive for green. Using a Pantone chart, Bartalos chose spot colors for all of his elements. The 3M adhesive film output more efficiently matches Pantone spot colors than CMYK process colors. During the final output process, the spot colors were converted to 3M equivalents (**Figure 35**).

Step 16: Making final color adjustments. Bartalos deleted the art template, grouped the elements on each layer, locked all his layers, and emailed a copy to his client for approval. Because of the pure vector nature of this file, it was tiny in size—a mere 292K. Vogt loved the design, but asked Bartalos to change the colors of a few elements. Bartalos brightened the palette, and replaced some large black fills with color. He phased out purple and added

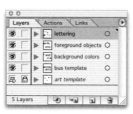

Figure 32

Figure 33

teal. He replaced olive with dark green and light green. The color adjustments gave the composition more contrast and balance (**Figure 36**).

Step 17: Adding some finishing touches. The client decided to minimize the type and make more space for illustration. He had Bartalos move the leaf graphic to the vacated space on the bus's right side and restore a submarine that was dropped from the early pencil sketch. As he did with the frogs, Bartalos once again incorporated the window in his design. In this case, the

Figure 34

Figure 36

Figure 35

window ledge acted as a natural water line and he placed the periscope over the window as if it were peering inside the bus. Whereas some artists would view elements such as windows as an undesirable interruption in their design, Bartalos found it fun to use the bus as his canvas (including those windows), and liked the fact that he had to consider the dimensions of the bus when making his design decisions. "I love to design for objects. Having to accommodate the dimension of an object is difficult, but also fun. It's my favorite kind of project." At this stage, the color palette was nearly established but still a bit on the dark side (**Figure 37**).

He repositioned the type so that it was below the gears and alligator, adding rhythm to the composition. He brightened the colors overall and slightly rearranged their placement.

Figure 37

Figure 38

Bartalos still felt that something was a little off. Vogt suggested changing the submarine from dark to light, which suddenly brought the composition to light. Changing the color field above the dark green to yellow further enhanced the effect (**Figure 38**).

Step 18: Using the real template. When Bartalos was able to get his hands on the confirmed bus template with final specs (**Figure 39**), he adjusted the graphic elements to fit the template. In this file, the bus outline measured 44 inches in length by 9.5 inches in height. He also resolved the colors of the roof. Bartalos flattened the layers (keeping a copy with the layers intact for archiving purposes) down into a single layer and grouped the elements on each side of the bus—left, right, top, back and front. He emailed the final file to Vogt (**Figure 40**).

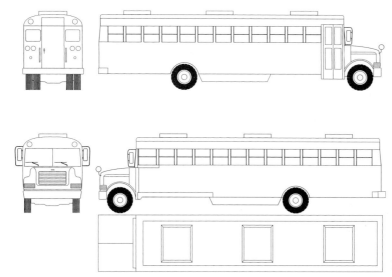

Figure 39

Figure 40

Step 19: Vogt blessed the final design, and scaled it up to the actual size of the bus. He then emailed the file to a service bureau in the Midwest that output the file to 3M-approved electrostatic adhesive film coated with protective laminates via a process called Scotchprint Graphics. Interestingly, the material appears opaque over windows from the outside, yet is transparent from the inside. As stated earlier, the service bureau converted the Pantone colors into 3M equivalents and then matched using a combination of films and over-laminates. The service bureau reassembled the individual elements onto the bus exterior in layers, similar to Bartalos' original Illustrator file—applying large background shapes first, followed by layers of progressively smaller shapes (**Figure 41**). The Scotchprint Graphics process, although capable of reproducing bitmap images, works best with vector graphics due to the small file sizes and ability to scale up the art dramatically without losing quality. In the Discovery Bus project, the viewer's close proximity to the bus required the large, yet clean, high-resolution imagery of Illustrator's vector graphics. Of the final product Bartalos says, "The only noticeable change was the series of the roof vents which differed from the template. Otherwise I was very pleased that the illustration on the bus was remarkably faithful to my Illustrator file" (**Figures 42 and 43**).

Figure 41

Figure 42

Figure 43

Scaling Illustrator Drawings

If you've been around Illustrator for any length of time, you've no doubt been faced with the task of scaling objects. Most people will scale with the bounding box, following these steps: Set the View to Show Bounding Box, grab either the Selection Tool or the Free Transform tool, and grab a handle. Then, hold the Shift key down to constrain proportions and drag diagonally to your desired size. To scale from the Center of the bounding box, press Alt or Option. You can also use the Scale tool, which allows you greater flexibility in setting new points of origin around which you can scale. For visual sizing these methods work fast and easy.

If you design objects at a small percentage of actual print size and you need to have stroke weights sized along with the objects, be sure to select the Scale Strokes and Effects option in the General Preferences dialog box. Only then will using the Selection tool, the Scale tool, or the Free Transform tool scale stroke weights. You can also scale the strokes along with the objects by specifying scale percentages. Select all objects to be scaled, and then double click the Scale tool in the Toolbox. In the Scale dialog box which appears, check the Scale Strokes & Effects option. Enter the percentage of scale and click OK. You can also access the Scale dialog box by choosing Object > Transform > Scale.

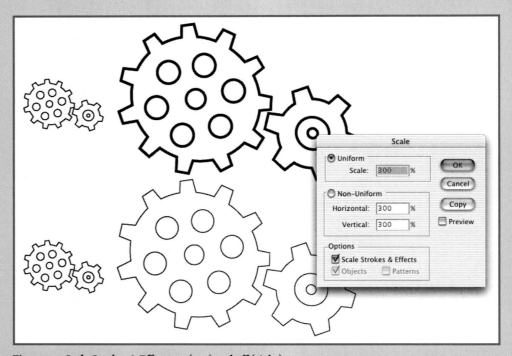

Figure 44   Scale Strokes & Effects on (top) and off (right).

At times you may wish to nudge the scaling up or down in point size to finesse a size. To do so, return to the dialog box and enter 99% to scale down in size 1 point. Enter 101% to scale up in size 1 point. Check the Scale Strokes & Effects option and then click OK. To continue nudging, you don't need to return to the Scale dialog box each time you want to scale another 1%. Press Control or Command-D on your keyboard or select Object > Transform again. Continue striking the modifier keys to repeat the transformation and you can nudge a size easily with the keystrokes. If you don't want to scale strokes, you can perform the first step in the Scale dialog box and leave the Scale Strokes & Effects checkbox disabled.

One of the most common problems experienced at imaging centers when clients ask technicians to scale drawings and images is that the documents are not always proportioned properly to yield the desired output size. For example, if you have a 10-by-12-inch image and tell the imaging technicians that you want a 20-by-30 inch print, the original image will have to be clipped or masked to yield the final print size. When sending files off to imaging centers, always try to size your files to fit exact proportions of the desired output. To be safe, try to keep your images at increments of 100 percent (100, 200, 300, etc.) of size. It will make it easy on the service center and eliminate problems arising from incorrectly sized files.

Chapter 10
Logo Design

Artist
Doug Panton
Toronto, Canada
Designer, Illustrator, Creative Director, Educator
www.dougpanton.com

Project
Logo

Client
Ridpath's Fine Furniture of Toronto

Illustrator Tools and Techniques
Pen Tool, Layers, Pathfinder commands, Mesh tool,
Blend Tool, Gradients

Opposite: Dot.com Revolution | *Time Magazine,*
illustration for magazine article

Doug Panton
Logo Design

When Doug Panton creates a new look for a client, he offers his client a complete package consisting of a logo and anything from corporate identity, package design, and branding to Web site design. A Doug Panton logo is often extracted and refined from a more complex illustration. In other cases, an elaborate and complex illustration may become a company logo. As an award-winning artist with many years of experience, Panton's work is intricate, unique, and recognizable.

Safetyman | Nexfor, illustration for a newsletter article on safety in the workplace

Doug Panton's credits include awards from almost every art director's club on the planet for both illustration and design. A principal and partner of Daigneault & Panton Inc., a graphic design firm in Cabbagetown, Toronto, Panton divides his time among owning and operating a successful studio, serving as illustrator and designer for that business, and teaching classes in graphic design and illustration at Sheridan College and the Ontario College of Art and Design. His client list is extensive, including companies such as Ralston Purina, NutraSweet, Budweiser, Air Canada, Tourism Canada, Bank of Montreal, Kimberly-Clark, Radio Bureau of Canada, Microsoft Corporation, and Kodak Canada to name just a few.

"I determine my thoughts and ideas before I get on the computer. Pencil sketches are well-defined and thought through before I place them into my Illustrator page. If you rely on the computer and the software to bail you out, you're doing yourself a disservice."

NCE icons | NCE Energy Trust, oil and gas company annual report

Panton has created award-winning illustrations and designs for more than twenty-five years, starting out as an illustrator and art director in large advertising agencies and now owner and chief designer and illustrator at his own design firm. He has moved from a traditional illustration technique to a completely digital environment, using Adobe Illustrator and Adobe Photoshop.

Panton decided to start the decade of the '90s with a computer system. He purchased a Macintosh IIcx with 8MB of RAM and an 8MB hard drive along with Adobe Illustrator 88. "Illustrator actually sat on my shelf for nearly six months before I launched the program. I think it was fear factor mostly—a condition very common to illustrators."

Big Band | The Santa Fe Natural Tobacco Company, package design

Rap | The Santa Fe Natural Tobacco Company, collectible cards

Using the computer resulted in no change in his design approach. Panton is a purist in regard to illustration. "I determine my thoughts and ideas before I get on the computer. Pencil sketches are well defined and thought through before I place them into my Illustrator page. I think if you rely on the computer and the software to bail you out, you are doing yourself a disservice. Once a tight comp is on the Illustrator page, you can pretty much have your own way with the design execution."

Panton begins a new project by spending ample time developing the concept, which includes doing research and reviewing reference material. He makes sure he's thoroughly familiar with his client's product or service before he begins to sketch some roughs. He reads and re-reads relevant text, takes notes, and ponders the subject. Rough thumbnails help him refine the concept. He creates 10 to 20 viewpoints and from these sketches, he selects a single composition and sketches an illustration in pencil that's 150 to 200 percent of actual size of the

RadioXM | *American Lawyer Magazine*, **magazine illustration**

NEW YORK'S HOTTEST DESIGNER IS NOW AVAILABLE IN TORONTO.
THE THOMAS O'BRIEN COLLECTION. EXCLUSIVELY BY HICKORY CHAIR, AT RIDPATH'S.

WE'RE LOCATED
AT 906 YONGE STREET
JUST NORTH OF BLOOR
TORONTO ONTARIO
CANADA M4W 2J2
[416] 920.4441

RIDPATH'S
CREATING NEW TRADITIONS EVERY DAY

Ridpath's advertisement | Ridpath's Fine Furniture of Toronto, Canada; ad for an exclusive line of furnishings final project. "Fundamentally I rely on my drawing skills to create my images. Later, in Illustrator, I take advantage of the ease of trying out different positions for elements or compositions with just the click of the mouse."

"It's important to plan out my images beforehand, using scanned sketches as templates. To do that, I open up an image and choose Template from the Layers palette. I like to start off simple and build up complexity in stages. When I create my illustrations, I block large shapes of color first, and add details on separate layers. This way I can break down the illustration into manageable chunks. Working with layers helps me manage my work as I go."

Recession | *InfoSystems Magazine*, illustration

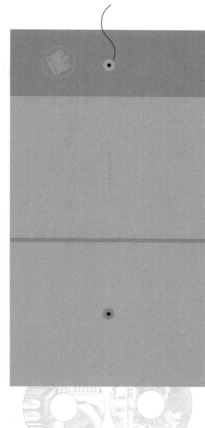

**Ridpath's Media Kit |
Folder design for a
media kit**

Ridpath's billboard | An outdoor billboard at the rear
of the Ridpath's store

Ridpath's CD Art | Part of a media kit for Ridpath's
new identity

The first challenge in Adobe Illustrator for Panton was mastering the Pen tool. Like most traditional artists, Panton struggled in the beginning with this tool. "As long as you're patient, persistent, and choose to use a mouse as your weapon of choice, you will succeed! It's important not to expect this tool to respond the same way as a Gilotte 303-nib would." For him, the initial struggle was worth the time it took to adapt to a new medium. The advantage of finessing layers, using blends to create merged shapes, and changing perspective with a few mouse clicks enables him to create multiple variations easily. "Blends are great for creating multiples of the same shape, or for merging one shape into another. You can also blend groups of objects—great for creating animations."

UpCountry Logo

The Project

Ridpath's Fine Furniture of Toronto, Canada, needed a new look. The company has worked with Panton for more than 15 years for all of their design, illustration, and advertising needs. They asked Panton to give a new look to the image that had been a part of their identity since the early 1900s. Ridpath's wanted to create an upscale image that would continue to serve their mature clientele while embracing a younger group. Because Panton creates many different types of designs for the client, he was commissioned to create a logo, as well as imagery that could be applied to multiple uses. "The client wanted something with a whole range of elements from which we could pull segments and apply different images for different purposes." Panton was to design the project as a single piece that would contain various images. Those images had to be able to stand alone and be suitable for various uses of the company brand, such as packaging, point-of-purchase material, newspaper and magazine advertising, billboard displays, corporate identity documents, and multimedia.

"Coloring is what I like best about Illustrator. It's like using my first coloring book. If it could manage my assignments, sort and account for my time on a project, do my billing, and collect on overdue invoices, I think you might have perfection."

—DOUG PANTON

The Steps

Step 1: Creating the concept. Panton always begins a new concept by developing pencil sketches. He often has two stages for developing the initial concept. The first stage is finalizing three to five rough sketches, which he selects from 10 to 20 pencil drawings. The second stage is meeting with the client to discuss the sketches and finalize the direction and the design. Ridpath's chose one of the roughs (**Figure 15**) and Panton went to work right away, completing the entire project in one week.

Step 2: Creating a template. Panton scanned the rough drawing and placed it on a new Illustrator art board. He created a template layer and used the default value of 50% for the Dim Images setting (**Figure 16**).

Step 3: Drawing the central image. Throughout the drawing, Panton used geometric shapes that he reshaped and manipulated by adjusting strokes or using Pathfinder effects. The first object he drew was the chair. He wanted to create a woodcut effect with strong contrast in the design. He drew circles and rectangles over the template and modified them

Figure 15

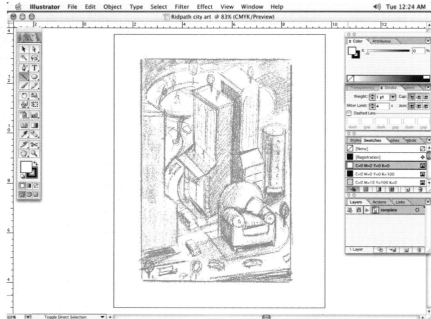

Figure 16

with the Pen tool and the Pathfinder effects. He modified rectangular objects by eliminating points, averaging paths, and joining points. He duplicated the lines on the chair surface and joined end points to create single paths that could be filled. By holding the Option (or Alt) key down and dragging, he duplicated a shape. To join the end points he used Control or Command-J (Object > Path > Join). After he created additional objects, he grouped them to make them easier to select and move around the art board (**Figure 17**).

Step 4: Creating the perspective. Panton developed the perspective for the drawing from the chair object. He doesn't create a vanishing point and align objects to guides. Instead, he uses more of a look-and-feel approach, placing individual objects adjacent to each other, keeping the overall perspective in mind. He may duplicate paths and drag a path to obtain the same perspective or he may just illustrate freehand while paying attention to the perspective view (**Figure 18**). After creating the chair, he drew the streets around it. He would later segment the lines used for the streets with the Pathfinder palette as he placed objects in front of these lines, using the Minus Back Pathfinder command.

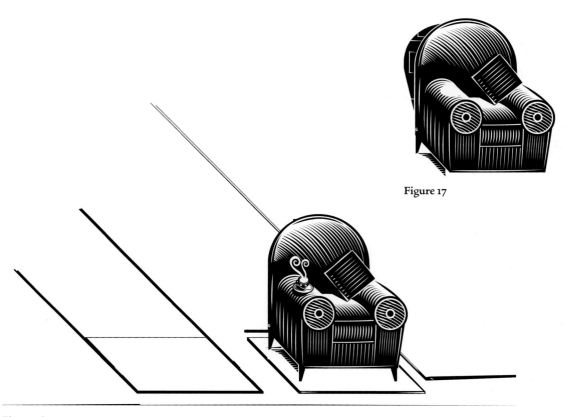

Figure 17

Figure 18

Step 5: Modifying the drawing. "Modifying designs really depends on the client. In some cases, I have complete artistic freedom. In other cases, I need to develop tight comps and stick religiously to the original design with little or no deviation. Fortunately with Ridpath's, they pretty much go along with whatever I do. As I worked on the piece, the two tall towers appearing behind the chair didn't feel right (**Figure 19**). I played with the design a little and modified it as I went along." Panton again created geometric shapes and aligned the sides to the perspective he had created for the chair and sidewalks (**Figure 20**).

Step 6: Creating the logo. What evolved out of the drawing was an image—the dresser— that Ridpath's adopted as their logo. He created the dresser by, again, first drawing geometric shapes and modifying rectangles and circles to obtain the right dimension and perspective. Panton duplicated the drawers by holding the Option (or Alt) key and shift-dragging new copies (**Figure 21**). He pulled the final image out of the drawing and included it in the client's identity package (**Figure 22**).

Figure 21

Figure 19

Figure 20

Figure 22

Step 7: Drawing the background elements and icons. For objects in the background, he followed the same process of creating geometric shapes and duplicating the shapes to create the background buildings. He added the sky lights, helicopter, and other background symbols to communicate the message that "we've been here for a long time, but we're not above having some fun with what we do." Panton added a humorous side to the piece with the background elements and the icons assembled in the foreground. He created some symbols in the drawing and copied some from other artwork he had on hand. The final piece (**Figure 24**) has won many awards and Ridpath's is delighted with the new look. They have used assorted objects from the design for various advertising campaigns—some of which appear here in the Gallery section.

Figure 23a   Old Logo

Figure 24   New Look

Figure 23b   New Logo

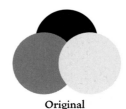

Original

Add

Subtract

Intersect

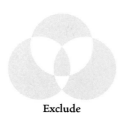

Exclude

Using the Pathfinder Effects

The Pathfinder palette offers many commands that allow you to add, subtract, intersect, divide, crop, and otherwise manipulate multiple paths. The Pathfinder commands let you easily start out with simple paths and create complex paths and shapes that would be time-consuming and tedious to create manually.

The Pathfinder palette is divided into two sections—Shape Modes and Pathfinders. The Shape Modes let you create and modify compound shapes, which are comprised of two or more paths, compound paths, groups, blends, envelopes, warps, text, or other compound shapes that interact to create a new editable shape. The Pathfinders, on the other hand, are designed to combine paths. Compound paths are made of two or more paths that interact to create a new editable path.

In the Shape Modes section you will find the following commands:

Add to shape area. Combines all selected shapes into a single shape. It deletes all overlapping areas. The shape is then filled and stroked with the fill and stroke from the top-most shape.

Subtract from shape area. Removes the front-most shape from the back-most shape.

Intersect shape areas. Keeps the overlapping areas of selected shapes and hides the non-overlapping areas from view.

Exclude overlapping shape areas. Retains non-overlapping areas and makes overlapping areas transparent. When there's an even number of objects overlapping, the overlap is transparent. When there's an odd number of objects, the overlap is filled.

In the Pathfinders section you will find these commands:

Divide. Breaks overlapping objects into separate objects.

Trim. Removes any areas of a filled object that are hidden. Removes strokes and doesn't merge objects of the same color.

Merge. Removes any areas of a filled object that are hidden. Removes strokes and merges overlapping paths filled with the same color.

Crop. Uses the front-most object to crop all other objects in a selection. Removes any strokes.

Outline. Breaks objects into separate line segments with no fill colors. Instead, it colors the strokes with the old fill color.

Minus Back. Removes the rear-most objects from the front-most object. The opposite of Subtract.

A final command, Trap, is in the Pathfinder palette pop-up menu. Trap allows you to overlap shapes slightly to avoid gaps in the printing process. Note: When you use Trap, be certain to check with your service center or print shop to be certain they want Trap included in the file. If your vendor provides trapping when the file is printed, they won't want you to trap your artwork. Trapping a trapped file can present problems when separating color.

All of the commands in the Shape Modes section of the palette produce shapes that are *live*. This means compound shapes are still editable and you can also *release* (undo) a Pathfinder command by choosing Release Compound Shapes from the palette pop-up menu. You can still select the original, individual shapes within the compound shape with the Direct Selection or Group Selection tools. The Expand command flattens the compound shape into a single path, thereby converting the live shapes into *dead* ones—shapes that cannot be released or edited.

Note that you will also find the above Pathfinder commands, along with Hard Mix and Soft Mix, under the Effects menu. You can Hard Mix and Soft Mix colors in areas that overlap. The commands under the Effects menu change the appearance of an object without changing the underlying structure of the object itself. You can apply them to groups of objects, layers, and type rather than simple shapes.

Divide

Trim

Merge

Crop

Outline

Minus Back

The Advertising Age®

InterActive

HALL of FAME

Chapter 11
CD Packaging

Artist

Michael Doret

Hollywood, California

Designer, Illustrator, Lettering Artist

http://MichaelDoret.com

Project

Bedlam Ballroom CD Packaging

Client

Squirrel Nut Zippers, Mammoth Records

Illustrator Tools and Techniques

Pen Tool, Filters, Pathfinder commands, Transparency

Opposite: Ad Age/Interactive Hall of Fame | *Advertising Age Magazine*, Logo

Michael Doret
Sign of the Times

You've no doubt seen artwork created in one form or another by Michael Doret. Perhaps you were browsing a newsstand and picked up a *Time* magazine. The cover might be a Doret design—he has six *Time* covers to his credit. You toss *Time* aside and browse the latest *TV Guide*—there's another Doret design on the cover. No, you're not in the mood for reading. Perhaps you want to pick up a music CD. You thumb through CD recordings and lift the Squirrel Nut Zipper's latest CD from the tray. The CD cover was yet another Doret design.

Doret, like several other artists profiled in this book, has an ongoing love affair with letterforms. Although the uses for his art are wide-ranging—magazine covers, signage, logos, editorial illustrations, t-shirts, baseball caps, and almost anything else that can be printed or silk-screened—the common element among all of his pieces is a unique blend of shapes and illustrative design with carefully carved letterforms. Doret begins with lettering in each

Hollywood and Vine Diner | Logo for a 1940's style restaurant in Los Angeles

new piece and then integrates the illustration to work in concert with the lettering. Doret developed his affinity with letterforms and illustration at The Cooper Union, where he earned a BFA (Bachelor of Fine Arts) degree. The first five years out of school,

"My projects are almost always letterform-related. I first look at the specific sequence of letters and how those letterforms might relate to each other."

he held different staff positions, the first of which was as Edward Benguiat's assistant. Benguiat designed 47 different font families—many well-known faces, including the one named Benguiat. Doret worked many years in his native home in New York City as a free-lance artist serving a prestigious client list that included the National Basketball Associa-tion, Major League Baseball, Walt Disney Imagineering, Warner Bros., Universal Studios, Nike, Adidas, *Time* magazine, *TV Guide*, United States Postal Service, Graphic Artists Guild, Red Sky Interactive, *Playboy*, Capitol Records, and Columbia Records.

Coolsville | Logo for Coolsville Records

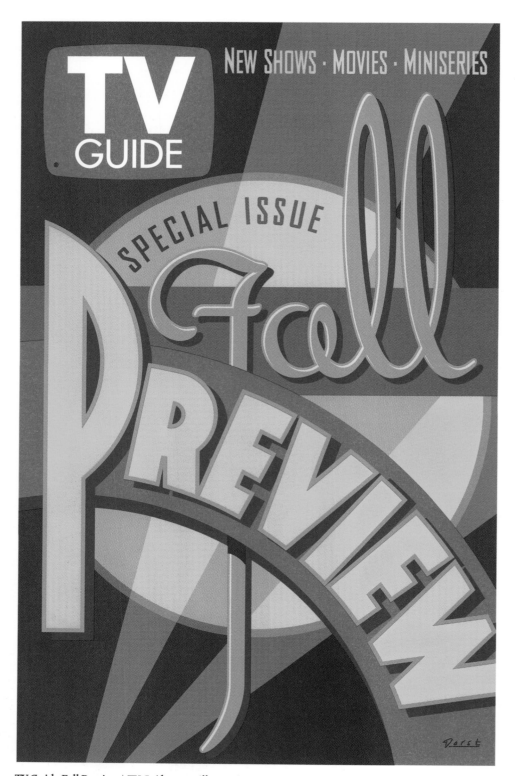

TV Guide Fall Preview | *TV Guide*, cover illustration

Doret decided to leave the Big Apple and moved, set up his studio in Hollywood, California. From college graduation until around 1995, Doret's methods were traditional. He hand-illustrated letterforms and design on frosted mylar with ink and drafting instruments. It wasn't until 1995 that Doret's illustrator-wife Laura Smith encouraged him to start working on a computer.

Doret purchased his first Macintosh computer in 1995 along with Adobe Illustrator 5.5. He's used Illustrator in every version to date and has found the computer to be a marvelous tool. "The part that I really like about using a computer and Illustrator is being able to visualize the finished product before printing. I used to produce pre-separated art for my finishes—black ink on frosted mylar. I would call out either Pantone colors or CMYK equivalents for each overlay that the printers would plug into their separations. So, I could never really 'see' my art before it was printed. That all changed with Adobe Illustrator."

When Doret begins a new project, clients typically contact him by phone. In the beginning of his career almost all initial contacts with clients were face-to-face. "Today face-to-face meetings are getting rare. My most frequent contact is over the phone. Sometimes I receive

Welcome to the Hollywood Dell | Sign for a Los Angeles neighborhood

initial requests through email, but a phone conversation is generally the first step in beginning a new project."

With such a broad range of design work and client requests, Doret varies his method for starting each project. "Since all my projects are different, there is no one method that I use. Generally, my projects are almost always letterform related, so I first look at the specific sequence of letters and how those letterforms might relate to each other. I look to see if there are any interesting combinations, and if there are, how I can capitalize on them to bring out the ideas a client wants to communicate."

After an interview with the client, Doret uses a tracing pad and pencil to sketch out rough ideas. From his extensive background in traditional media, he'll work with a sketchpad, creating thumbnails, roughs, and tight comps before he begins to work in Illustrator. "I usually start with rough thumbnail sketches, gradually tightening them up in successive versions as I emphasize the elements and relationships that I like. At the same time, I minimize or eliminate those components that don't work for me. Once I have a general design fairly pinned down, I might take out some colored pencils and create a rough color sketch for myself—where I start adding the dimensionality that the use of color might allow. I start playing with elements such as outline, dimension, highlight, and drop-shadow."

New York Knicks | NBA basketball team, logo, © 2002 NBAP

Carolina Courage | Women's soccer team from the WUSA (Women's United Soccer Association), logo

When Doret finishes a tight tracing, he scans the drawing and begins to work in Illustrator. He places the scanned artwork in Illustrator as a template and traces the template to begin the drawing.

Not all concepts are easily developed. If he finds a challenge along the way, he steps back from the project and puts it aside. Doret may share thoughts with his wife and others as he works out a concept in his head. For other means of inspiration, Doret researches period art and designs created for many different purposes. "If an idea doesn't immediately spring into my head, I almost always start looking through my files and books for old material that might inspire me. I am an avid fan of the graphics of the early to mid-20th century, and it is there that I look for inspiration: matchbooks, poster stamps, posters, old signage, showcard art, theater marquees, petroliana, and collections of old logos. I might find something as simple and general as a color combination that could spark an idea, or it might be something as specific as letterforms. It can literally be anything that might give me inspiration."

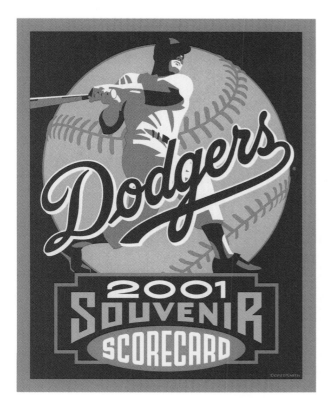

Dodgers Scorecard | Los Angeles Dodgers, cover illustration

Graphic Artists Guild | logo

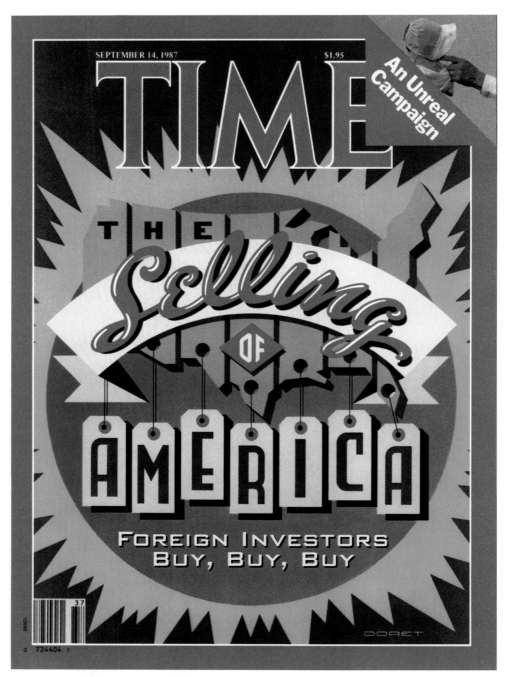

The Selling of America | *Time* magazine, cover illustration, © Time Inc.

The Colombian Connection | *Time* magazine, cover illustration, © Time Inc.

The Project

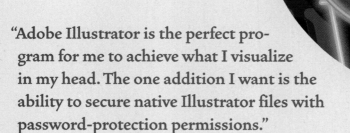

Lane Wurster, art director for Mammoth Records, was familiar with Doret's work and thought he would be perfect for the job of creating CD packaging for the Squirrel Nut Zippers, a band who performs swing music. Doret, in turn, was a fan of the band and their previous CD covers, all of which sport a vintage look and feel. The art director gave Doret a few guidelines. He wanted a roadside neon sign look—like those advertising roadhouses, honky-tonk bars, or old motels from the 40s and 50s. In fact, there would be an animated component to the illustration—an animation on the enhanced CD and a *lenticular* (picture with plastic coating that gives the effect of motion) special edition CD package. He also wanted the package to be highly typographic. Vintage and typographic? Two words that warm Micheal Doret's creative heart.

"Adobe Illustrator is the perfect program for me to achieve what I visualize in my head. The one addition I want is the ability to secure native Illustrator files with password-protection permissions."

—MICHAEL DORET

The Steps

Step 1: Exploring concepts. Doret's first steps were to sketch out some concepts. His initial idea was to use a playful strip tease theme with the name of the CD in the middle and the stripper on either side (**Figure 13**). He thought it would be great to have the woman appear in neon in alternate poses of dress and undress (**Figure 14**). The art director loved the idea, but a female member of the Squirrel Nut Zippers band was adamantly opposed to the idea, so it was scrapped.

Step 2: Nailing the concept. Doret then came up with the idea of a crazed character, dubbed "King Leer," as the focal point, with lettering around him. Doret made some rough sketches and showed them to the art director, who loved the new direction (**Figure 15**).

Step 3: Developing the main character. Doret, who grew up in Brooklyn, was a frequent visitor as a child to Coney Island in the 50s. There were three amusement parks there that were built at the turn of the century—Dreamland, Luna Park, and Steeplechase-The Funny Place. While Dreamland and Luna Park burned down in the 20s or 30s, Steeplechase survived. "The logo for Steeplechase was this leering face of a guy with a huge grin (**Figure 16**). I have had this image in my head ever since I was a child. I thought something along those lines would be good for the CD

Figure 13

Figure 15

Figure 14

Figure 16

illustration. A demonic, cartoony, smiling face to symbolize bedlam, craziness, and madness. It seemed to fit (**Figure 17**)." Doret then played with the face, making it progressively rounder, more geometric, and less naturalistic (**Figures 18 and 19**). Since he knew there would be some animation to the illustration, he developed King Leer in two poses.

Step 4: Tightening the comps. Eventually the two poses evolved into a placid King Leer who yanks on the chain of the neon sign, turns it on, and gets zapped. The zapped King Leer is winking and grinning, and his hat and monocle have flown off. Doret tightened up the comp for King Leer (**Figure 20**), as well as for the typographic components (**Figure 21**).

Step 5: Creating the tracing scans. For his final sketches, Doret added, as he always does in his illustrations, measurements and angles for all of his elements. "All of my work is geometrically related, so precision is necessary," says Doret. He then scanned these sketches into Photoshop and saved them as TIFFs. Doret calls the scans of his final sketches "tracing scans" because he uses them as templates in the Illustrator file (**Figures 22–25**).

Step 6: Starting the Illustrator files. Doret created a new 11-by-8.5-inch CMYK file in Illustrator. He then placed the main lettering tracing scan on the bottom layer (**Figure 26**). Next, he added not one, but four layers of guidelines to ensure proper placement and alignment of his elements (**Figure 27**). Doret hid and showed these guides as needed.

Figure 17

Figure 18

Figure 19

Figure 20

Figure 22

Figure 23

Figure 21

Figure 24

Figure 25

Step 7: Starting King Leer. Doret usually starts with the most difficult element first, which in this project was King Leer. He created a new 11 by 8.5, CMYK Illustrator file in which to create the King. "I find that it is easier in a complicated illustration with so many elements to draw things in separate files and then copy and paste them into the main illustration." Doret imported the three tracing scans for King Leer and placed them each on a sublayer under a Templates layer. He placed each tracing scan on top of the other to ensure proper alignment for the animated version of the illustration (**Figure 28**). Doret then added his essential guidelines layer. He also created what he calls a safety layer, which consisted of a black rectangle that he could display when creating elements such as white glows. "I usually have several safety layers where I put type before converting it to outlines. I also add shapes before applying pathfinder commands or strokes and converting them to shapes. It makes editing later much easier."

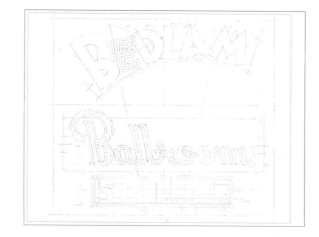

Figure 26

Next, he created a new layer for what he called Base Leer—the dark, shadowy image of King Leer, which would be under the neon versions, akin to the metal sign under the neon tubes. He then displayed only the tracing scan for Base Leer (**Figure 29**). He began by first creating a circle with the Ellipse tool for the Head. He then created a shape with the Pen tool for the left ear and copied and reflected it using the Reflect tool for the right ear. Doret is a die-hard mouse aficionado. "I don't use a stylus and pressure sensitive tablet like a lot of other illustrators. I guess I just started with the mouse and got used to it. It is all I use."

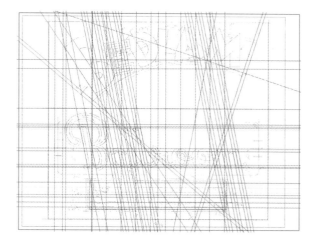

Figure 27

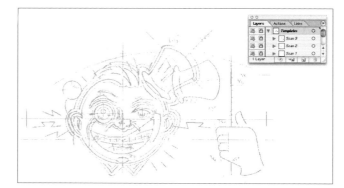

Figure 28

Figure 29

Figure 30

Next, he created the highlight for the top hat (**Figure 29**). Doret selected all of the elements and used the Add to shape area command in the Pathfinder palette to unite the separate elements into a single shape.

Step 8: Creating Base Leer. Using the Ellipse and Pen tools, Doret created the shapes for the detail elements of the Base Leer. Again, he used the Reflect tool to create the collar, ears, mouth, nose, and chin shapes, first drawing one side and then copying and reflecting to produce the opposite side. He also applied the Add to shape area command to these pairs of elements (except for the ears) to unite them into single shapes. He created the holes in the monocle, collar, and hat by making the shapes with the Ellipse and Pen tools and then using the Subtract from shape area command in the Pathfinder palette (**Figure 30**).

Step 9: Creating Placid Leer. Doret then continued on to what he called the Placid Neon Leer layer. On a sublayer, using the Pen tool, he drew Leer's shocked face in 4-point strokes of Pantone (PMS) 3125 CVC. He then set the Opacity of the strokes to 12% in the Transparency palette to create a ghosted effect (**Figure 31**). On another sublayer, he created Leer's placid face using 4-point white strokes, to which he applied a 2.0-pixel Gaussian Blur Effect. This created a neon glow effect (**Figure 32**, shown against the safety layer for display purposes).

Step 10: Finishing Placid Leer. On another sublayer and, again, using the Pen tool, he drew another copy of placid Leer, using a 4-point stroke. He applied a process gold color to the strokes, which he mixed using the CMYK color sliders (**Figure 33** top). On the last sublayer for this layer, Doret created another copy of placid Leer, using a 2-point white stroke. These two sublayers viewed together create an unlit neon tube effect (**Figure 33** bottom). The entire layer is shown in **Figure 34**.

Figure 31

Figure 32

Figure 33

Figure 34

Step 11: Creating Neon Leer. This layer, called Neon Leer, required several additional sublayers. Doret started by copying the gold-colored, placid Leer from the previous layer. He set the Opacity of the strokes to 12 percent in the Transparency palette. Next, he created another sublayer, which consisted of a copy of the face elements of the aqua-colored, shocked Leer from the previous layer. He changed the stroke color to PMS 369 CVC and applied a Gaussian Blur effect of 2.0 pixels. He copied the monocle, collar, hat, and hand to another sublayer, while he copied the shock marks to yet another sublayer. He gave the strokes on both sublayers 2-pixel Gaussian Blur effects and colored them, using the process gold and Pantone 3125 CVC that he used earlier (**Figure 35**).

Figure 35

Step 12: Finishing Neon Leer. Doret created three more sublayers. Again, using a copy of the shocked face, he applied a 4-point stroke of PMS 369 CVC on the first sublayer. On the next sublayer, he applied a 2-point process light-green colored stroke. On the third sublayer, he applied a .5-point stroke of PMS 389 CVC. The effect of the three sublayers together is one of a neon tube (**Figure 36**). Doret repeated the process for the shock marks, using white and PMS 3125 at 50% and 100% (**Figure 37**). Doret finally added two last sublayers, which contained the monocle, collar, hat, and hand. He created the sublayers, using a 4-point process gold stroke and a 2-point white stroke to produce the same neon tube effect created on the Placid Leer layer (**Figure 38**). The total King Leer illustration appears in **Figure 39**.

Figure 36

Step 13: Creating the base Bedlam lettering. Doret copied and pasted the King Leer art into the main Illustrator file and then moved on to the base Bedlam lettering. Using the Pen tool, he drew each letter of Bedlam separately, based on the angles

Figure 37

Figure 38

Figure 39

Figure 40

Figure 41

noted on the tracing template. "When I am creating angles, I like to repeat the angles. It provides synchronicity and symmetry." He filled the letters using a process burgundy and brown, which he mixed using the CMYK sliders in the Color palette and stored in the Swatches palette.

Step 14: Creating the base Ballroom letttering. On the same layer, Doret created the base Ballroom lettering, using the Pen tool. He filled the lettering with the same process brown he used for the Bedlam lettering (**Figure 41**).

Step 15: Creating the dimensionality. To create the drop shadows for the base Bedlam and Ballroom lettering, Doret first made a copy of the separate Bedlam letters and then united them using the Add to shape layer command in the Pathfinder palette. He then used the Direct Selection tool to tweak the tops of the letters to give more of a sense of dimension to the lettering. He filled the shadow with a process black. He copied and pasted the Ballroom lettering and filled it with the same process black. Doret created a safety layer and put copies of the Bedlam shadow, Ballroom lettering (and later the Squirrel Nut Zippers type) on the layer in case he needed to use them for revisions (**Figure 42**).

Step 16: Drawing the background. The last element Doret added on this layer was a background behind the lettering. Using the Rounded Rectangle and Pen tools, he created two separate shapes, filled them with a process dark blue, and placed them behind the base lettering and shadows. He then duplicated the shapes, filled them with a darker blue, and placed them on the very bottom to act as a drop shadow.

Figure 42

Figure 43

Step 17: Producing the Bedlam neon lettering. On a new layer, Doret created the neon Bedlam lettering, using the same methodology he used with King Leer. He created the initial paths of the lettering with the Pen tool, using a stroke of .5 points. He then grouped the strokes, made a copy, pasted them in back, and applied a weight of 2 points. He repeated the process, creating two more strokes of 4 points and 6 points. For the 6-point stroke, he applied a Gaussian Blur Effect of 3 pixels. He colored each set of strokes with varying shades of process yellow, red, and green, which he mixed using the CMYK sliders in the Color palette and stored in the Swatches palette (**Figure 44**).

Step 18: Producing the Ballroom neon lettering. On a new layer, Doret repeated the process with the Ballroom lettering (**Figure 45**).

Step 19: Creating the ghosted elements. Next Doret created a layer that contained copies of the Bedlam neon lettering and the shocked King Leer. He set the opacity of these elements to 12 percent in the Transparency palette.

Figure 44

Figure 45

Figure 46

Figure 47

Step 20: Drawing the Tonite lettering. Using his tracing scan as a template, Doret created the Tonite lettering, using the Pen tool and filling the paths with the same process black used in earlier elements. He created the lettering in a separate Illustrator file (**Figure 47**).

Step 21: Creating the illuminated panel. After creating a second copy of the Tonite lettering and coloring it with a process red with an 86% Opacity, Doret drew two rectangles with the Rectangle tool to create the frame of the sign. He tweaked the rear rectangle with the Direct Selection tool to create a bevel in the corner, and then filled both with two shades of process brown. Next, Doret created another rectangle for the illuminated panel. He chose Object › Create Gradient Mesh to create a rectangular gradient mesh in the panel. He applied various shades of process light-yellow to the mesh patches to create the illusion that the panel was backlit. "I wanted the panel to display different densities, as though some light bulbs were brighter than others." (**Figure 48**)

Step 22: Finishing the illuminated panel. Doret created a series of 1-point process black strokes with the Pen tool. These strokes created the grid over the illuminated panel. Next, he added a series of small circles that he created with the Ellipse tool. He then made a copy of the circles, pasted them in back, and applied a 3-pixel Gaussian Blur Effect (**Figure 49**). He divided the entire set of circles among six layers so that circles would appear to move

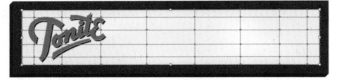

Figure 48

Figure 49

Figure 50

around the marquee in the animated version of the illustration. Doret finished the panel by adding the Squirrel Nut Zippers type. He created the type, in process black, using Franklin Gothic. He then converted the type to outlines. He moved a few of the letters so that they wouldn't be perfectly aligned and used a number 7 in place of the letter L. He also substituted a lower case d, which was rotated, for an uppercase P. He then filled the E, U, and p with a process brown that he created using the Color palette sliders, and set the Opacity to 90 percent in the Transparency palette (**Figure 50**).

Step 23: Adding the background. The last element to be added was the background (**Figure 51**). Doret simply created a rectangle and filled it with process black. He then created a polygon with the Pen tool and filled it with a process burgundy. He made a copy of the polygon, tweaked the corner to create a bevel for dimension, filled with a darker shade of the process burgundy, and sent it behind the first polygon. After creating crop marks and then placing his signature in the bottom right corner, Doret was finished with the main illustration.

Step 24: Creating the animated GIF. To create the animated version for the enhanced CD, Doret selectively hid and displayed certain layers. He then chose File > Save for Web and saved the image as a GIF (bedlam01.gif). He repeated the process, hiding and displaying various layers each time until he created 12 separate GIFs (four GIFs are shown in **Figure 53**). He then built an animated GIF using GIF Builder. See the animated version of the illustration at www.michaeldoret.com/doret/artwork/bedlamcd.html.

Figure 51

Figure 52

Figure 53

Step 25: Sending it to the client. After getting approval from the client, Doret burned a CD containing the illustration and animated GIF files, and delivered it to Mammoth Records. Mammoth used the illustration for both a regular CD cover and also for a limited edition lenticular CD package, which gave the cover an animated feel. As an offshoot of the CD packaging, Doret created supplemental illustrations for T-shirts (**Figures 54 and 55**) and concert-tour banners (**Figure 56**). The Bedlam Ballroom CD Package was nominated for the Best Recording Package for the 44th Annual Grammy Awards.

Figure 54

Figure 55

Figure 56

Securing Illustrator Artwork

The one feature Doret wants most in Adobe Illustrator is the ability to secure Illustrator files for digital-rights protection. Doret's ideal Illustrator would have the ability to password-protect files with various levels of protection, including locking artwork, restricting printing, and opening a file. In its current version, Adobe Illustrator does not have security methods built into the program to protect your digital rights. However, with the help of other Adobe software, you can protect your files from unauthorized viewing and printing. Adobe Acrobat is one of the programs that can help you preserve your digital rights. You can save an Illustrator file directly to PDF format, then open, edit, and secure the PDF with Acrobat.

To protect a file with password security using Acrobat, first select File > Save As in Adobe Illustrator. From the Format pull-down menu, select Adobe PDF (PDF). When the Adobe PDF Format Options dialog box opens, be certain the checkbox for Preserve Illustrator Editing Capabilities is checked and the file compatibility is Acrobat 5.0 (**Figure 57**).

Open the file in Acrobat 5 or greater. (Note: if you don't have Acrobat, you need to purchase it. The following steps cannot be performed with Acrobat Reader.) Select File > Document Security. The Document Security dialog box opens. From the Security Options pull-down menu, select Acrobat Standard Security (**Figure 58**).

When the Standard Security dialog box opens (**Figure 59**), enter a password in the User Password field. This password will permit a user to open your file, but, any editing restrictions will remain in effect.

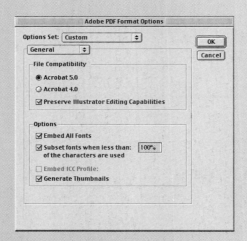

Figure 57

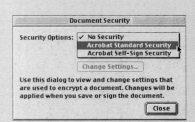

Figure 58

Also, enter a Master Password. This password enables you to open the file, change permissions, and unsecure the file, which is essential if you need to edit the file in Illustrator.

Check the permissions options you wish to use. If you don't want anyone to change your document in any way, select None from the Changes Allowed pull down menu. If you want to restrict printing to a low resolution, set the Encryption Level to 128-bit RC4 (Acrobat 5.0) and select Low Resolution from the Printing pull down menu. You can also use 128-bit encryption to protect the document against changes and permit only low-resolution printing while still offering users the ability to add comment notes. If you wish to enable comment authoring, select Comment Authoring, Form Field Fill-in or Signing from the Changes Allowed pull down menu. Click OK and save the file. (Note that if you secure files with 128-bit encryption, it will require Acrobat viewers 5.0 or greater to open the files).

In the above example, no user can open the document without knowing the user password. When a user password is supplied and the file opens in Acrobat, the user cannot change restrictions or disable security. The user won't be able to open the file in Illustrator either. The security needs to be removed in Acrobat before an Illustrator user can open the file.

Acrobat provides other means of securing documents with the Acrobat Self-Sign Security method, which lets you secure files for selected members of a workgroup and provide different permissions for different users. To learn more about Acrobat Security, see the Acrobat Help document installed with Adobe Acrobat software.

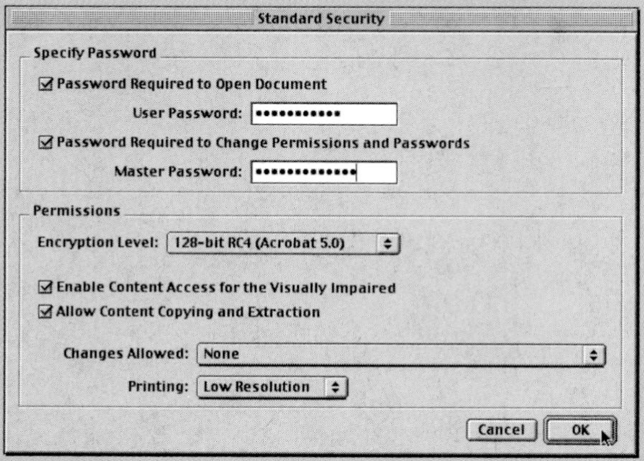

Figure 59

Chapter 12
Editorial

Artist
Louis Fishauf
Kettleby, Ontario, Canada
Designer, Illustrator, Typographer
www.fishauf.com

Project
Editorial Illustration

Client
Business Week magazine

Illustrator Tools and Techniques
Pen Tool, Pattern Brush, Transparency, Gradients,
Pathfinder commands

Tech Buying Guide | *Business Week* **magazine**

Photo: Jackson Fishauf

Louis Fishauf
The Medium is the Message

Louis Fishauf thinks of himself as a graphic designer first and foremost. But this has not kept him from becoming, almost unintentionally, an equally distinguished illustrator. His work is recognizable for its clean lines over complex textures, attention to minute details, and a dry, subtle sense of humor evident in his most serious work.

He was born in Germany, but has lived in Toronto, Canada since he was one. After graduating from the Ontario College of Art, he worked in the studio of Les Usherwood, a well-known typographer and printer whose eponymous typeface designs are still widely available. Fishauf

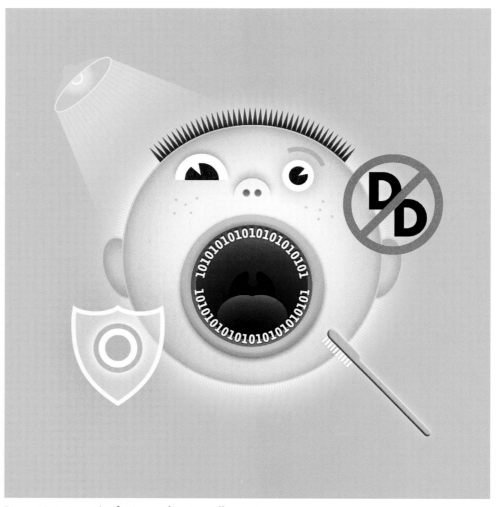

Prevent Data Decay | Infotriever, advertising illustration

then became art director for a succession of Canadian magazines including *Chatelaine, The City, City Woman, Executive, T.O. Magazine,* and *Saturday Night.* His work at the magazines won numerous awards and medals.

"I'm not the kind of guy who will sit down with a pad of paper and develop three or four sketches to choose from. I usually begin working right on the computer, rather than sketching on paper."

In 1991, he received the ADCT's Les Usherwood Award for "a lifetime of excellence in the field of communication arts." In 1997, he was invited by Apple Computer to become one of

Buying Guide | *Business Week* magazine

Editorial Illustration | *Business Week* magazine

the first 40 AppleMasters, an international group of recognized visionaries from various fields. His association with the Macintosh computer began in 1984 with one of the first Macs manufactured. "I didn't grow up with computers but adopted them early in my career. I would say that working on the computer was a turning point in how I approach design projects."

When Fishauf begins a new project he flirts, struggles, and toys with his computer. "For illustration projects, I rarely have a set idea when I begin working. I need to let the piece evolve organically until I feel it's ready to present to the client. That usually means it's any-where from 70-90 percent complete before I show it. I then make any alterations based on client feedback, and proceed to final art." By contrast, for design projects such as logos or Web sites, he presents a number of directions on his Web site, and arrives at the final solu-tion through a collaborative process with the client. Through subsequent interaction with the client, he arrives at the final solution and he's on to the next project.

Economy Section | *New York Times*

While Fishauf's early work was based in traditional print media, a world of pen and ink, T-squares and triangles, X-acto knives, and hand-specified type, this did not keep him from becoming an early adopter of the Macintosh. "I could work very quickly in MacPaint and MacDraw on an early Mac," he comments. But he was still using traditional photographic reproduction methods for his final output.

Soon after the introduction Apple's LaserWriter printer, a group from Apple toured some Toronto design studios. One of the visitors to Fishauf's studio, Reactor Art & Design, was Jan Davis, wife of Russell Brown—Adobe's first art director and a distinguished AppleMaster himself. She told him about a soon-to-be-released drawing program called Adobe Illustrator.

Logo | Pen Equity Management Corporation

"As soon as I got my hands on it, I thought it was very cool," said Fishauf. "It changed my concept of computer graphics because I could draw free-form lines and shapes using Béziers and get high-quality graphics out of the LaserWriter printer."

Fishauf began a long association with Adobe Systems and Apple Computer. He was a beta tester of Adobe's first version of Photoshop, which, along with Illustrator, is his main work environment. He's used every version of both programs and his work has developed two distinct styles, "a more graphic, Illustrator style, and a more collagey style, for which I work more often in Photoshop." Inevitably, he ends up combining features of both programs to produce a collage-like fusion of semi-realistic elements over highly patterned, colorful backgrounds.

Fishauf starts a project by sitting down to his computer with little or no concept in mind. "I find that just putting something—anything—down will start the creative juices flowing. Sometimes though, they flow a lot slower than I'd like. I often go to bed after the first day's work on an illustration, hating what I've done and thinking I'll have to start all over in the morning. After a night's sleep, and the benefit of relatively fresh eyes in the morning, I can usually salvage something from the day's work and forge ahead. I just keep pushing and pulling, trying this and that until at some point in the process something clicks, and the piece that wasn't working a minute ago suddenly comes into focus. Once that happens, the hard part is over, and the rest is pure enjoyment."

Everywhere You Look | Adobe Systems

Magazine Cover | *NetWare Connection* magazine

Cover Design | *Business Week* **magazine**

To help prepare for a new assignment, Fishauf researches a project, then puts his mind to rest for a few days before he starts illustrating on the computer. Each design is an evolution of background and free association as a concept begins to develop. "I read the brief and ask the client any pertinent questions. If research is required, I do it online or at the Toronto Central Reference Library, which has an extensive and well-organized picture collection (mostly magazine clippings from the past 50 years). I have a huge library of my own illustration pieces. I may review many of my previous drawings for elements to use in a new illustration. I'll copy and paste graphic elements, rework them, and adapt them to the current project. Then, if time permits, I like to not think too hard about the job for a couple of days, but just let it percolate in the back of my mind until some ideas start to bubble up. I usually begin working right on the computer, rather than sketching on paper."

"For me it's rare that I ever have a concept worked out when I work on a piece. I'll usually have some half-baked ideas about an assignment, some reference material, icons, or bits and pieces of things that I've done. I'll incorporate some of these into a new drawing, but my initial start is to open Illustrator and let the final image evolve as I work. I'd have to say that my creative process is not starting with a concept —the concept is generally developed through trial and error. I'm not the kind of guy who will sit down with a pad of paper and develop three or four sketches to choose from, then when one concept is approved by a

Personal Finance | *Sympatico NetLife* **magazine**

Buying Guide | *Business Week* **magazine**

client, go ahead and get started. I wish that I could work that way, but unfortunately that's just not how I execute new project designs."

Whichever way Fishauf's work goes, toward Illustrator or Photoshop, it has a brilliant sense of layout and design, and the typographic elements are precisely placed and set. His impressive knowledge of traditional design and typography is matched by his skill with Illustrator's tools and applying his own techniques.

Champagne | *Computer Artist* magazine

The Project

"I have a relationship with *Business Week*. I won't say I do a lot of work with them, but in the course of a year, I'll do three or four designs for them. I received a call from one of the art directors who asked if I was available to begin a new project." The art director wanted a piece for a story on global capitalism. She asked for a kind of *yin* and *yang* view of capitalism in a global economy, illustrating the good and bad aspects of capitalism." The project description was simple and there was no need to do extensive research. Fishauf had his own view of the effects of global capitalism, so he let the project sit on hold for a few days before beginning the design.

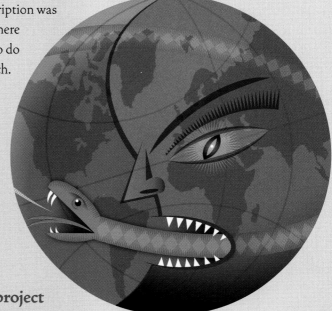

"The ability to execute a project from conception to final art in one seamless digital environment on my desktop is what I like about Illustrator. If I could ask for more , two features I'd love to have are type style sheets and basic 3D effects like extrusion and perspective."

— **LOUIS FISHAUF**

The Steps

Step 1: Developing the concept. True to Fishauf's style, he launched Illustrator and created an artboard first. He used no scans as templates and introduced no elements to help him with the initial concept. He created a keyline for the final print size on a tabloid page. The client wanted an illustration with two opposing views—the *yin* and *yang* of global capitalism. Fishauf drew a circle on the page with the idea that he would later introduce a scanned map of the globe. The globe needed to be divided into two objects that would represent positive and negative views. He drew a Bézier curve to divide the map and chose the Divide button in the Pathfinder palette (**Figure 14**). "The placed scan came at a much later stage. I knew I would use a map to represent the global view, but first I wanted to play with the *yin* and *yang* concept."

Step 2: Applying color. As an extension of moving toward representation of polar opposites, Fishauf added color gradients, choosing warm and cool colors to define the opposing views of capitalism (**Figure 15**). He created a number of custom gradients and experimented with different views, while letting the concept develop in his mind.

Step 3: Creating the character. "When I drew the globe I had the idea of making a face out of it. The shape of the Bézier curve was drawn to conform to a facial profile that would later have more detail to illustrate a face." Fishauf then added a few objects that he drew by hand to illustrate the face. Using a combination of Pen tool paths and Pathfinder tools he added facial features to create the central character (**Figure 16**).

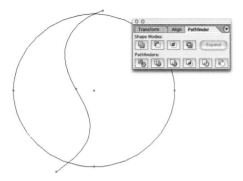

Figure 14

Figure 15

Figure 16

Step 4: Using custom brushes. Fishauf first drew a simple snake shape with a green fill, then saved it as an art brush, which he applied to an ellipse. For the diamond pattern, he created another art brush and applied it to a copy of the same ellipse. Selecting the snake brushstroke, he converted it to outlines using the "Expand Appearance" command in the Object menu. He redrew the snake's head to make it larger and more dramatic. Then he made copies of each edge of the snake's body separately, pasted them in front, and painted them with a custom pattern brush to create the ribbed effect (**Figure 17**). He then experimented with different colors, opacity levels and blend modes to achieve the final effect (**Figure 18**).

Step 5: Adding detail. The globe was the central focus for the design. Before dividing the globe circle into the yin and yang sections, Fishauf made a copy of the object, which he saved in a new layer for future use. After adding the facial features to the globe, he used copies of this circle object as a mask for the placed map scan, as well as for the glow effect around the outside of the globe. The glow is made up of two layers pasted behind the globe, one painted with a zigzag pattern brush, and the other a 12pt white stroke with a 4.5-pixel Gaussian Blur applied (Filter > Blur > Gaussian Blur). Fishauf then added the top hat, the devil horn, and the longitude and latitude lines (**Figure 19**).

Step 6: Adding the background. To further centralize the globe in the drawing, Fishauf created multiple rectangles, transformed the objects to triangles and trapezoids, and moved points at the corners to shape them. He moved one point of each object behind the globe and added gradients to render an effect that made the objects appear to focus at the center of the globe. Fishauf wanted to keep the viewer's eye toward the globe, which he

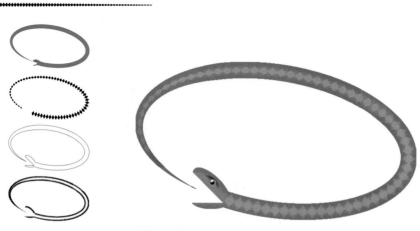

Figure 17   Figure 18

Figure 19

ultimately positioned off center in the drawing. After drawing simple rectangular objects and making manipulations to paths, he moved objects until he had a feeling for the final composition of the lines (**Figure 20**). To add a more devilish appearance to the face, he added a horn, which he created with the Pen tool, to the top right side of the globe.

Step 7: Adding blended objects. To create the satellite rings in the drawing (Figure 21), Fishauf first drew two circles with white stroke and no fill, holding down the Option key to draw them both from the same center point. He then assigned opacities of 33 percent and 4 percent respectively to the small and larger circles, and used the Blend tool to create a blend of 33 steps between the two. Using the Transparency palette, he applied an "Overlay" blending mode to the resulting pattern of concentric circles. The rings added another focal point to the image.

Step 8: Adding objects from archived illustrations.
Fishauf found icons in his library of images that could complement his message. He copied and pasted the icons and objects assembled throughout the background from other files in his personal library of images. He edited objects for color and transformed them to accommodate scaling and perspective (**Figure 22**).

Figure 20

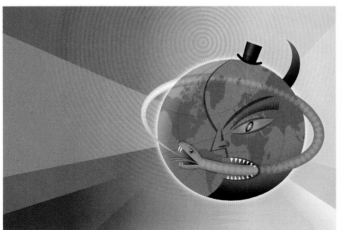

Figure 21

Figure 22

Step 9: Adding shadows. The two dark clouds at the top left of the design are vector objects that he drew in Illustrator. Fishauf again rasterized the clouds and applied a Gaussian Blur (**Figure 23**). Fishauf admits, "I added my own bias to the drawing. As I was developing the piece there was an obvious slant on the negative view of global capitalism." Dead fish on the background, dark clouds, and industrial waste all contributed to the view Fishauf had as he created the artwork.

Step 10: Adding type. The client determined the type for the headline, tag line, and body copy. Fishauf had no input on the typeface or positioning of the type. He added the text as prescribed by the client and converted the headline and tagline type to outlines. He sent the final piece to the client via email as an Illustrator file.

The art director at *Business Week* liked the design. However, after it was submitted to the magazine editors, they felt there was too much focus on the negative. Fishauf was asked to add a little more balance to the overall look (**Figure 24**). He did so and *Business Week* published a modified design. The artwork illustrated here was more to Fishauf's liking and he's pleased to see the original illustration published as he first designed it (**Figure 25**).

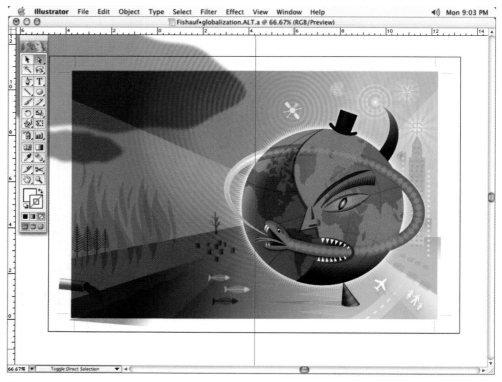

Figure 23

Figure 24   Final Image—Approved by *Business Week*

Figure 25   Final Image—Fishauf's Preference

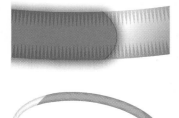

Figure 26

Creating Custom Brushes

Brushes are creative stroke patterns you can apply to Illustrator paths. When you use repeating patterns with objects, you'll find custom brushes a great asset in simplifying the illustration of complex objects. Illustrator offers you a huge library of several hundred brushes from preset illustrations in four different categories: Art Brushes, Scatter Brushes, Calligraphic Brushes, and Pattern Brushes. If none of the Illustrator presets suit a particular job, you can create your own pattern design and define the pattern as a new brush. The new brush is then applied to a path.

Fishauf created several Custom Brush Patterns he used in the artwork for the *Business Week* piece. One particular object containing brush patterns is the snake (**Figure 26**).

The diamond shape in the snake body is an Art Brush and the ribbing is a Pattern Brush. To create a similar effect for your own artwork, you first need to illustrate an object contained within the brush shape. To create a shape similar to the diamond shape inside the snake body, create a diamond and duplicate it several times. Each subsequent shape should be sized smaller than the previous object.

You can select the objects with any of the selection tools. To create the brush, either drag the selection to the Brushes palette or select New Brush from the Brushes palette flyaway menu (**Figure 27**).

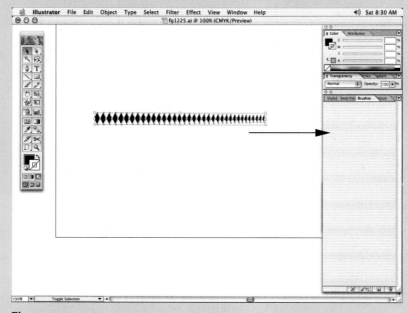

Figure 27

Illustrator opens a dialog box from which you can select a type of brush from multiple choices. In this example, Fishauf used the Art Brush (**Figure 28**).

After clicking OK in the New Brush dialog box, the Art Brush Options dialog box opens. You assign attributes in this dialog box for direction of the pattern, sizes, rotations, and color attributes. When you select Tints from the Method pull down menu, you can change colors in the Illustrator toolbox and you can adjust transparency in the Transparency palette (**Figure 29**).

In the example illustration, Fishauf created a stroke with the Pen tool. He selected the stroke, clicked on the brush pattern in the Brushes palette, and the pattern was applied to the selected stroke (**Figure 30**).

Figure 28

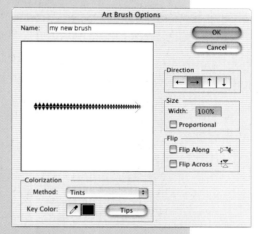

Figure 29

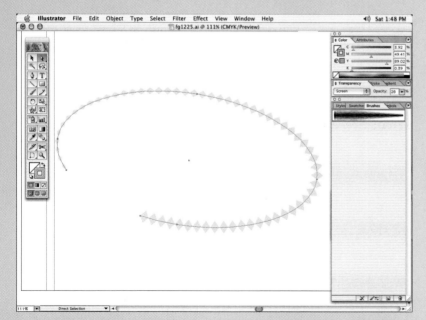

Figure 30

Using the same example illustration, the ribbing on each side of the snake body contains a Pattern Brush. You create Pattern Brushes in the same manner as the Art Brushes. First, draw the pattern and select the objects, then drag to the Brushes palette (**Figure 31**). When the New Brush dialog box opens, select New Pattern Brush.

The Pattern Brush options contain a number of attribute choices for the way a pattern is ultimately displayed along a path. You can specify different shapes on inside and outside corners, as well as, the beginning and ending points on the path. For this example, Fishauf used the default selection for *Side Tile* (**Figure 32**). The Side Tile is the first icon appearing under the brush name in the Pattern Brush Options dialog box.

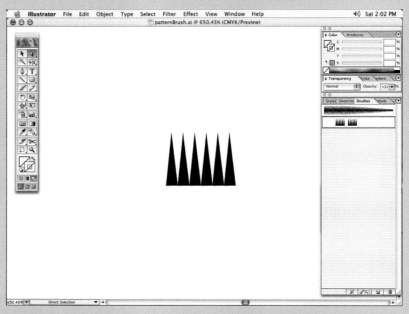

Figure 31

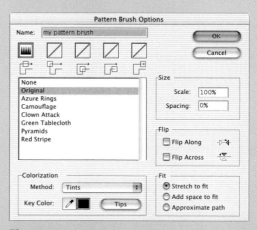

Figure 32

In Fishauf's illustration, he drew several strokes. He selected the outer path and clicked on a Pattern Brush. He copied and scaled a second stroke and flipped it, then applied the same brush stroke.(**Figure 33**).

The final image contained duplicate paths without strokes, which he used as a mask. When you select the Object > Clipping Mask > Make menu command, the top path masks the underlying objects to its path. It's easiest to see the effect of applying the mask by looking at the difference in the tail of the snake between Figure 33 above and (**Figure 34**) below.

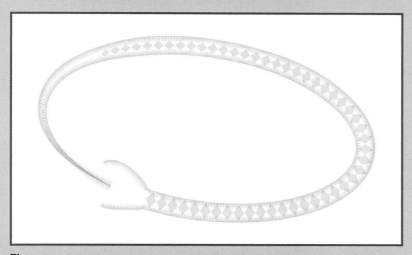

Figure 33

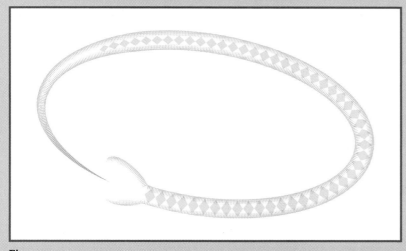

Figure 34

Chapter 13
Cartoon Illustration

Artist
Nick Diggory
Brisbane, Australia
Designer, Illustrator, Cartoonist, Art Director
www.nickdiggory.com

Project
Cat and Dog for 2002 Calendar

Client
Origin Design, Bristol, England

Illustrator Tools and Techniques
Pencil Tool, Layers, Stroke palette

Opposite: Lady in tub | Self promotion

Nick Diggory
Cartoons from Down Under

Where does a 21st-century artist live? If you're Nick Diggory, the answer is, anywhere in the world you want. For Diggory, that place is the beautiful Gold Coast of Australia. Originally from England, Diggory moved to Australia and found no work available in the area he chose to live. Thankfully, he kept his English phone number, had his calls routed to his home in Australia, and talks to his English clients as if he were sitting across town from

Cow | *American Showcase,* a journal for illustrators

them. "It's funny. When I talk to new clients in the UK, they think that I'm just down the road a bit. After I tell them I am actually located in Australia, they are quite surprised." Diggory quickly reassures his clients that they are only paying for a local call. "Technology certainly has made the business end of things easy to deal with." Diggory found that with his computer, a high-speed connection, and call forwarding, he could serve clients anywhere in the world.

Diggory has had a passion for doodling and illustration since he was a kid. He couldn't wait for high school graduation to start a career in illustration, so at the age of sixteen, he dropped out of school and went straight to art college. He enrolled in the Cheshire School of Art and Design where he graduated with a Distinction in Exhibition and Design. Since then— over 20 years ago—Diggory has delivered more than 16,000 commissioned illustrations without ever missing a deadline.

Diggory tried the job market for a while after graduating from art college. His first job was with a fashion photographer in Manchester, England, where he worked as a finishing artist. Shortly thereafter he moved on to work as a visualizer for an advertising agency and later became an art director at another agency. His five-year career as an employed artist ended when he was given the boot for spending more time on a fast-growing freelance business than

"Errors can improve the finished article. I often send the client three or four versions of the finished artwork because I prefer the look of some of the illustrations with errors. I love the flexibility of Illustrator."

he did at his "real job." The consequence of being asked to leave was a blessing, and he's never looked back. His freelance business has grown to the point that he creates illustrations for package designs and brand advertising for clients all over the world.

The freelance work that occupied his time during his last employment was drawing the character Oddbins, a French peasant who popped up all over the place to represent a wine distributor in the United Kingdom. Other artists have depicted Oddbins since then, but Diggory was the bloke who drew the first illustrations of the French peasant logo.

When artwork started to become computer generated, he balked. "I held off using computers for ages. I actually told my wife that if that was the way things were going, I'd do something else for a living." Then one day he was introduced to Adobe Photoshop and he learned what people were talking about. He bought his first Mac with Photoshop 3. It wasn't until version 6 that he started using Adobe Illustrator. A client wanted a billboard design, and Illustrator was the obvious choice.

Snake | *Contact*, a
UK advertising journal
for illustrators

Dog on leash | Self promotion

Diggory begins a project with a pencil sketch. His clients are relatively firm about the kind of design they want, so he creates only three or four sketches and sends the scanned pencil drawings to the client. "Occasionally I'm called into an agency at the design stage to give some input of my own. More often than not, the designers know exactly what they want but can't draw it. That's where I come in. Nine times out of ten I can hit the mark in a couple of sketches." For Diggory, a 48-hour turnaround is a luxury he seldom experiences. His clients typically want something within 24 hours. Following client approval, he creates the illustration in Illustrator and emails it to the client. Then it's off to another job.

Computer Collage | *Internet Advisor* **magazine**

Sports | *Internet Advisor* **magazine**

Sometimes a client, such as an ad agency, will provide Diggory with visuals of the concept they want to pursue. They then ask Diggory to put his spin on it. When he has to work from just a written brief, it's harder to predict what the client wants. In fact, occasionally a client will reject his sketches, but use them to refine their needs, saying, "No, that's not it, but now that I have seen something, I think I know what I want." Clients such as Warner Brothers and Disney are extremely specific about what they want. "They will go so far as to say, we want you to use a 1.4 stroke here and a 2.5 stroke here. Those types of jobs are not very fun—they're too restrictive."

Pig | Ad for Graphics International

"With Illustrator I can actually be more creative. There's more room to explore the possibilities. Sometimes errors I make can improve the finished article. I often send the client three or four versions of the finished artwork because I prefer the look of some of the illustrations with errors. I love the flexibility of Illustrator. It's so easy to try out new styles."

Cowboy | *American Showcase,* **a journal for illustrators**

The Project

Origin Design, a small design studio in Bristol, England, and also one of Diggory's existing clients, commissioned him to create an illustration for a 2002 calendar. The theme was a play off the two number 2s in that year's number. Origin Design had a list of clever pairings, such as hook and eye, sticks and stones, cat and mouse, chicken and egg, yin and yang, night and day, and so on. They told Diggory to choose one and he picked the pairing of cat and mouse. Other than the size, Origin gave Diggory no other direction. He had free creative reign. " When a client trusts you enough to say, 'do what you like,' that's when the job is both easy and fun." The calendar also featured illustrations and photographs from eleven other artists and went on to win a Certificate of Merit at the National Business Calendar Awards 2002.

"I love the flexibility of Illustrator, which enables me to easily create several versions of a drawing. If I could ask for one more feature it would be an airbrush tool."

—NICK DIGGORY

The Steps

Step 1: Creating a good sketch. Diggory created the initial concept pencil sketch for the project in a mere half-hour. "Sometimes the concept comes to me immediately. Other times it takes a long time. If I get the feeling that it just won't happen, I get up and go fishing, clear my head, and then come back and try it again. You can just feel it not happening and you know you have to walk away. Sometimes you can get too close to it and try too hard to think of something clever." Satisfied with his first crack at a concept, Diggory tightened up the rough and drew the final pencil sketch. He scanned the sketch at 300 dpi into Photoshop and saved it as a JPEG, which he then emailed to Origin Design. They approved it right away without changes.

Concept Sketch

Final Sketch

Step 2: Making a template. Upon approval from Origin, he created a new, A4-size CMYK file in Illustrator and placed the scanned sketch on his base layer. He then dimmed the sketch layer to 50%. Diggory uses Illustrator for his projects because, as he puts it, "Illustrator allows you to experiment with different styles. Photoshop is more restrictive in that you know you can always replicate a style. I mean, if I can put a reflection on a shape, then anyone can. I guess if there's a downside to using the computer as a tool for illustrations, it's that you see a lot of art that looks the same. You can spot someone who has just started using Illustrator or Photoshop from a mile away."

Step 3: Starting the cat drawing. He started the illustration by concentrating on the main characters first, beginning with the cat. "I tend to concentrate on the main characters first. If I started with the background first I could easily go overboard and then the focus would shift to the background rather than the characters." On a new layer, using a Wacom tablet and Illustrator's Pencil tool, a stroke weight of 2.6, and Pantone 161 CVU (a dark brown) as the stroke color, he drew the paths that composite the head. Diggory didn't worry about creating closed paths (see the inset figure in **Figure 14**), but instead concentrated on just the stroke line. "I tend to avoid the Pen tool and work with Bezier curves. Because I work so quickly, the Pencil tool is ideal."

Step 4: Filling in gaps. On the same layer, Diggory created the fill shape for the cat's face and also added the jaggy highlights, using a 1-point stroke. The fill shape would fill in the gaps left by the open paths. For any shapes that would later contain just a fill color and no

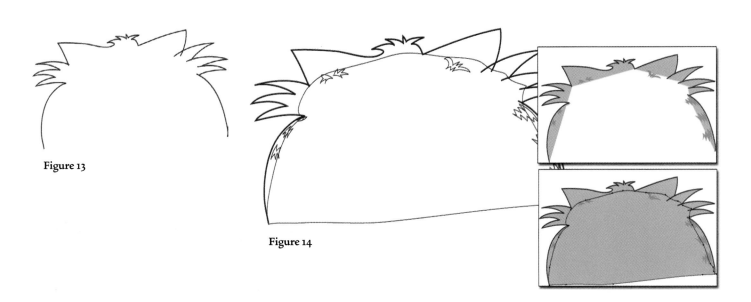

Figure 13

Figure 14

stroke, Diggory set the stroke weight to 1 point and then later, when he applied color, he set the stroke weight to None.

Step 5: Adding the facial features. On a new layer, he added the nose, mouth, eyes, and insides of the ears. The stroke weight ranged from 1 point for the teeth to 2.2 points for the eyes and 2.6 points for the nose. For shapes that would ultimately have no stroke color, but just a fill, Diggory used a 1-point stroke.

Step 6: Finishing the face. Diggory created a separate layer and added the shadows in the eyes and mouth. Again, using a 1-point stroke, he drew the brows, the pupils, and the nose reflection, each on its own layer. On yet another layer, he created the nose shadow, the soon to be white ruff, and the jaggy highlights of the ears and fur.

To complete the face, Diggory created another layer and added the whiskers, using a 1-point stroke. He then used the Ellipse tool and created the pores.

Step 7: Drawing the cat's appendages. Diggory created another layer and drew the tail, using a stroke of 1.7 points (**Figure 17**). He created the stroke layer for the left paw, using a stroke of 3.2 points. Using the stroke layer as a guide, he drew the paw shapes that would contain the fill colors, and then moved the fill layer under the stroke layer (**Figure 18**). He repeated the process with the right paw.

Figure 15

Figure 16

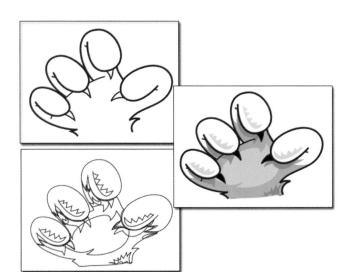

Figure 18

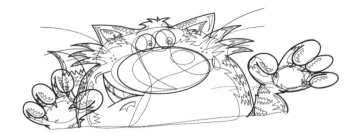

Figure 17

Step 8: Drawing the mouse. The mouse wasn't as complex as the cat, so he created the entire mouse on one layer. He drew the stroke outline of the mouse using 80% Black and a stroke weight of 2 points for the outside body outline and .7 to 1.5 points for the thinner detail strokes. Diggory then created another layer and made the shapes that would contain the fill areas of the mouse. He used a 1-point stroke that he would later set to a color of None once he filled the areas.

Step 9: Creating the background elements. To begin creating the background, Diggory started with the background rectangle and shadow areas (for the objects in the background) on a single layer. He then created another layer and drew the objects in the background, such as the door, the picture, the lamp, and the window and curtains. He drew all the objects with a 1-point black stroke (**Figure 20**).

Step 10: Creating additional elements and details. Next came the flower pot and the cup and saucer, each on its own layer. Since he wanted to fill and stroke the cup and saucer, he used a 1.7-point stroke for those elements. He then created a couple more layers and

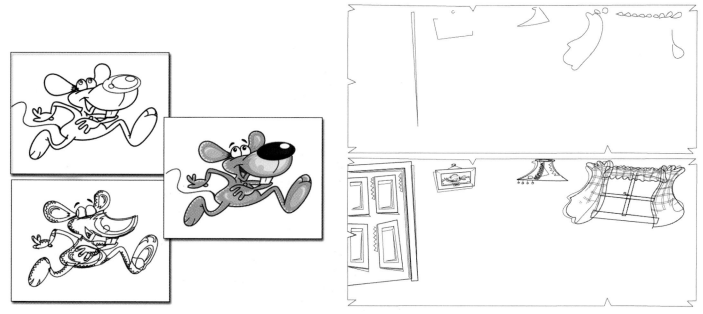

Figure 19

Figure 20

created the table with the Pen tool. He switched to the Pencil tool and created the saucer and mouse shadows. Back to the Pen tool and a new layer, Diggory drew the 3-point strokes that would make up the stripes on the tablecloth (**Figure 21**).

Step 11: Finishing the line drawings. Finally, to complete the background, he made a layer and drew five circles with the Ellipse tool to create a paw print. He grouped the separate circles, selected them and then Option-dragged (Alt-drag to do this on a Windows machine) to clone a second print. He repeated the process, randomly placing the paw prints on the background wall. Diggory added detail elements to the background, such as the paw prints and the fish in the picture frame that were not in the original sketch. "I tend to keep the background in the sketch very loose. The clients don't seem to mind if I embellish the background somewhat in the final illustration. I call this little bit of extra detail the 'selling layer.' The client sees new elements I've added and thinks, 'I didn't ask for that, but it's really nice.' They feel like they're getting a little more for their money."

Figure 21

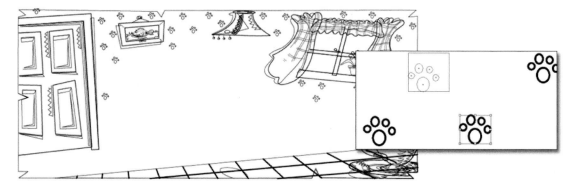

Figure 22

Step 12: Adding color. After he finished the line work, Diggory chose his color palette. He used Illustrator 9's PANTONE Uncoated Swatch Library for all of his colors (**Figure 23**). While he tends to use intuition to select his colors, he did consciously choose more subdued, pastel colors for his background elements, so as not to detract from the foreground characters. Diggory says, "One of the most frustrating things to me about working on a computer is the difference in how colors appear between monitors. I have two G3s and the colors look different even between the two monitors!" Diggory painstakingly selected each of his elements and filled them with color. Some shapes were both filled and stroked with color. Others were just filled, with the stroke set to None, while yet others were stroked with color and without a fill. To get the stacking order of the shapes correct, he chose Arrange from the Object menu and made the appropriate selections. In some instances, he had to rearrange layers to get the compositing correct.

Figure 23

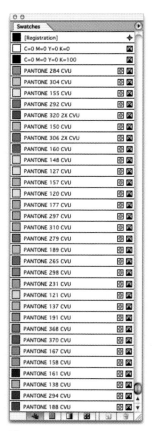

Figure 23

Step 13: Framing the picture. As a final touch, Diggory created two more layers. Using the Pen tool and a 3-point black stroke, he created a frame around the entire illustration. The final layer contained an additional black stroke to touch up the bottom portion of the frame.

Step 14: Final adjustments in Photoshop. Once Diggory completed the illustration, he opened the Illustrator file in Photoshop, rasterized it as a 300-dpi CMYK image, and applied a drop shadow behind the cat to "liven it up a bit and bring the characters off the background." The entire project took Diggory only 3.5 hours. "I work very quickly. And because I'm so busy, I also like to get each job out of the way so I can move on to the next one. I prefer a deadline of three hours rather than three months. If I have three months, it's too easy to wait until the last day to do the job."

Diggory saved a copy of the file as a low-resolution, 72-dpi JPEG file. He emailed the JPEG to Origin Design for final approval. Once Origin gave the okay, he flattened the layers, saved it in Photoshop's native file format and emailed the 20-MB file to the client. "Unless the client specifically asks me not to, I always flatten the final file before I email it. That way, no changes can be made. I have had some pieces where alterations were made after I submitted the final and I wasn't told about it." In this case unfortunately, the size of the calendar was changed at the last minute and therefore the printer resized the entire illustration, keeping approximately the same height, but elongating it quite a bit. Says Diggory without irritation, "I preferred the original size, but who I am to argue with a printer?"

Figure 25

Working Between Illustrator and Photoshop

Nick Diggory, like many of the other artists in this book, often uses Photoshop in concert with Illustrator for embellishments that Photoshop handles better. Among the most common uses of Photoshop for Illustrator artists are applying soft, blended drop shadows and rasterizing artwork for printing.

Nick Diggory used Photoshop for both these purposes. He applied the drop shadow in Photoshop at the final production stage. In some circumstances you may wish to add Photoshop elements, such as drop shadows, in Illustrator and preserve the vector artwork while adding some raster images to the final drawing. It's not hard to do since Adobe developed Illustrator and Photoshop to work together.

If you want to add a drop shadow to an element or an entire drawing and preserve the vector objects that you created in Illustrator, open Photoshop and create a new document, being careful to specify a color model and image resolution when you create the new file. If your artwork is to be printed in CMYK color at 175 lpi, for example, be certain to create a new document large enough in physical size to accommodate the Illustrator elements at CMYK and 350-dpi resolution. (Note: use two times the halftone frequency for image resolution as a standard rule of thumb.)

Open both Illustrator and Photoshop and place the document windows side by side. With a new document in the Photoshop window appearing as a blank page, select all the elements to be shadowed in the Illustrator window and drag them to the Photoshop document window (**Figure 26**).

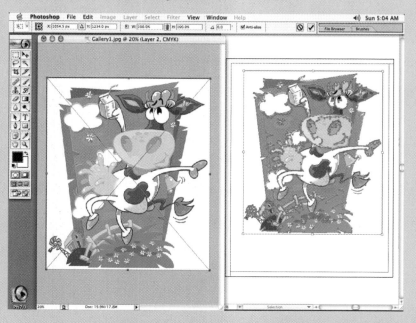

Figure 26: Drag and drop Illustrator vector art from the Illustrator document window to the Photoshop document window.

When the objects appear in Photoshop, the artwork has not yet been rasterized. You can freely size or transform the vector objects without affecting image resolution. As long as the vector-bounding box is visible around the objects, the objects are still in vector rather than raster format. However, in the case of drop shadows, you'll want to be certain not to scale the objects, so leave the size alone.

To rasterize the objects, strike the Enter or Return key on your keyboard. The result will be a rasterized version of the objects on a new separate layer. Hit the slash (/) key to lock the layer's transparent pixels, and then fill the layer with white. When transparent pixels are locked, only the layer's nontransparent areas will be filled with white. Use the Layer Style dialog box (Layers > Layer Style > Drop Shadow) to apply a drop shadow and set the distance and size (**Figure 27**).

Figure 27: **Open the Blending Options dialog box and check the box for Drop Shadow. Set the size and distance to create the shadow desired.**

Click OK in the Blending Options dialog box. Drag the layer with the shadow to your Illustrator drawing and send the shadow behind the objects (**Figure 28**). By preserving the type and objects and only adding smaller raster images to the design, you'll use less memory than rasterizing the entire illustration.

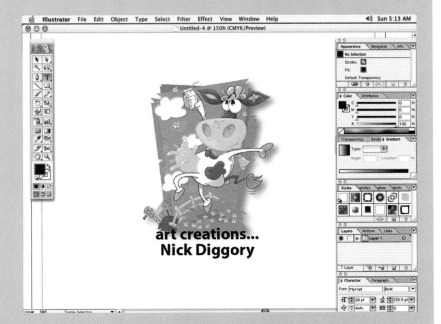

Figure 28: **The final artwork after the Photoshop shadow has been introduced in the Illustrator drawing.**

Chapter 14
Portrait Illustration

Artist

Tiffany Larsen

Seattle, Washington

Designer, Illustrator, Web Designer, Fine Artist, Computer Geek

www.uberpop.com

Project

Shirley Manson portrait

Client

Flaunt magazine

Illustrator Tools and Techniques

Pen Tool, Layers, Liquify Tools, Symbols, Adobe Streamline

Opposite: James Legros | *Flaunt* magazine (top left); Chris Kattan | *Flaunt* magazine (top right); Ashcroft | Self-promotion (bottom left); Outkast | Self-promotion (bottom right)

Tiffany Larsen
Whiz Kid to Professional Illustrator

What happens when you combine the qualities of an illustrator with those of a super geek? It's quite simple. You get Tiffany Larsen. However, this woman is anything but simple. Her background in computers dates back to days when most of us thought computers were game machines for kids. As a matter of fact, she was just ten years old when she started using computers.

"My first legitimate computer was an Atari 520ST. The graphics were great for the time. I'd spend hours using the shareware paint programs. Such a little geek. I guess using a computer to create art is second nature at this point." Combining fine art with her computer graphics, Larsen began to develop her unique style.

Horoscope Icons | ChickClick.com

Larsen was equally passionate about computer illustration and painting in the fine arts. She began her college career at the University of California at Davis where she earned a degree in Studio Art in 1996. Her first job out of college was with Metro Newspapers in San Jose, California, where she created ads for magazines, then moved on to creating cover designs. Larsen was on a fast track and soon became the first Webmaster (online art director) at Sanrio, home of "Hello Kitty," where she managed the sanrio.com and sanriostore.com Web sites. Larsen then worked as editorial art director for ChickClick.com, a Web site for teen girls. Although ChickClick was interesting and

"Some pieces create themselves. There seems to be a set progression and only one possible outcome. Although, with other pieces you're forced to rework it over and over again."

Paul Reubens | Self-promotion

very hip, she wanted something more akin to a dream job —something that would let her use her skills in fine art, her love of bright and exotic colors, and her talents as an illustrator. In true Larsen style, she set her sights, focused her aim, and targeted companies that could give her the freedom to do the work she wanted. Her efforts led to jobs with *Flaunt* magazine and clothing manufacturer Joe Boxer.

To begin a new project, Larsen may jump right in and develop a concept as she begins to illustrate. "Some pieces create themselves. There seems to be a set progression and only one possible outcome. It's not always so easy, though. Sometimes you're forced to rework a piece over and over again. The problem could be related to anything—the palette is wrong, or the amount of detail is excessive, or there's a problem you just can't put your finger on. These are the pieces that drive an artist mad. These can also be the most gratifying."

Golfer, "Pivot Rules" | Joe Boxer

Golfer 1, "Pivot Rules" | Joe Boxer

When it comes to research and inspiration, she floods herself with information. "I create a separate folder on my desktop for images and other inspiration. Sometimes I feel like the altavista.com image search is my best friend. I grab as many interesting pictures relating to my subject as possible." If she's not struck with the perfect palette, she goes to the bookshelf and flips through a collection of 1950's *Better Homes and Garden* magazines, niche books, old space books, and children's books. If those don't do the trick, she moves on to Japanese design books and other favorites like Stenberg Brothers poster books, *Tokion* magazine, and *Juxtapoz* magazine. If all the research from magazines and printed artwork don't create the right inspiration, Larsen gets more active in her search and visits a thrift store, museum, or art gallery.

Once inspired, she scans artwork from sketches and views an image on one monitor while working in Adobe Illustrator on another monitor. She applies color to many layers and

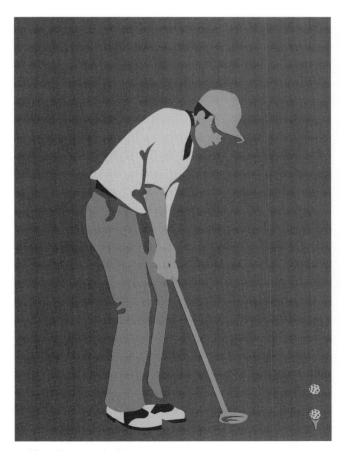

Golfer 2, "Pivot Rules" | Joe Boxer

Golfer 3, "Pivot Rules" | Joe Boxer

builds up the design. Each layer contains its own color with large shapes and color models evident in her pop art style. She builds up color and layers to produce the final piece, much as she would if she were creating a painting. Larsen is also particularly fond of creative tools in Illustrator, like distortion and warping.

When she left her last job and began freelancing, she acquired Fox as a client. "I created Flash animations using original illustrations for 'Ally McBeal'. The pieces were for an advice column called 'Woe of the Week,' and were each one to three minutes long. I worked on a one-week-per-episode deadline. The pace was remarkably fast, but it gave me the opportunity to use Illustrator in several different ways. I would sketch the illustrations out

Anchor | Self-promotion

TIFFANY

Nelly Furtado | Self-promotion

on paper and ink them in. Then, I scanned them, cleaned them up in Photoshop, and saved them as TIFFs. Next, I opened the scans in Streamline and converted the images to vectors. Now that they were .ai files, I could open them in Illustrator, remove any 'tweaky' extraneous points that Streamline added, and add color. Once the character art was finalized, I exported the document as a .swf and imported it into Flash."

Concurrent to her work with Fox, Larsen used Illustrator 10 for a new series of animated fairy tales for a broadband educational company. "Illustrator 10, with its enhanced SWF export, works great. The ability to move Illustrator drawings to Flash allows me to work fast and without any interruption to my creative flow."

Franka Potente | Self-promotion

Benicio Del Toro | Self-promotion

The Project

Larsen designed and mailed a series of promotional postcards, featuring portraits of celebrities, to select clients for whom she wanted to work. "I chose specific magazines that I wanted to illustrate for and sent the creative directors a barrage of postcards—one each week for four consecutive weeks. I was excited that it paid off with *Flaunt*, because they were the publication that I wanted to work for most." To date, Larsen has created seven illustrations for *Flaunt*, a Hollywood-based cultural magazine, featuring art, entertainment, and fashion. She continues to provide a portrait for each monthly issue's celebrity feature story, despite the fact that she usually has only a few days per project. Her assignment for the Spring 2002 issue was to do a portrait of Shirley Manson, lead singer for the band Garbage. She cranked out the illustration in two days. Larsen's "clean yet hip" approach to these portraits is a perfect match for *Flaunt*'s cutting-edge, urban style.

"Adobe has played the software game well. Over the years they've appropriated and created some key user-friendly features. I love the Symbol Sprayer. What I'd like to see next is multiple pages."
—TIFFANY LARSEN

The Steps

Step 1: Developing a color palette. *Flaunt* emailed Larsen a scanned photo of Shirley Manson. The photo was a PR shot provided by Garbage's agent. Larsen opened a new 8.5-by-11 document in Illustrator and placed the scanned image on a new layer, which she then hid. Larsen used the photo for reference only. Unlike many illustrators, she doesn't use the scan as a template. "I don't draw directly from the photo. It just doesn't look right. It sounds cheesy, but what I'm trying to do in my illustration is capture the *feeling* of the person."

After studying the photo, Larsen developed the color palette before doing any drawing. Using the CMYK color sliders, she mixed and stored her colors in the Swatches palette. "When I look at a photo, I see the shapes in color. I associate those colors with a feeling, which I try to capture." For Shirley Manson, she decided on shades of purple accented with white and gray (**Figure 17**).

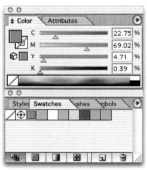

Figure 17

Figure 16

Step 2: Building the first layer. After she established the color palette, Larsen decided which parts of the illustration should contain the midtones, or flat color areas. She created a new layer and drew the arms, the head, and the neck. She used the Pen tool to draw the shapes in the Illustrator document window on one monitor while using a second monitor to view the scanned pencil drawing —she used the scan only as a reference point without tracing the image. She then filled the shapes with a medium purple. "I start with the middle tone and slowly build the illustration up. I place different colors each on their own layer, so I can hide them as I build the piece. I add the darkest, lightest, and complementary colors last."

Step 3: Beginning the build-up of layers. Because the photo of Shirley included her body, Larsen created a new layer and drew the clothes next, filling them with white. She then put the clothes layer under the light midtones layer (**Figure 19**).

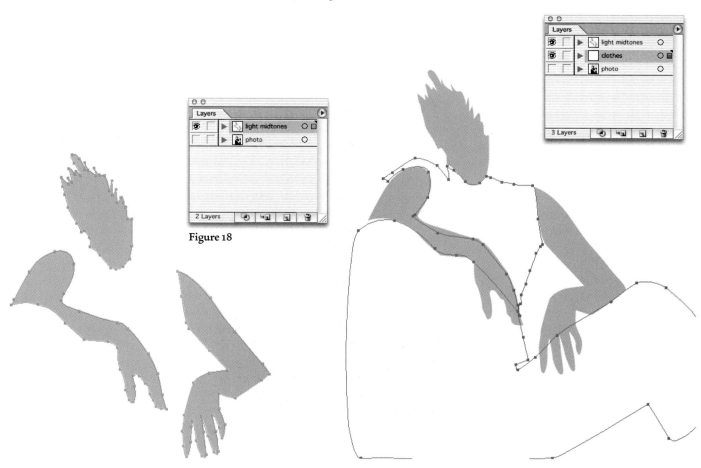

Figure 18

Figure 19

Step 4: Many layers for many details. From there, Larsen moved to the shapes that would make up the darker midtone areas. She created a new layer and drew the eyelashes, eyebrows, nostrils, and inside of the mouth. She then filled them with a darker purple. She also created a separate layer for the hair, which she filled with the same shade of purple. She placed the hair layer under the light midtones layer, and placed the dark midtone layer above it. Larsen confesses, "I have a tendency to create too many details. Putting each color on a separate layer makes it easier for me to delete elements and simplify the illustration."

Step 5: Creating the highlights. Larsen created a new layer for the highlights. She created the highlights on the side of the nose and filled them with a light purple. She created five separate shapes for the lips, using a lighter shade of purple for the plumpest part of the lips and a darker shade for the outside corners and the shadow under the bottom lip, giving the lips some dimension. She created two shapes for the highlight on the neck and filled them with the same shade as the nose highlight. Larsen then created Shirley's fingernails and filled them with the same shade of purple as the outer lips. To complete the highlights, Larsen drew the whites of the eyes and filled them with the lightest shade of purple.

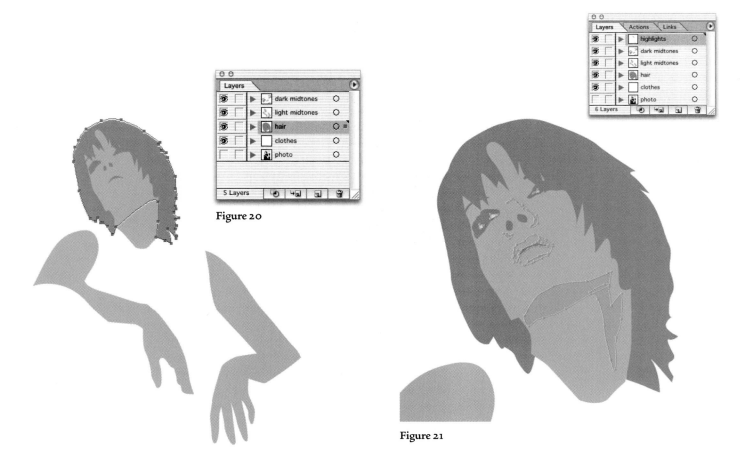

Figure 20

Figure 21

Step 6: Final touches. She finished the illustration by adding the last layer, which she moved to the bottom of the stack of layers. On that layer, Larsen drew a rectangle and filled it with a medium gray. This made the white of Shirley's clothes pop.

Once she finished the illustration, she deleted the scanned photo, flattened the layers, and saved the file as an Illustrator EPS. Since the file size was small, she emailed it to *Flaunt*. She says of the prepress process, "The most difficult thing for me right now is preparing files for print. I got sidetracked in the Web world for several years. Retraining myself to think in a print frame of mind has been a challenge. Sending a file out is so final—with the Web, you can swap things on the fly. You're bound to the decisions you make with print." Anyone who has created artwork for print can appreciate the many issues related to prepress, output, getting color right and last-minute changes. For a Web artist like Larsen, illustrating for screen displays is a breath of fresh air, not only because it comes out like you expect it will, but those last-minute changes can be made without losing your wallet at the printer.

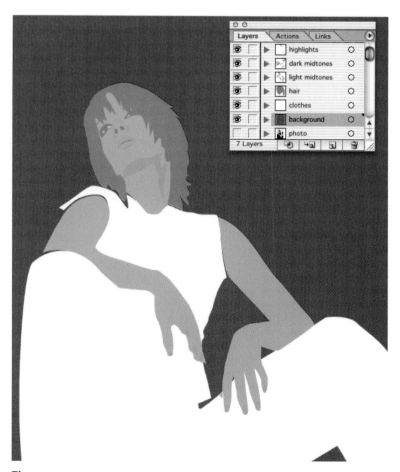

Figure 22

Building a Color Palette and Creating Tints

Larsen begins her work by creating a color palette. Once the colors have been created and nestled away in the Illustrator Swatches palette, she can start illustrating. When you build a color palette, there are many ways to approach creating colors for an illustration. You can use a Pantone Process color chart to select hues for work destined to be color separated in process color. You can use scanned images, access color values in Photoshop, and transport the values to Illustrator. Or you can choose one of the many swatch libraries included with Adobe Illustrator.

Creating tints of a color is not always intuitive, especially for those converts from other illustration programs, such as Macromedia Freehand and CorelDraw, since each illustration program uses a different method for specifying color. In older versions of Illustrator, you were forced to create a spot color in order to use tints. This was problematic if you were printing color separations and limited to the four process colors of C,M,Y, and K. And of course, converting spot colors to process can cause unwanted color shifts.

Luckily, those days are long behind us with the advent of global color. Illustrator now makes it easy to create tints of process colors. First, create your base process color using the CMYK sliders in the color palette. Next, open the Swatches palette, click on the pop-up menu, and select New Swatch. The New Swatch dialog box opens (**Figure 23**). Name your swatch and, for the Color Type, make sure Process Color is selected.

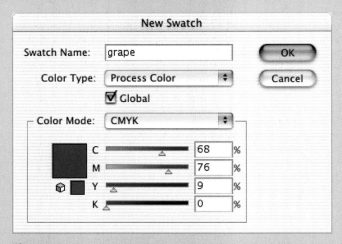

Figure 23

Then, most importantly, check the Global option, since only Global colors can be tinted. Click OK to leave the Spot Color dialog box and return to the document window. When you select the color in the Swatches palette, the Color palette will display the Tint slider bar rather than the separate C, M, Y, and K slider bars. This makes it easy for you to define any tint percentage of that process color. Once you define a tint, you can simply drag that color from the swatch in the Color palette or from the Fill swatch in the Tool palette onto the Swatches palette. The tint will be stored for later use (**Figure 24**). Repeat the steps to build your process color palette of both base colors and tints.

Some artists choose to store their colors using the Swatches palette. Others, such as Sarajo Frieden (see Chapter 6) like to use small (¼-inch or so) rectangles, or "color chips," filled with colors and stored on the pasteboard for easy access with the Eyedropper tool. A similar method you can use, without storing the chips on the pasteboard, is to store them in a separate document altogether. But keep in mind that the advantage of applying global swatches from the Swatches palette (as opposed to the color chip method) is that if you edit a global base color, that color and all of the tints based on it automatically update. If you use the color chip method with non-global colors and later change your mind, you have to change each object's color manually or you need to choose Select > Same.

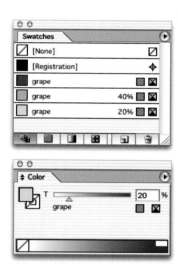

Figure 24

Chapter 15
Textile Design

Artist

Helle Abild
Illustrator, Lecturer, Instructor
Copenhagen, Denmark
www.abild.com

Project

Digitally designed and printed pillows

Client

Self Promotion for Danish Crafts Collection #6

Illustrator Tools and Techniques

Pen Tool, Blend Tool, Gradients, Envelope Distort,
Transformations

Opposite: Floral String | Crane's, a design for notebook and greeting card

Helle Abild
New Directions in Pattern Designs

What happens when Thor meets Disney? In the world of Helle Abild it's a transatlantic juxtaposition of two diverse cultures—Danish and American—stemming from a dual life in two countries. She studied in Denmark at the Textile Department of the Danish Design College in Copenhagen and at the Furniture and Product Department of The Danish Royal Academy and moved to the U.S. to experiment with new techniques and technologies in pattern design. The manifestation of her dual identity shows in recent fabric panels she designed with a viking helmet and a Mickey Mouse hat blended together on a brilliant multi-colored background. Such designs have received accolades

Jingle Bells | Pottery Barn Kids, infant bedding design concept sketches

from Danish newspapers that describe her work as wild, beautiful, and amazing. Her client list is equally impressive. Among Abild's clients are Dansk, Esprit, Walt Disney, Warner Bros., Crane's, DuPont, Nicole Miller, Scandinavian Airlines, and several textile companies. She has accumulated credits, awards, and praise in both Denmark and the U.S., although winning awards is not her primary interest. "I think all that award stuff is a very American thing."

"Most people in the textile industry are intimidated by Illustrator. I find it brilliant for what we do."

Jingle Bells | **Pottery Barn Kids, concept sketches for plates, silverware, and mugs**

Jingle Bells | **Pottery Barn Kids, rug design concept sketches**

It's not the awards that motivate Abild, it's experimentation, creativity, and sharing methods. Besides creating designs, she also teaches new methods and techniques to people who use traditional design methods. She's presented workshops and lectures at schools including the San Francisco Design Academy of Art College, the Danish Design College, and the Iceland Academy of Arts.

Textile and pattern designers often use vertical market applications that cost over $15,000 US. But those who are using off-the-shelf software tend to gravitate to Adobe Photoshop. "Most people in my industry use Adobe Photoshop. But in every class I teach, I convince most people how intelligent Illustrator is for what we do, and they fall in love with the program. I like the clean look. It reminds me of the simple Scandinavian design I grew up with."

Jingle Bells | Pottery Barn Kids, concept sketches for children's clothing

Leaves | Dupont, design for a line of silk scarves

**Flowers in Color | Crane's,
design for notebook and greeting card**

Abild began using computers in 1990 with a Macintosh IIcx. In 1992, when she moved to New York, she purchased a color PowerBook, which she named Oliver. Helle and Oliver took a menswear design job at Jhane Barnes in New York where everyone was working on computers . It wasn't until 1995, when Abild and Oliver moved to CNET in San Francisco, that they were introduced to Adobe Illustrator starting with version 5.5. "I was in love with the program and I loved making illustrations in it. It just seemed like a natural tool for me. I always liked the cut paper look and found the pen perfect for that style."

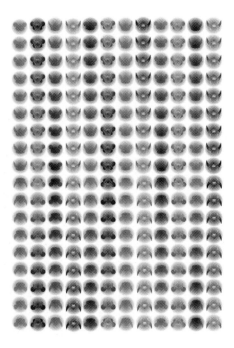
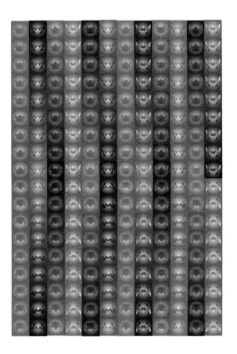

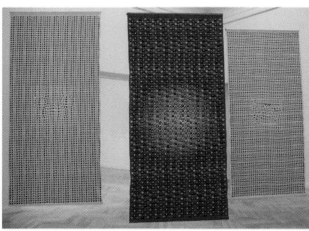

Transatlantic-Transformation | Design for two-sided, digitally-printed textile panels for the Fall exhibition in Charlottenborg, Denmark. Abild distorted the illustration in Illustrator to give the appearance of a 3D form lying underneath the fabric.

Using Illustrator dramatically changed the way Abild worked as a textile and pattern designer. "Before the computer, people used to glue photocopies together. With Illustrator, all the design elements are exact and the file can be emailed right to production."

Abild creates her designs either by starting with sketches or by using tools in Illustrator and adapting designs to features she uses in Illustrator. For work that begins with sketches, she makes hand drawings. She creates small sketches, usually 50 or more, over a period of several days. She experiments with variations and combinations. The sketches are like free

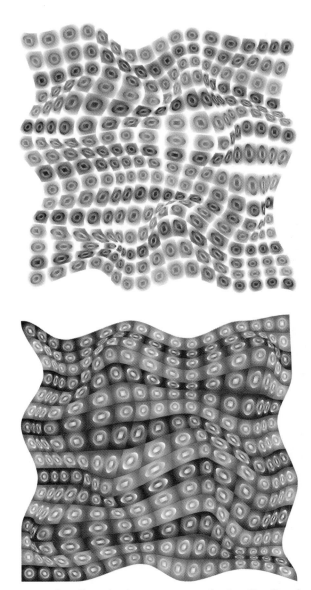

Design for pillows (preliminary concept for the Alfe pillows)

Y2K Quilt | a pre-pattern study for a DuPont project

**Basic Flowers |
Dansk, designs for
tableware (five plates)**

association on paper. From the sketches, she ultimately decides which ones to use in a new pattern and scans them. She uses Adobe Streamline to convert the sketched scans to vector objects.

Having the freedom to reshape objects and use different transformation tools provides great opportunities to draw in Illustrator without templates and pencil sketches. As another approach, Abild may launch Illustrator and begin using objects, transforming them and applying different filters to render results on individual shapes that will collectively produce a new pattern design. She continues to work and rework the shapes until she decides on the perfect combination. When creating Web site designs, she often works this way, usually picking a particular feature she likes and applying that feature to different

Offline Notifier | CNET, Web site icons

Mixed illustration | CNET, Web site icons for story on modems

shapes. "When designing Web sites, I like to make them in Illustrator first. That is the fastest way to communicate with the client and to show the ideas quickly."

Illustrator gives Abild a great advantage. "I really enjoy being able to save files and open them again, not to mention reuse elements that I've copied from one file to another. That's great for what I do—it's like having a library of shapes. And because they're vector illustrations, I can take any little object out of a file and resize it."

missAbild | Illustration for abild.com, Self promotion

Professor Modem | CNET, Web site icons

Career | Økonomen business magazine, illustration for the cover of a Danish magazine about career and family life

The Project

A curator for a Danish government organization that promotes Danish design had seen Abild's work at the "Transatlantic-Transformation" art exhibition in Copenhagen. He asked her if she would make something innovative for a collection that would appear at the Ambiente home furnishings trade show in Frankfurt, Germany. She was given free rein and decided to create a digital illustration for a line of pillows. Not only did she create the design digitally, but she had the fabric printed digitally as well.

The illustrations went from concept to finished pieces quickly. Printing and manufacturing the pillows took up the bulk of the time. Abild adds, "I sometimes name my designs. I named the pillows Alfe, after my boyfriend. Alf also means Elf in Danish."

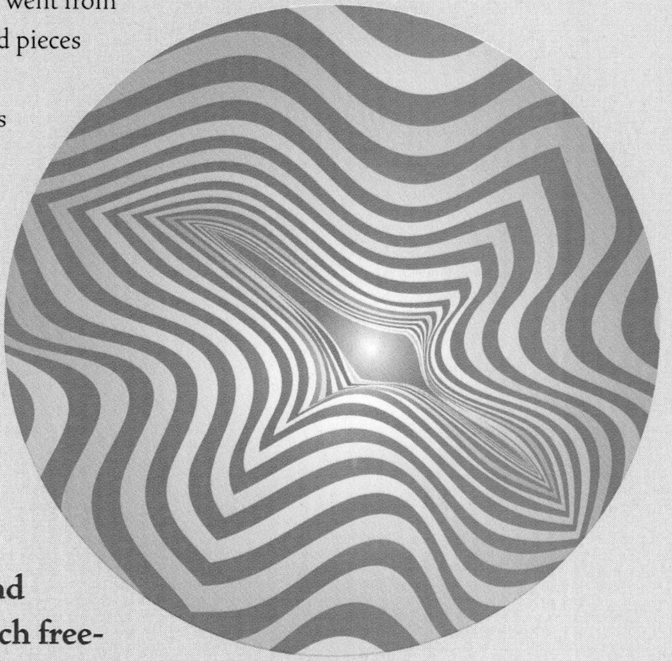

"I love Illustrator. It's elegant and intelligent and gives me so much freedom to move things around and change them. One thing I'd like to have is the ability to draw in repeat with a set amount of distance between objects so I could easily make a seamless pattern."

—HELLE ABILD

The Steps

Step 1: Laying the foundation. Abild began by creating a new tabloid-sized RGB document in Illustrator, with the units of measurement set to centimeters. She recalls, "When I start a project, I usually do several pencil sketches, but with this piece, I developed the concept directly in Illustrator." Setting her colors to no fill with a black stroke, she created a square by double-clicking the Rectangle tool on the page and entering a dimension of 27cm by 27cm in the Rectangle tool dialog box. She then scaled the square by double-clicking the Scale tool in the toolbox, entering 90%, and clicking the Copy button. Abild then selected Object › Transform › Transform Again, which created a third square at 90% of the previous square. She repeated that command 24 times (Command-D or Control-D), creating a nested box-within-a-box effect (**Figure 20**).

Step 2: Applying gradients. Abild created a two-color radial gradient in the Gradient palette, using purple (which she mixed in the Color palette with the RGB sliders) and white, with the midpoint slider set to 50%. She stored the gradient in the Swatches palette.

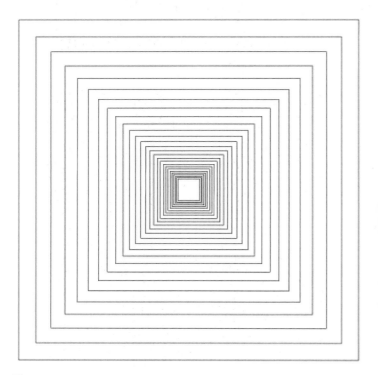

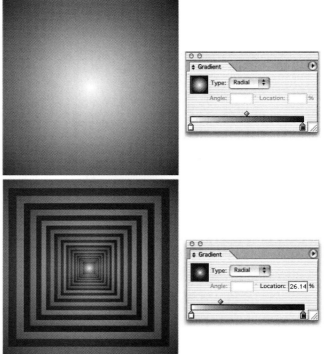

Figure 20

Figure 21

She selected the largest rectangle and filled it with the gradient. Abild then chose the Gradient tool and dragged diagonally from the center of the square to just past the left corner. She repeated the filling and dragging process on every other rectangle. Using the same gradient, she moved the midpoint slider to 17% to mix the gradient so that purple was the more dominant color. Next, she selected the second square and, with the Gradient tool, filled the square with that gradient, again dragging from the center to just past the left corner. Abild used the same gradient for the remaining squares, but adjusted the midpoint slider to various locations, ranging from 17% to 50%. She again repeated the filling and dragging process to fill those squares.

Step 3: Creating a folded-fabric illusion. After she completed the nested squares, Abild selected them all and created two copies, which she pasted into two new files. She then created gradients, using green and white and red and white, and filled the squares using the same procedure she used for the purple squares. On her color choices, Abild says, "While the designs are more or less the same for the home furnishings market, the colors used in Europe tend to be brighter and lighter. The colors in the U.S. are darker. They like more earth tone colors." After she completed the fills, Abild selected the Object > Envelope Distort > Make with Mesh command. She entered four rows and four columns in the Envelope Mesh dialog box (**Figure 22**). Abild used the Envelope Distort command to give the illustration the illusion of folded fabric (**Figure 23**). She repeatedly pushed and pulled the anchor points on the mesh grid to get the wrinkles where she wanted them. "I love the Envelope tool. It's so easy to create a draping effect. You can make it seem like the fabric is moving." While you might think Abild would have used the distorted illustration as a comp to show the client how the design would appear in a fabric form, she actually used the distorted squares as her final design for the pillows, giving them a very whimsical feel.

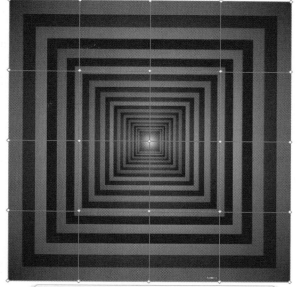

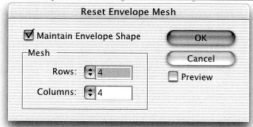

Figure 22

Figure 23

Step 4: Apply an Envelope distortion. Abild applied the Envelope Distort to the red and green squares as well, creating the same wavy style. She then selected and copied the purple squares, created a new file, and pasted the squares. She chose Object > Envelope Distort > Release, and deleted the wavy mesh. She then chose Object > Envelope Distort > Make with Mesh and created another design—this time going for a more linear, skewed look. Abild repeated the process with the red and green squares. These linear designs were also used for the pillows. For the back of the pillows, Abild saved copies of all the illustrations and reversed the order of the dark and light gradients. Once she was satisfied with the distortions, she chose Object > Envelope Distort > Expand. This command permanently applied the distortion, replacing the mesh grid with anchor points Expanding the envelope distort caused a loss of editability—a good thing if you want to ensure that no one else manipulates your design. It also allowed the original illustration to be opened in older versions of Illustrator, if necessary.

Figure 24

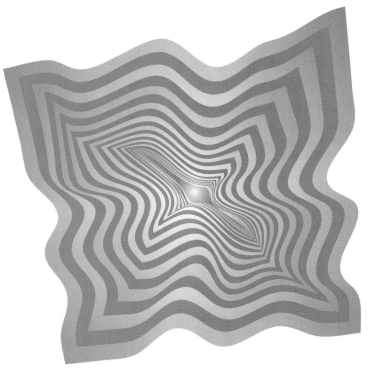

Figure 25

Step 5: Rasterizing in Photoshop. Abild then opened the files in Photoshop, rasterized them in RGB, changed the color mode to Lab (a requirement established by the printer), and saved them as TIFFs. After she showed the finished illustrations to the curator and received approval, she burned them onto a CD and mailed them to RA Smart in England, one of the few vendors that uses a Mimaki large inkjet printer to print on fabric. "Digital printing is a very new thing in the textiles industry." While the technology has evolved—it is now possible to print millions of colors, rather than the previous limit of 15—the process is an expensive one. The printer was able to print only one yard of fabric per hour. The newer printers today are able to produce around 12 yards per hour. RA Smart mailed the printed fabric back to Abild and she had the actual 40-centimeter-square pillows made in Denmark.

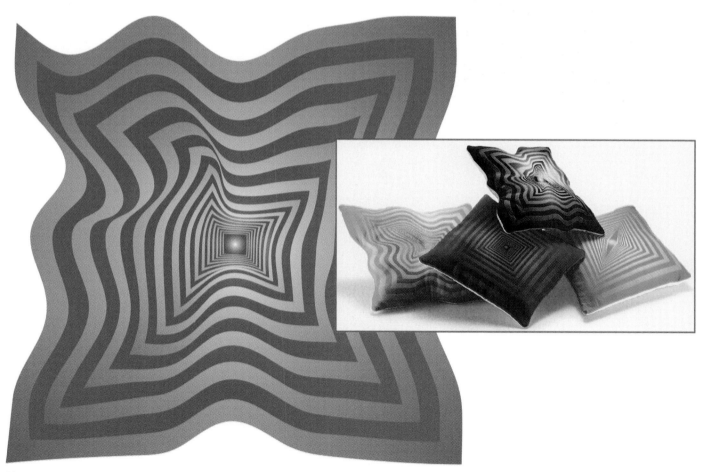

Figure 26

Creating a Gradient Mesh

The Gradient Mesh is not only a useful design tool, it's fun to use and lets you experiment with creating different shapes. Yet, surprisingly, many artists shy away from the tool—perhaps because it seems less intuitive than other Illustrator tools. Here are some tips to make this tool a little less confusing.

When you create gradient meshes, there are a few things to keep in mind. First, the points you create in a mesh can be changed after you establish the number of points in the Gradient Mesh dialog box. When you create the mesh, you use a dialog box to choose the number of anchor points to be placed in the mesh. You can add additional points with the Add Anchor Point tool and delete points using the Delete Anchor Point tool. The entire shape of the object can be reformed after you initially create the mesh when you select Object > Create Gradient Mesh. It's also important to remember that unlike Bezier curves, anchor points can individually accept color changes. With the Direct Select tool, you can select an anchor point and apply color to the anchor point with either the Paint Bucket or by selecting a color from the Swatches or Color Palettes.

To understand how to create a gradient mesh, start by creating a shape with either one of the geometric tools (such as the Rectangle tool), or a freeform shape that you draw with the Pen tool. Select Object > Create Gradient Mesh to open the Create Gradient Mesh dialog box (**Figure 27**).

In the Create Gradient Mesh dialog box, enter the number of rows and columns you want. When you first start experimenting with the tool, use lower values for the rows

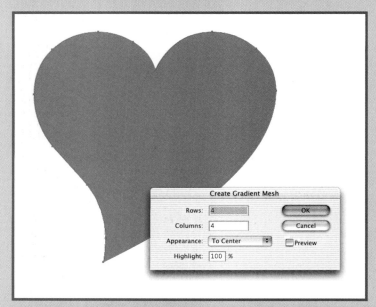

Figure 27 Draw a shape in the document window and fill the shape with a color.
Then select Object > Create Gradient Mesh to open the Create Gradient Mesh
dialog box.

and columns, say two to four for each. You have several choices from the pull-down menu for Appearance. If you choose Flat, the mesh will be formed like a uniform grid. If you choose To Center, the mesh will appear similar to a radial gradient. To Edge gives you a similar appearance as To Center with the gradient reversed. To gain more insight, check the preview box see how the color blending is applied with the various Appearance settings. Choose the number of rows and columns and the Appearance you want and click OK. The initial shape should look like our example (**Figure 28**).

All the anchor points in the mesh behave much like anchor points on Bezier curves. Click on a point with the Direct Select tool and move it to reshape the object. If you need more points on paths, use the Add Anchor Point tool. Conversely, if you need to delete a point, use the Delete Anchor point tool.

To change color transitions, select an anchor point and apply color with either the Paint Bucket or by selecting a new color from the Color or Swatches palette. (For applying custom colors to a color guide file, see the sidebar in Chapter 14.)

Let your imagination go wild and fiddle with the points and color transitions to understand more on how this tool can be an effective instrument when creating your own illustrations. We began with a simple shape and reworked the points and beziers to produce the result you see below (**Figure 29**).

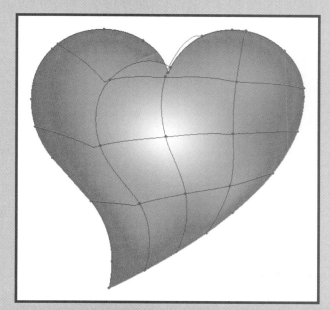

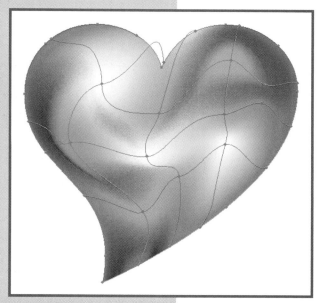

Figure 28   You can create a mesh shape with anchor points and lines using the Create Gradient Mesh dialog box.

Figure 29   The final shape appears after reworking points on paths and applying different color transitions.

EARTHWORKS
EARTHWORKS

THE BIRD SCULPTURE

Climbing & Balance
LOOKOUT FORT
Solar fountain
PUEBLITO DE ADOBE
POND & ECOSYSTEM
Rabbit 8
Meadow
Greenhouse
Montaña de la Mariposa
Rainwater Catchment
Museum Building

Compost Demonstration
Music Plaza
Garden House
Whisper Dishes
Swale Crossing
HORNO/ BAKE OVEN
Children's Garden
Sand & Water Play
Turtle Habitat
Building Entrance

Rainwater Catchment
Acequia

Welcome to Earthworks – a magical place where families play and learn together as they discover the natural world. Smell a flower • climb our lookout fort • create a sand castle • watch a butterfly • make music • plant a seed • laugh, discover, and dream. Be gentle and respectful as you make your way and come back often to see the wonderful changes nature brings year round.

SANTA FE
CHILDREN'S
MUSEUM

Chapter 16
Cartography

Artist
Bruce Daniel
International Mapping Associates
Palm Springs, California
Director of Design & Multimedia Production
www.ima-maps.com

Project
Bike Map

Client
City of Albuquerque

Illustrator Tools and Techniques
Pen Tool, Layers, Transparency, Blend Modes, Effects,
Appearance Palette, Layer Styles, Symbols

Opposite: SFCM | Santa Fe Children's Museum

Bruce Daniel
Maps with Pizzazz

What's so exciting about a map design? After all, you can log on to www.maps.com, enter your location and destination, and a map with some lines, street names, and maybe a few icons appears with a trail to get from point A to point B. Most likely, you pay little attention to the lines, icons, and symbols and just want to get to your destination.

A Bruce Daniel map, however, contains detail you can't possibly ignore. His designs have much more impact than those of maps you find on Web sites and local service stations. They serve a wide range of uses. For instance, his maps have been used to help the World Court's international judges decide on territorial boundary disputes. Or, you might find a Bruce

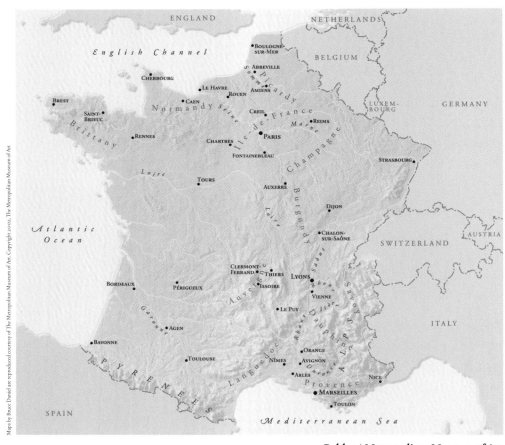

Baldus | Metropolitan Museum of Art

Daniel map for a resort community —including detail about culture, architecture, and points of interest—and precise typography to emphasize the ambiance of the community.

One doesn't necessarily plan on being a cartographer in college. It comes to you perhaps as a matter of coincidence or an alternative for earning a living while pursuing that dream career. For Daniel, that dream was performing arts. Upon graduating with a major in theater from Oberlin College in Ohio, he traveled to Baltimore, where he worked in set design and production for experimental theater groups. Soon after he headed to New York to work in off-off-Broadway and off-Broadway theater.

"Being able to vary the opacities of different layers is really important in creating maps. It enables a person to see information above and below. I can show lines for counties, campuses, and malls, lines for arroyos and roads and so on, and still be able to see the underlying terrain due to transparency abilities."

Like many performing artists, Daniel needed to earn a living while pursuing his dream. He decided to work part time for a design firm where much of his work was devoted to design. Early in college he'd had fantasies of being an architect, until one of his theatre mentors pointed out, "You make a mistake in a set design and the mistake is destroyed when the play ends. You make a mistake in architecture and the mistake outlives you." So Daniel decided to use his background in set design in combination with his other talents to enter a field that let him create illustrations related to environmental settings.

Nob Hill | © Nob Hill—Highland Renaissance Corporation

Daniel was a computer graphics pioneer who began illustrating on an early Macintosh computer with Aldus FreeHand. He preferred FreeHand to earlier versions of Illustrator because of FreeHand's support of layers, multiple undos, and ability to draw in preview mode. For Daniel, using layers is a vital part of creating illustrations. It wasn't until version 5 that he tried to use Illustrator, when layers, drawing in preview mode, and multiple undos were included in the Macintosh version. He still favored FreeHand and went back and forth between the programs until the release of Illustrator 9. Today, his tool of choice is Adobe Illustrator 10. "The raster effects, transparency, blend modes, and symbols in Illustrator 10 just blew open the artistic capabilities for the type of work I do."

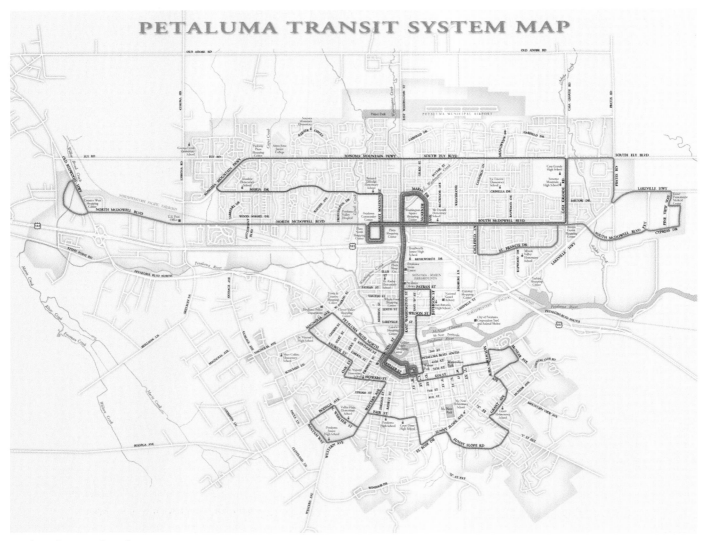

PETALUMA TRANSIT SYSTEM MAP

Petaluma | © City of Petaluma

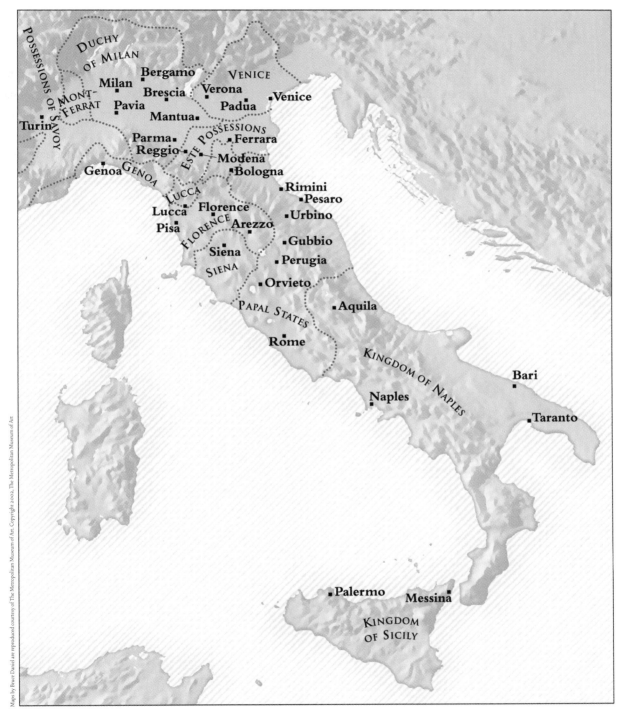

15th Century Italy | Metropolitan Museum of Art

When Daniel begins a new project, he first asks his clients and himself a few questions. "How much data does the map need to show, what kind of manipulation of that data is required, how much tracing is needed, how available and how clean is the source material? What is the overall look and feel that the client is asking for? Is this a high-end product for public marketing and way-finding, or is it a map to show the intricacies of a piece of land?" Through discussions with the client, he sets a general approach and process. Inspiration comes from various places, depending on the project—sometimes from the client, sometimes from observing a place, sometimes from research or ancillary materials. Data and vision work together.

Daniel spends a lot of time discussing the project with his client and tries to visualize the image he'll illustrate, keeping in mind the feeling and sentiment he wants to capture. He may visit the area that the map will cover, research the demographics and history of the

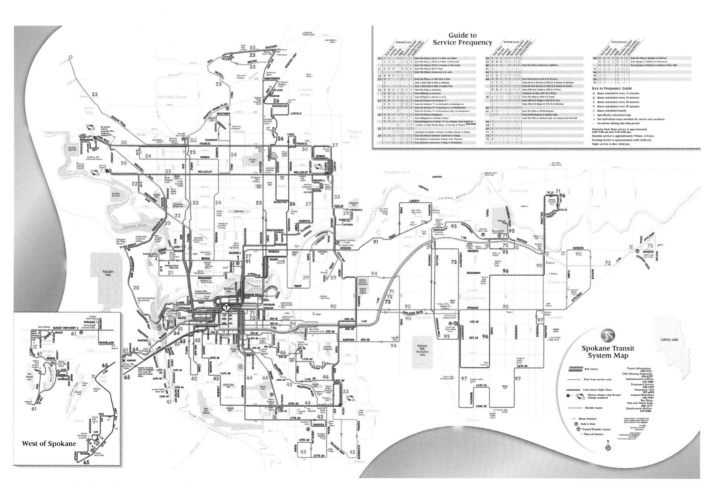

Spokane | © **Spokane Transit Authority**

area, and study cultural symbols relevant to the location. "Developing the design standards for each project is by far the most enjoyable part for me. Taking a sample area of a map and playing with attributes, appearances, transparency, and effects can be magical or frustrating depending on your knowledge of Illustrator. Since almost all of my work begins and ends in the vector environment, I know the program pretty well. As I work towards a certain style, I delve deeper and deeper into the program's artistic strengths.

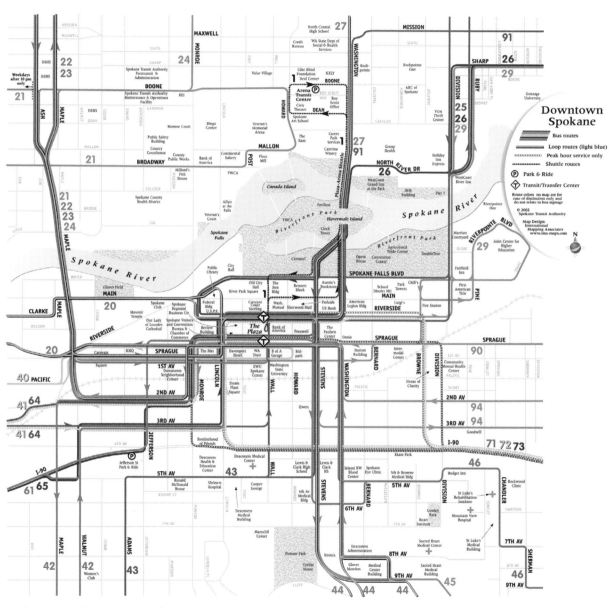

Spokane | © Spokane Transit Authority

"The most difficult project I have worked on was maps of 45 venues for the Atlanta Olympics. The bureaucracy of trying to acquire the data was a bear. The most complex in terms of technical design has to be the Houston Metro Bus map." Sometimes Illustrator's performance frustrates him. As he draws very complex maps with many layers and elements, the program can slow down. "The most difficult part of the design process in Illustrator is how slowly the program displays some of the effects

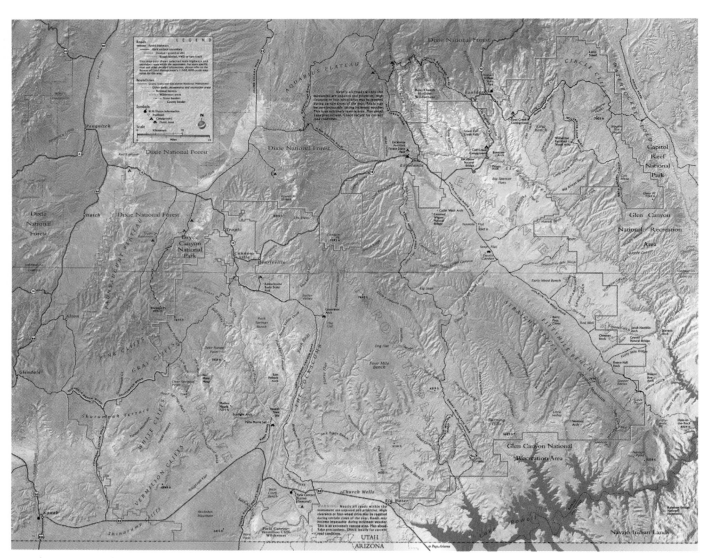

Grand Staircase Escalante | Bureau of Land Management

and appearances. I wouldn't want the program to dumb down, but I do want it to display faster. Every once in a while, I'll have to open a file in an early version of Adobe Illustrator, and I'm stunned at how fast it works—that is if I can remember how to work around the lack of features." With the advantages of transparency and newer feature-rich tools, Daniel returns to version 10.

GS/E Model | © **International Mapping Associates**

The Project

The City of Albuquerque contacted Bruce Daniel's company, American Custom Maps (now part of International Mapping Associates), about doing a bike map for the city and then put the project on hold for four years waiting for budget approval. At the start of the project, Daniel asked the client about the look they wanted. Would it be high tech? Nostalgic? Did they want to highlight a specific feature or quality of the region? That direction helped to provide a graphic focus for the map. From there, Daniel derived inspiration from the locale itself. He got a sense of the environmental color to arrive at a color palette. Since Daniel has been a resident of New Mexico for 16 years, he was very familiar with the area and had a strong feel for the color, topography, climate, and culture of the region.

"I have no 'signature' look per se. The richness and uniqueness I bring to each project provides some continuity in my work." He likes to explore different aspects of design and of a program's features and tends to employ certain design elements based on what he's interested in at the moment. For the Albuquerque bike map, Daniel used drop shadows, glows, blurs, varying transparencies, and different blend modes to provide a map that visually separates layers of tightly packed information yet still provides an aesthetic feel. "I want people to be able to find the information they are most interested in and visually forget the rest. They should be able to hone in and focus on what they want quickly," says Daniel. At press time, the project has taken 220 hours (finishing touches are all that's left). And the number of paths contained in the map? A mere 3,074.

"**Illustrator 10's transparency and blending mode capabilities have greatly impacted map making. Its ability to import various data formats, and the industry's increasing compatibility with GIS [Geographical Information System] and other technical data formats makes the workflow smoother than ever before. My only wish is for complex Illustrator files to print easily.**"

—BRUCE DANIEL

The Steps

Step 1: Acquiring data from important sources. In the days of old, Daniel had to start a map project by tediously tracing every highway, street, road, culvert—well, you get the picture. Now his job is a little easier because his clients supply him with Geographical Information System (GIS) files. Most cities have a GIS, which provides geographically referenced data (to real-world coordinates) from a multi-layered database of everything from property to sewer lines. Daniel first made a list of all of the information he wanted to include in the map. Then using an Illustrator plug-in called MAPublisher ($849) from Avenza Systems (www.avenza.com),

Daniel was able to easily import the city's GIS data (which was in a .dxf format) and place each file on a separate layer in an 8.5-by-11-inch Illustrator file. "Before computers, I used to have many layers of Mylar over my board. So it was a natural progression for me to use layers in Illustrator. Now I wonder how I ever lived without them."

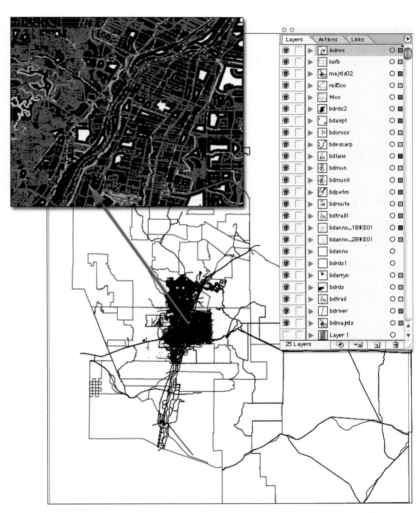

He imported the GIS data as vector paths of 1-point black strokes. And while Daniel may consider himself extremely fortunate to have access to this data, non-cartographers may gasp at the rat's nest of paths (**Figure 12**).

Step 2: Coloring and texturizing the background image. With the converted GIS files in vector format, Daniel brought the layers into his 25-by-33-inch RGB Illustrator file, which contained nothing but guidelines, and scaled the layers to fit the document size. He then moved on to importing the next set of data—the background terrain image. He acquired this image from the Earth Data Analysis Center in New Mexico, which provided

Figure 12

high-resolution Digital Elevation Model (DEM) files (**Figure 13**). He had to first open the DEM files in an application called Natural Scene Designer from Natural Graphics. In this program, Daniel was able to render the shaded relief. He also applied custom colors, using white for the highest elevations, tan for the medium elevations, pink for the low elevations and light green for the lowest elevations. "I felt it was important to graphically show the different elevations, especially for a bike map. I chose the colors I did because I wanted to give a sense of the valley rising to the mountains toward the east and leveling off to the mesa toward the west." He then brought the file into Photoshop and added a slight texture and softening with a couple of filters. This not only added visual interest, but also hid the artifacts and seam lines that were inherent in the DEM file. He then applied a Hue/Saturation adjustment layer to richen the overall color (**Figure 14**). He saved the final 30-by-43-inch, 150-dpi RGB file (all 84.2 megabytes' worth) as a TIFF and imported it into Illustrator.

Step 3: Marrying vector and raster data. Next Daniel sized the terrain TIFF to fit the page. Amazingly the vector data fit the raster background terrain image almost to a T.

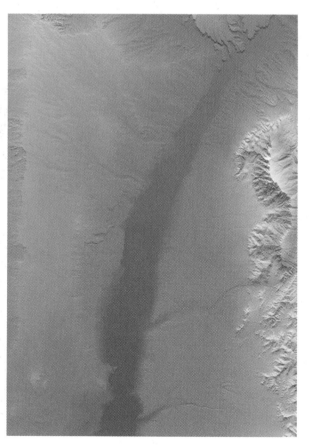

Figure 13

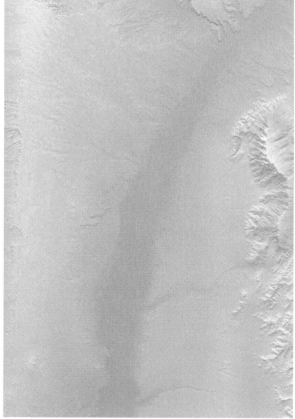

Figure 14

"It was quite amazing that two different projections of data from two different sources fit so well. All I had to do was rotate the terrain image ¾ of a degree."

Step 4: Organizing the layers of data. Even though the GIS data and the terrain image provided the skeletal components of the map, there was still the enormous task of sorting out all the information and stylizing it to look map-worthy. Daniel started by assigning a different selection color to each layer in the Layer Options dialog box, which he opened by double-clicking each layer in the Layers palette. The color was just a working color so he could distinguish one group of elements from another. The look and feel for each element would be developed later. Because map elements were on separate layers, Daniel could play with the stacking order. "For example, for this map, municipal boundaries are low priority. So, I can move that layer to the back and make it less prominent. On the other hand, if this were a map for a developer, those boundaries would be more important and could be moved up in the stack." Next, Daniel made the small roads image layer (the grid of tiny city streets) the only visible layer and exported it as a TIFF with a resolution of 300 dpi. He opened it in Photoshop, chose Image > Adjustments > Invert (**Figure 15**). Then he placed it back into Illustrator as a linked TIFF. On that layer he set the Transparency to 43% and set the blend Mode to Lighten. He rasterized that particular layer in Photoshop beforehand in order to eliminate the complexity of the many paths and the numerous anchor points on that layer (**Figure 16**).

Step 5: Highlighting bike paths with neon multistrokes. Next, Daniel tackled the most important element of the map—the bike designations (bike routes, lanes, and trails). "I wanted the bike designations to lift right off the page, so I made gave them a neon effect." Starting off with lines of 1.5 points in yellow, green, and blue, he created this neon effect by applying multiple strokes in the Appearance palette. Daniel selected the stroke and chose Add New Stroke from the Appearance palette pop-up menu. Each

Figure 15

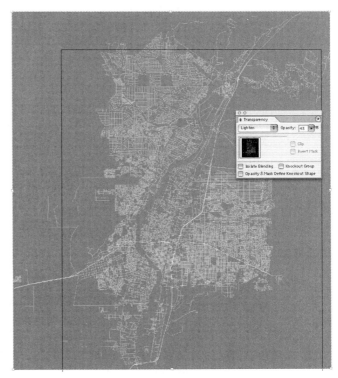

Figure 16

path for a bike designation contains three strokes of .75 points, 2 points, and 3 points with rounded end caps. He colored each stroke in a different shade. For example, for bike routes, he used yellow for the .75-point stroke, light orange for the 2-point stroke, and dark orange for the 3-point stroke. He repeated this method using blues for bike lanes and greens for bike trails. The varying stroke weights and shades of color created the look of a neon tube (**Figure 17**). Once Daniel created these multi-strokes, he saved them as a new style in the Styles palette by selecting the stroke and choosing New Style from the Styles palette pop-up menu. He did this with all of the custom strokes in the map. This allowed him to easily apply a particular style to any paths he created later. Daniel made the bike routes, bike lanes, and bike trails sub layers under the main layer of bike designations. "It's nice to use layers with sub-layers. It provides better organization for highly informational works that map makers and technical illustrators have to tackle. You can group and name components and you can apply effects on a layer basis rather than an object basis." With 26 layers and 35 sub-layers in the final file, it's easy to see why organization is a key element in Daniel's work. In addition to organization, Daniel will often hide his most complex layers, such as those containing objects which use rasterizing Effects, and even remove his layer styles temporarily to improve Illustrator's performance and speed up Illustrator's screen refresh. Since the styles are saved in the Styles palette, they're quick and easy to reapply at the illustration's completion (**Figure 18**).

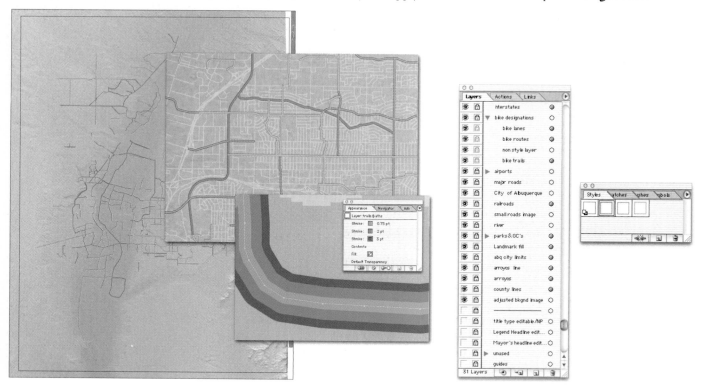

Figure 17   Figure 18

Step 6: Applying blurs and blends to arroyos. He then moved to the county lines layer, which consisted of just a single path dividing two counties. The path consisted of a .5-point black dashed line set to an opacity of 61%. From there he worked on the *arroyos* (drainage lines). On this layer, Daniel wanted to give the impression of a slight scoop in the terrain. To do this, he took the vector path, which was a 6-point brown stroke and applied a 6-pixel blur effect (Effect > Blur > Gaussian Blur). In the Transparency palette, he adjusted the transparency to 30% and set the blend mode to Luminosity (**Figure 19**). He felt the shaded depression alone looked like just a variation on the terrain and didn't offer quite enough definition, so he added a 1-point dashed turquoise line with an opacity of 43% through the center of the depression (**Figure 20**). "It's amazing, some of the things that can be done to simple line work," says Daniel.

Step 7: Softening the city limits. For the Albuquerque city limits layer, Daniel used a soft purple line for the boundaries. Again, making that layer the only visible one, he exported the original data as a TIFF and brought it into Photoshop. There, he created an alpha channel mask by selecting all of the interior areas. He then colored the line purple and applied a Gaussian blur of 25 pixels to blur the inside of the city boundaries (**Figure 21**). He then placed it back into the Illustrator file as a linked JPEG, to try to keep the file size small. With this particular image, the need for quality was minor, so

Figure 19

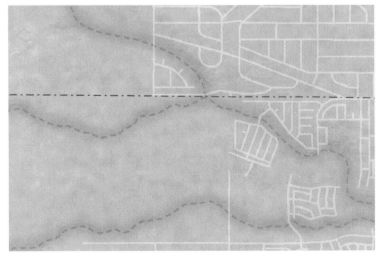

Figure 20

Figure 21

Figure 22

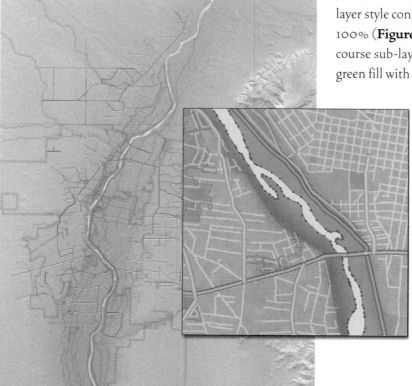

Figure 23

saving it as a JPEG, rather than a TIFF or EPS, was not detrimental. In Illustrator's Transparency palette, he set the transparency to 60% and the blend mode to Multiply. He then added back the original vector data as a .5-point light-purple stroke on a separate layer. "Being able to vary the opacities of different layers is really important in creating maps. It enables a person to see information above and below. I can show lines for counties, campuses, and malls, lines for arroyos and roads and so on, and still be able to see the underlying terrain due to transparency abilities."

Step 8: Stylizing landmarks, parks, and golf courses. Daniel then worked with the landmark layer, which he filled with a light red and set to an opacity of 25%. Next, he created a layer called Parks and GCs (Golf Courses), to which he applied a 25% Opacity. He then made a parks sub-layer and created and applied a layer style to the park areas. The layer style consisted of a light green fill with an opacity of 100% (**Figure 22**). He repeated the process with the golf course sub-layer, also using a layer style, that consisted of a green fill with 30% opacity. "I like to apply styles to the layer level rather than the object level. That way the layer style supercedes the object style and acts as a shell."

Step 9: Filling the river with water. Next, he added the river layer, which wasn't a path, but a shape. Daniel applied a medium blue stroke of .4 points and a light blue fill, indicating water (**Figure 23**).

Step 10: Working on the railroads. From there, Daniel tackled the railroad layer. For the paths indicating railroads, he once again employed multiple strokes (similar to the bike routes in

Step 5) of a 4-point dashed brown line, a 1.5-point white line, and a 2.5-point brown line (**Figure 24**). He set the blend Mode to Darken. Daniel created a style from the multiple strokes and saved it in his Styles palette.

Step 11: Stroking roads and filling airports. Next he worked on the major roads layer, where he applied a white 1.75-point stroke to the paths (**Figure 25**). Then Daniel filled the basic airport shapes with a black fill at 30% opacity and a .5-point black stroke, and filled the buildings within the airport area with brown and stroked them with a .5 brown stroke (**Figure 26**).

Step 12: Creating a multi-stroke path for the interstates. Daniel created another multiple stroke for the path in the interstates layer. It consisted of a 1.75-point white stroke and a 2.5-point black stroke. He then applied a drop-shadow effect to the multi-stroke and saved it as a layer style in the Layers palette (**Figure 27**).

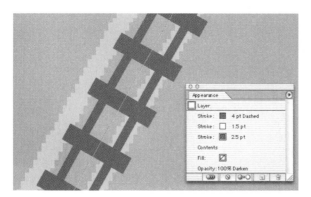

Figure 24

Figure 25

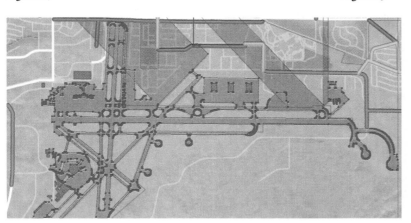

Figure 26

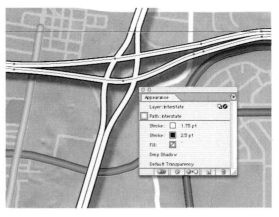

Figure 27

Step 13: Creating symbols. Daniel's next step was to add the icons that would appear throughout the map. These icons included highway numbers, bridges, high schools, places of interest, recreational facilities, trail parking places, and, of course, bike shops. He numbered the bike shop icons so that they corresponded with a chart on the back of the map, giving exact addresses of the shops. To create these icons, Daniel drew the various shapes with the Ellipse, Rectangle, and Pen tools, and filled and stroked them using various bright colors. He then selected each shape and chose New Symbol from the Symbols palette (**Figure 28**). Saving the icons as symbols gave Daniel a couple of great advantages. First, it kept the file size small, since each symbol was counted only once in terms of memory, no matter how many instances of the symbol appeared. Most importantly, any time he revised a symbol (color, stroke weight, and so on), all instances of the symbol dynamically updated, saving a tremendous amount of revision time. Daniel took advantage of this and redid the original bridge, parking, and bike shop symbols. "I wanted to make the stroke on the bridge icon just a little thicker. Because it was a symbol, I revised it and then Option-dragged it over the old bridge symbol in the Symbols palette. All instances of the bridge were updated in a couple of seconds, and they even kept their rotations intact. If the icon hadn't been a symbol, I probably would have left it as is. It would have been too time consuming for such a minor change. Symbols give you the ability to fine-tune and tweak quickly."

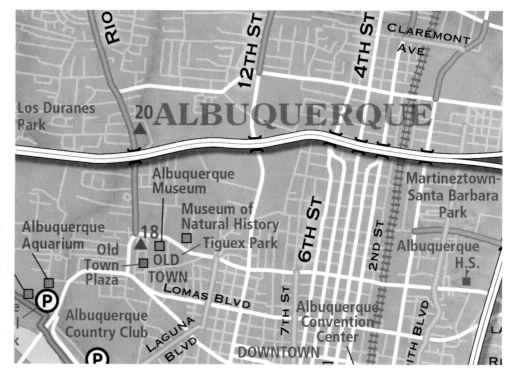

Figure 28

Figure 29

Step 14: Adding the text. Next, he added the type for various elements of the map. He added the type as either point type or type on a path (if the road was curved). He chose Alexa for the map title and mayor's statement headline, ITC Clearface Heavy for the city (gray) and county (black) names, Copperplate Gothic for the roads (black) and trails (brown) and Frutiger for the points of interest (burgundy), parks (green), high schools (burgundy), landmarks (green), rivers (blue), and bike shops (burgundy). He then added a .5-point stroke in brown, black, and green, if the name needed a leader (**Figure 29**). After viewing the first comp, the client felt that the type for the roads needed to be divided into two sizes for better differentiation between the major roads and the rest of the street. Daniel did that making the major roads 8.5 points and the other roads 7 points. He also added an Outer Glow effect (Effect > Stylize > Outer Glow) around the type for the major roads, which he made into a new style and saved in the Styles palette.

Step 15: Creating folding guides. Daniel added guidelines to indicate the fold lines for the map (**Figure 30**). The final 24-by-32-inch map would be folded to a finished size of 4 by 8 inches.

Step 16: Adding the mayor's statement and photo. Next, he added the Mayor's statement, headline, caption, and photo. The photo was a four-color image placed as a linked TIFF. He created the caption and paragraph text with 10-point Frutiger in black, while the headline was in Alexa and enhanced with a soft drop shadow.

Step 17: Creating the compass rose. Colleague Judy Nielsen, who assisted Daniel in making some of the initial choices of color and style for the map, created the burgundy, white, gray, and black compass rose using the Ellipse, Star, and Pen tools. The outer circle was another multiple stroke of 1-point light gray, 2-point medium gray, and 3-point black. The spokes of the compass were also a multiple stroke of .5-point light gray and 2-point dark gray. She made both of these multiple strokes into layer styles and saved them in the Styles palette. Nielsen filled the center circle with a dark gray-to-white radial gradient

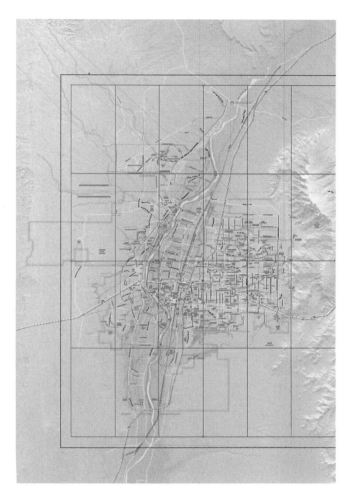

Figure 30

Welcome To Bicycling In Albuquerque

Bicycling is both an important element of the City's multimodal transportation system and a very popular recreation activity. Our temperate climate and sunshine allow for year-round bicycling opportunities. Taking advantage of these opportunities can result in significant benefits to your health and physical fitness. Bicycle commuting is strongly encouraged as a means of reducing traffic congestion and improving the City's air quality.

Albuquerque bicycle programs strive to provide a safe environment for bicycle riders of all levels. There are over 300 miles of on-street bicycle facilities and multi-use trails in the City, and what you see represented on this map is only the beginning. The City is committed to the continued expansion of the system to make bicycling accessible to everyone.

On behalf of the City of Albuquerque, I invite you to explore the routes and destinations identified on this map. I sincerely hope you enjoy your bicycling experience in Albuquerque. Please bicycle responsibly, obey traffic laws and share our multi-use trails.

Martin J. Chavez,
Mayor

Figure 31

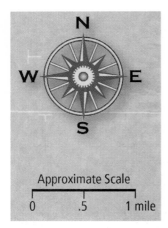

Figure 32

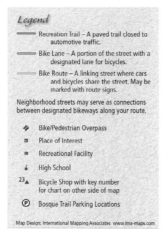

Figure 33

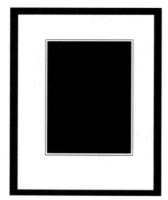

Figure 34

that she created in the Gradient Editor in the Gradient palette. The direction letters were 13.79-point Copperplate Gothic. Once completed, she grouped all elements. She then added the Scale element, using 10-point Frutiger for the type and .75-point and 2-point black strokes for the graphic (**Figure 32**).

Step 18: Creating the legend. The legend was the next element that Daniel added, using three layers. First he placed a textured background as a linked TIFF. He then applied a drop shadow (which he saved as a layer style). Finally, he added the type (10-point Frutiger) and icons describing the bike route designations, places of interest, bike shops, and so forth. He then added the legend title in burgundy, using the font Alexa and adding a slight drop shadow behind the title.

Step 19: Adding titles and a clipping mask. The final two steps for this side of the map were to add the map title (Alexa, burgundy, with a slight drop shadow) and frame to neatly encase the map. He created the frame by using two rectangles, one for the outside and one for the inside. Daniel then selected both and clicked on the Subtract from shape area button in the Pathfinder palette. He filled the frame white (shown against black for display purposes only in **Figure 34**). The frame neatly encased the contents of the map and hid the edges of the various placed TIFFs. He then added trim marks to indicate where the map was to be trimmed, leaving 1/8-inch bleed around the map (**Figure 35**).

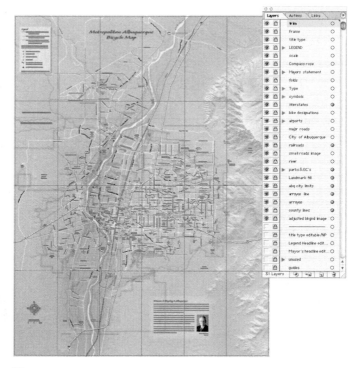

Figure 35

Step 20: Creating guides and text. "I really dread doing the backs of maps. I don't have a love affair with blocks of text and it's a challenge to get a large amount of text to fit within the panels of the folds." Daniel, with initial assistance from Nielsen, started the back of the map by placing guidelines where the folds would be (**Figure 36**). He then created his body text within those guidelines, being extremely careful to avoid the fold lines. He created body text in Frutiger and created headlines in Copperplate Gothic.

Step 21: Giving photos pizzazz. The challenge Daniel faced for the back of the map was to take mediocre photos and somehow make them compelling. Daniel opened the three larger bike shots in Procreate's Painter, color-enhanced them, and applied a zoom filter and texture to them, giving them some movement and life (**Figure 37**).

Step 22: Adding icons and text. The icons for the safety and rules section were stock infographics (in vector format) provided by the city of Calgary in Canada for a credit line. Nielsen enhanced these infographics to give them more visual interest. She placed a white, rounded rectangle with a light purple drop shadow behind each icon to help lift the element off the background. She added type to the right of each icon in 11.7-point Copperplate Gothic for the heads and 9-point Frutiger for the body text (**Figure 38**). Nielsen also added the skater and safety circle graphics (again from Calgary) and applied the same soft purple drop shadow (**Figure 39**).

Figure 36

Figure 37

ONE PERSON PER BIKE
Riding double is only permitted when carrying a child in an approved carrier or when riding on a tandem bicycle. Children should always wear a helmet.

RIDE IN SINGLE FILE
Ride in single file when riding in a group except when overtaking or passing.

OBEY TRAFFIC SIGNS AND SIGNALS
As a vehicle, bicycles must obey all the Rules of the Road. Cyclists have the same privileges and duties as other traffic.

Figure 38

Figure 39

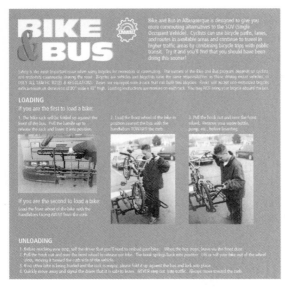

Figure 40

Figure 41

Figure 42

Step 23: Creating an advertisement. The next step was to design the transit ad from an initial layout provided by SunTran, which showed how to safely load and unload bikes from the city buses (**Figure 40**). He started by creating a square with the Rectangle tool, filling it with a light purple and adding headline type. He then added an inner bevel effect to the head type and a soft drop shadow to the turquoise ampersand. He placed three four -color images as linked TIFFs and added the type (Frutiger, 9.5 points).

Step 24: Applying headlines. He added headlines in the Alexa font with the same drop shadows that he used for side one of the map. He then added lines to visually divide the densely packed information (**Figure 41**). The lines were 3.39-point, light-purple strokes, which he roughened (Effect > Distort & Transform > Roughen) and shadowed.

Figure 25: Placing the cover photo. To add the cover image, Daniel first placed the four-color image as a linked TIFF and then created an opacity mask in the Transparency palette. He created the opacity mask by making a rectangle, which he filled with the default white-to-black linear gradient. This allowed the photo to gradually fade to transparency and blend nicely with the city seal graphic (**Figure 42**).

Step 26: Adding the background image. Nielsen created the 25-by-33-inch textured background in Photoshop at 150 dpi (**Figure 43**). Daniel took the image into Painter, where he reworked the textureusing the Effects > Apply surface texture and Effects > Focus > Glass Distortion commands. He then placed the background as a linked TIFF in the Illustrator file and positioned it just above the guidelines layer in the Layers palette.

Step 27: Getting ready for print. The final step entailed adding trim marks (**Figure 44**). Daniel does all of his work in RGB color mode. "I prefer working in RGB, even though much of my work is printed on a CMYK press. Illustrator 10 seems to have more flexibility in the RGB space for working with filters and effects. Straightforward Photoshop conversion of RGB to CMYK gives me unremarkable conversion, so I'd rather work with the printer or service bureau in a conversion process that is tweaked specifically to their equipment and materials. I don't really like the fact that you have to choose an RGB or CMYK color space in Illustrator.

I wish you could create a CMYK color that would retain its numerical settings when converting back and forth. But, in general, I'm happy with the final look and balance of color when processed by competent printers and service bureaus." Daniel burned the final file, consisting of 14.2 MB for two Illustrator files and 209.3 MB of linked TIFFs and JPEGs, to a CD, and gave it to the City, which took it to their contract printer. The color proof was a Kodak Approval print, which Daniel checked carefully for any prepress snafus. Daniel was confident that a file this complex, with 3,074 paths and many more anchor points, would print. But he said he can always pasteurize a complex vector illustration at a high resolution as a failsafe. "There is always the need to balance time, accuracy, and production needs, but it seems printing is always the bottleneck," laments Daniel. Due to the complexity of the map, Daniel was present at the press check to verify that all of the components printed correctly and that the color was correct.

Figure 43

Figure 44

Figure 45

Working with Symbols

Bruce Daniel creates small icons and symbols that he reuses many times in a single drawing. Each icon is an illustrated work that's replicated throughout the design. Periodically he may decide to change an attribute for an icon. If he had drawn, duplicated, and placed the icons throughout the artwork, he would need to delete all duplicated icons and replace them with a new or revised icon. However in Illustrator 10, Daniel uses the Symbols palette to manage his icons so that he can freely change attributes and dynamically update changes on all instances of the icons.

A Symbol is an art object you store in the Symbols palette. In Daniel's work, it might be an icon for handicapped access, a sign for a bike path, or a traffic sign. When he creates an icon, he adds the artwork to the Symbols palette by selecting the paths and dragging them to the Symbols palette (**Figure 45**).

You can add a descriptive name for the symbol by double-clicking on the icon in the Symbols palette or by selecting the fly-out menu and choosing Symbol Options from the menu commands. When the Symbols Options dialog box opens, type the name for the new symbol (**Figure 46**). Illustrator 10 also offers eight symbolism tools that allow you to adjust the color, density, size, location, rotations, transparency, and style of symbol sets.

One advantage of using Symbols is the manner in which Illustrator handles them. Rather than interpreting Symbols as individually placed artwork, Illustrator sees

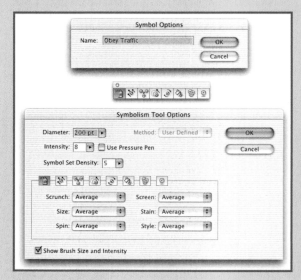

Figure 46

Symbols as an image link. The artwork is only used once and each instance is linked to the original artwork, which reduces file size and complexity in the design. To add a Symbol to the artwork, click on the Symbol in the Symbols palette and drag it to the document window.

When Daniel uses many different instances of a given Symbol and later wishes to change attributes, such as paths, strokes, or colors, he has to edit only a single Symbol on the page. To edit a Symbol, you first need to select one of the Symbols in the document page, then open the Symbols fly-out menu, and select Break Link to Symbol. The artwork ungroup and all objects become editable so you can make your changes. In **Figure** 47 the auto and grass colors have been changed from the original design.

The final step is to redefine the Symbol. Select all objects in the edited Symbol, keep the selection active, and open the Symbols fly-out menu. Select Redefine Symbol from the menu options (**Figure** 48). Even easier, simply Option or Alt-drag the revised symbol over the old one in the Symbols palette and the old one will be replaced.

Illustrator dynamically updates all Symbols in the document window to reflect changes in your edits. When working on Illustrator files that are 50 MB or larger, with 20 or more iterations of the same icons, an artist like Daniel finds using Symbols to be a great time saver.

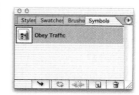

Figure 47

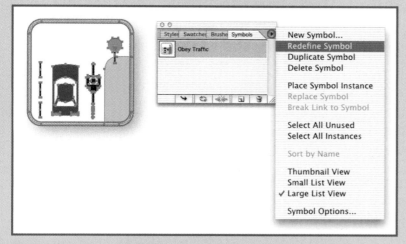

Figure 48

Index

Image Credits

All artwork, photographs, and images appearing in *Adobe Master Class: Illustrator Illuminated* are protected by the conventions of international copyright law and cannot be reproduced without the express written permission of the respective copyright holders. We thank the artists and copyright holders for their cooperation in making this production possible:

Cover

Downhill Skier, ©Martin French; Untitled, ©Amore Hirosuke; JustBee, ©Russell Benfanti; Boat Cutaway, ©Alan Raine; Unicef/Feliz Cumpleanos, ©Sarajo Frieden

Chapter 1: The Illustrator Way of Thinking

Page x. Just Bee, ©Russell Benfanti; "Multiplex" detail, ©Michael Bartalos; No Ordinary Bird, ©Sarajo Frieden; Canton Market, ©Daniel Pelavin

Page 2. Illustration ©Tiffany Larsen; image ©Sarajo Frieden

Page 3. Sketches ©Daniel Pelavin; sketches ©Michael Bartalos

Page 4. Downhill Skier, ©Martin French; "Global Capitalism," ©Louis Fishauf

Page 7. Illustration ©Russell Benfanti, courtesy Winslow Press

Page 8. Pillow design ©Helle Abild

Chapter 2: Technical Illustration

All artwork ©Alan Raine

Chapter 3: Children's Illustration

Page 28. Clyde, ©ipicturebooks, www.ipicturebooks.com.

Page 30. Yellowbloat, ©Russell Benfanti

Page 31. Octopus' Garden, ©ipicturebooks, www.ipicturebooks.com, courtesy Byron Preiss Visual Communications

Page 32. Mendola, cover ©Russell Benfanti

Page 33. Workbook (apple), ©Russell Benfanti, AdSource, ©Russell Benfanti

Page 34. Sheep, ©Concordia House Publishing; Groovy Tubes *Bug Blast* book illustration, by Russell Benfanti, ©2002 Innovative Kids. Reprinted with permission.

Page 35. COOTIE® & ©2002 Hasbro, Inc. Used with permission; Hasbro novelty compound, ©2002 Hasbro, Inc. HASBRO is a trademark of Hasbro and used with permission. ©2002 Hasbro All Rights Reserved; JustBee, ©Russell Benfanti

Page 36. Cootie Group, COOTIE® & ©2002 Hasbro, Inc. Used with permission

Page 37. Hide, Clyde ©ipicturebooks, www.ipicturebooks.com.

Pages 38–47. illustrations from *The Chair Where Bear Sits*, all ©Winslow Press.

Chapter 4: Trade Show Displays

All artwork ©Martin French

Chapter 5: Poster Design

Page 66. World Aids Day T-Shirt, ©Social Marketing Association/Population Services International. Used with permission.

Page 67. Earthlife Poster Expand ©Earthlife Africa. Used with permission.

Page 69. Haircut—Mandela Cool ©Ellen Papciak-Rose

Page 70. Happy Birthday Buskaid! ©Buskaid. Used with permission.

Page 71. AmeriCares HomeFront T-Shirt design ©AmeriCares®HomeFront®. Used with permission; "Lwazi's Life — birth to 3 years," "Gabriella Catches a Star and her friends find some stuff in the sky," and Ellen Promo Page ©Ellen Papciak-Rose

Page 72. Building Resiliency Among Children Affected by HIV/AIDS, ©Catholic AIDS Action, used with permission.

Page 73. My Soweto Township ABC's, ©Ellen Papciak-Rose

Page 74. Nelson Mandela House and Mandela House Postcard, ©Ellen Papciak-Rose

Page 75. ALP Covers and Spots, all images ©AIDS Law Project. Used with permission.

Page 76. GTZ Relationship Cover ©GTZ—German Technical Cooperation. Used with permission.

Page 77. Discovering Life Skills, ©Shuter & Shooter Publishers (Pty) Ltd., P.O. Box 109, Pietermaritzburg 3200 South Africa

Pages 78–83. "Prevent Malaria In Your Area" and "SupaNet is not for fishing," all ©Social Marketing Association/Population Services International. Used with permission.

Chapter 6: Greeting Cards

All artwork ©Sarajo Frieden

Chapter 7: Advertisement

All artwork ©Amore Hirosuke

Chapter 8: Typography

All artwork ©Daniel Pelavin

Chapter 9: Billboard/Large Format Designs
All artwork ©Michael Bartalos

Chapter 10: Logo Design
Page 176. Dot.com revolution, ©*Time* Magazine. Used with permission.
Page 178. Safetyman, ©Nexfor. Used with permission.
Page 179. NCE Icons, ©NCE Energy Trust. Used with permission.
Page 180. Biz Quiz, ©Microsoft Corp. Used with permission.
Page 181. Big Band and Rap, both ©The Santa Fe Natural Tobacco Company. Used with permission.
Page 182. RadioXM, ©*American Lawyer* Magazine. Used with permission.
Page 183. Ridpath's advertisement ©Ridpath's Fine Furniture of Toronto, Canada. Used with permission.
Page 184. Recession, ©*InfoSystems* magazine. Used with permission.
Page 185. Ridpath's Media Kit, Ridpath's billboard, and Ridpath's CD Art, all ©Ridpath's Fine Furniture of Toronto, Canada. Used with permission.
Page 186. UpCountry Logo ©UpCountry Canada. Used with permission.
Pages 187–191. all images ©Ridpath's Fine Furniture of Toronto, Canada. Used with permission.

Chapter 11: CD Packaging
All artwork ©Michael Doret. Design & Finished Artwork, www.MichaelDoret.com.

Chapter 12: Editorial
All artwork ©Louis Fishauf

Chapter 13: Cartoon Illustration
All artwork © Nick Diggory

Chapter 14: Portrait Illustration
Page 258. James Legros and Chris Kattan, ©*Flaunt* magazine. Used with permission; Ashcroft and Outkast ©Tiffany Larsen
Page 260. ChickClick Horoscopes ©IGN Entertainment, Inc. Used with permission.
Page 261. Paul Reubens, ©Tiffany Larsen
Pages 262–263. Pivot Rules illustrations ©2002 Windsong Allegiance Group LLC. Used with permission.
Page 264. Anchor, ©Tiffany Larsen
Page 265. Nelly Furtado, ©Tiffany Larsen
Page 266. Franka Potente and Benicio Del Toro, ©Tiffany Larsen
Pages 267–271. Shirley Manson illustrations, ©*Flaunt* magazine. Used with permission.

Chapter 15: Textile Design
All artwork ©Helle Abild, except:
Page 274. Floral string, ©Helle Abild/Crane's. Used with permission.
Page 280. Leaves, ©Helle Abild/Dupont. Used with permission.
Page 281. Flowers in Color, ©Helle Abild/Crane's. Used with permission.
Page 284. Basic Flowers designs ©Helle Abild/Dansk. Used with permission.
Page 285. Offline Notifier, Mixed illustration, ©Helle Abild/CNET.com. Used with permission.
Page 286. missAbild, ©Helle Abild; Professor Modem, ©Helle Abild/CNET.com. Used with permission; Career, ©Helle Abild
Pages287–291. pillow design project, ©Helle Abild

Chapter 16: Cartography
Page 294. SFCM, ©Santa Fe Children's Museum. Used with permission.
Page 296. Baldus, Map by Bruce Daniel, reproduced courtesy of The Metropolitan Museum of Art. ©2002, The Metropolitan Museum of Art
Page 297. Nob Hill, ©Nob Hill-Highland Renaissance Corp. Used with permission.
Page 298. Petaluma, ©City of Petaluma. Used with permission.
Page 299. 15th Century Italy, Map by Bruce Daniel, reproduced courtesy of The Metropolitan Museum of Art. ©2002, The Metropolitan Museum of Art
Pages 300–301. Spokane and Spokane detail, ©Spokane Transit Authority. Used with permission.
Page 302. Grand Staircase Escalante, prepared for Bureau of Land Management
Page 303. GS/E Model, ©Bruce Daniel, International Mapping Associates
Pages 304–317. Bike Map, all images ©City of Albuquerque. Used with permission.